PRAISE FOR *THE BOOK OF JAVASCRIPT*

"Real-world scripts that you can plug into your pages . . . [and] a patient tutor's explanation of how they work."

—Jim Heid, Conference Chair,
Thunder Lizard's "Web Design" conferences

"Thau's JavaScript tutorials at Webmonkey.com are so insanely popular, they've earned him a Plato-like following of devoted fans. . . .Thanks to this book/CD-ROM combo . . . Thau-mania is destined to grow to Elvis proportions."

—Evany Thomas, Managing Editor of Webmonkey.com

". . . an approachable introduction to contemporary JavaScript scripting practices. Its clear and concise examples make an intimidating subject seem quite friendly."

—Michael Masumoto, Multimedia Studies Program
Instructor at San Francisco State University

THE BOOK OF JAVASCRIPT

A PRACTICAL GUIDE TO INTERACTIVE WEB PAGES

thau!

No Starch Press
San Francisco

Printed in the United States of America
3 4 5 6 7 8 9 10—03 02 01

Trademarked names are used throughout this book. Rather than use a trademark symbol with every occurrence of a trademarked name, we are using the names only in an editorial fashion and to the benefit of the trademark owner, with no intention of infringement of the trademark.

Publisher: William Pollock
Project Editor: Karol Jurado
Assistant Editor: Nick Hoff
Editorial Production Assistant: Jennifer Arter
Cover and Interior Design: Octopod Studios
Composition: Magnolia Studio
Technical Editor: Nadav Savio
Copyeditor: Gail Nelson
Proofreader: Christine Sabooni
Indexer: Nancy Humphreys

Distributed to the book trade in the United States and Canada by Publishers Group West, 1700 Fourth Street, Berkeley, California 94710, phone: 800-788-3123 or 510-528-1444, fax: 510-528-3444

For information on translations or book distributors outside the United States, please contact No Starch Press directly:

No Starch Press
555 De Haro Street, Suite 250, San Francisco, CA 94107
phone: 415-863-9900; fax: 415-863-9950; info@nostarch.com; www.nostarch.com

The information in this book is distributed on an "As Is" basis, without warranty. While every precaution has been taken in the preparation of this work, neither the author nor No Starch Press shall have any liability to any person or entity with respect to any loss or damage caused or alleged to be caused directly or indirectly by the information contained in it.

Library of Congress Cataloging-in-Publication Data

```
Thau, Dave.
    The book of JavaScript / Dave Thau.
        p. cm.
    Includes index.
    ISBN 1-886411-36-0
        1. JavaScript (Computer program language)  I. Title.
QA76.73.J39 T37 2000
005.2'762--dc2                                    98-087609
```

DEDICATION

I dedicate this, my first book, to the first people in my life.
Thanks, mom and dad, for tricking me into becoming an engineer.
And for everything else as well.

ACKNOWLEDGMENTS

This book was truly a collaborative effort. Thanks to Nick Hoff for patiently editing my addled prose and giving me the various swift kicks I needed to finish this thing, William Pollock for talking me into writing this book and helping shape its overall direction, Nadav Savio for making sure my scripts actually worked, Karol Jurado and Gail Nelson for dotting my i's and crossing my t's, and Amanda Staab for getting the word out. And a big thanks to my sweetheart Kirsten, for tolerating the many missed weekends and the evening hours filled with the clamoring of this keyboard.

BRIEF CONTENTS

CONTENTS IN DETAIL

1

WELCOME TO JAVASCRIPT!

2

USING VARIABLES AND BUILT-IN FUNCTIONS
TO UPDATE YOUR WEB PAGES AUTOMATICALLY

3

GIVE THE BROWSERS WHAT THEY WANT

4

ROLLOVERS: EVERYONE'S FAVORITE JAVASCRIPT TRICK

5

OPENING AND MANIPULATING WINDOWS

6

GETTING FUNCTIONAL: WRITING
YOUR OWN JAVASCRIPT FUNCTIONS

7

GIVING AND TAKING INFORMATION WITH FORMS

8

KEEPING TRACK OF INFORMATION WITH ARRAYS AND LOOPS

9

TIMING EVENTS

10

FRAMES AND IMAGE MAPS

11

VALIDATING FORMS, MASSAGING
STRINGS, AND WORKING WITH CGI

12

COOKIES

13

DYNAMIC HTML

14

HOW TO FIX BROKEN CODE

Appendix A

BEYOND THE BROWSER: PLUG-INS, ACTIVEX, MAKING MUSIC, AND JAVA

Appendix B

REFERENCE TO JAVASCRIPT OBJECTS AND FUNCTIONS

309

Appendix C

ANSWERS TO ASSIGNMENTS

359

About the CD-ROM

377

Index

379

FOREWORD

I learned JavaScript completely on my own. There was no one to tell me about "event handlers" or how to set cookies. No one even explained what a variable is, let alone the best ways to name them. Of course I had reference books, but they were intimidating tomes, full of cryptic lists and tables, written by programmers for programmers.

David Thau is a remarkable combination of natural teacher and seasoned programmer. As a result, *The Book of JavaScript* not only teaches JavaScript thoroughly and enjoyably in a friendly, unintimidating tone, but it teaches programming as elegantly as any book I've seen. In fact, I've always thought of this as Thau's ulterior motive—he pretends he's just showing you how to make a rollover or validate the text in an HTML form, but before you know it you've learned how to code!

Perhaps the most telling thing I can say is that, reading this book, I can't help but wish I was learning JavaScript for the first time. If you are, then consider yourself lucky to have Thau as a teacher. You couldn't do better.

Happy JavaScripting!

Nadav Savio

PREFACE

You are about to begin a journey through JavaScript—a programming language that adds interactivity and spark to Web pages all over the Internet. This book, written primarily for nonprogrammers, provides scripts you can cut and paste into your Web site, but it also makes sure you understand how they work so you can write your *own* scripts. Each chapter in the book focuses on a few important JavaScript features, shows you how professional Web sites incorporate them, and takes you through examples of how you might add those features to your own Web pages.

Before you dive in, here is a quick overview of what you'll learn as you make your way through *The Book of JavaScript*.

Chapter 1 lays out the book's goals, describes JavaScript and compares it with other tools, explains some of the nifty ways in which JavaScript can enhance your Web pages, and takes you through writing your first JavaScript.

Chapter 2 describes how JavaScript figures out what day it is and writes that date to a Web page. Along the way you'll learn how JavaScript remembers things using variables and performs actions using functions.

Chapter 3 shows you how to direct someone to a Web page specifically designed for his or her browser. This involves figuring out what browser the visitor is using, then making a decision based on that information using if-then statements and their kin.

Chapter 4 covers that favorite JavaScript trick—an image swap. You'll also learn how to trigger JavaScript based on a viewer's actions.

Chapter 5 tells you everything you need to know about opening new browser windows—the second-favorite JavaScript trick. You'll also learn how JavaScript writes HTML to the new windows, closes them, and moves them around on screen.

Chapter 6 explains the magic of writing your own JavaScript functions. Functions are the major building blocks of any JavaScript program, so learning to write your own is a critical step to JavaScript mastery.

Chapter 7 shows you how JavaScript works with HTML forms to collect all kinds of information from your users and give them fancy ways to navigate your site.

Chapter 8 describes how JavaScript deals with lists, whether they're of all the images on a Web page or of all the friends in your address book. JavaScript calls lists *arrays*, and they come in very handy.

Chapter 9 discusses setting events to occur at specific times. For example, you can open a window and then close it in 5 seconds, or you can write a clock that updates every second. Once you know how to do this, you can create games and other interactive applications based on timed events.

Chapter 10 discusses how JavaScript works with HTML frames. It covers topics including changing two or more frames at once and preventing your Web pages from getting trapped in someone else's frame set.

Chapter 11 shows how to make sure people are filling out your HTML forms correctly. Along the way, you'll learn fancy ways to check user input—for example, you can check the formatting of an email address.

Chapter 12 covers cookies. These bits of code let your Web pages save information a visitor has provided even after he or she turns off the computer. This allows your site to greet guests by name whenever they visit (if they tell you their name, of course!).

Chapter 13 introduces Dynamic HTML, a feature of newer browsers that lets you animate entire Web pages.

Chapter 14 wraps things up by giving you tips on what to do when the JavaScript you've written isn't working correctly.

Appendix A covers how JavaScript can interact with other programs your browser may include—Java, ActiveX, and QuickTime, for example.

Appendix B provides a complete list of all the objects and functions that comprise JavaScript.

Appendix C offers answers to the assignments that end each chapter.

Have fun!

1

WELCOME TO JAVASCRIPT!

Welcome to *The Book of JavaScript*. JavaScript is one of the fastest and easiest ways to make your Web site truly dynamic. If you want to spruce up tired-looking pages, you've got the right book. This book will give you ready-made JavaScripts you can implement immediately on your Web site, and I'll take you step by step through sample scripts (both hypothetical and real-world examples) so you *understand* how JavaScript works. With this understanding, you can modify scripts to fit your specific needs as well as write scripts from scratch. Your knowledge of JavaScript will grow as you work through the book; each chapter introduces and explores in depth a new JavaScript topic by highlighting a real-life Web site that uses it.

Is JavaScript for You?

If you want a quick, easy way to add interactivity to your Web site, if the thought of using complex programs intimidates you, or if you're simply interested in programming but don't know where to start, JavaScript is for you.

JavaScript, a programming language built into your Web browser, is one of the best ways to add interactivity to your Web site because it's the only cross-browser language that works directly with Web browsers. Other languages, such as Java, Perl, and C, don't have direct access to the images, forms, and windows that make up a Web page.

JavaScript is also very easy to learn. You don't need any special hardware or software, you don't need access to a Web server, and you don't need a degree in computer science to get things working. All you need is a Web browser and a text editor such as SimpleText or Notepad.

Finally, JavaScript is a *complete* programming language, so if you want to learn more about programming, it provides a great introduction. If you don't give a hoot about programming, that's fine too. There are plenty of places—including this book and its bundled CD-ROM—where you can get prefab scripts to cut and paste right into your pages.

Is This Book for You?

This book assumes you don't have any programming background. Even if you have programmed before, you'll find enough that's new in JavaScript to keep you entertained. One of the best things about JavaScript is that you don't have to be mega-geeky to get it working on your Web pages right away. You *do* need a working knowledge of HTML, however.

The Goals of This Book

The main goal of this book is to get you to the point of writing your own Java-Scripts. Equally important, however, is the ability to read other people's scripts. JavaScript is a sprawling language, and you can learn thousands of little tricks from other scripts. In fact, once you've finished this book, you'll find viewing the source code of JavaScript Web pages the best way to increase your knowledge.

Each of the following chapters includes JavaScript examples from professional sites. You'll soon see there are many ways to script, and sometimes going through the site's code unearths interesting corners of JavaScript that I don't cover in this book.

Beyond learning how to write your own JavaScript and read other people's scripts, I also want you to learn where to look for additional information on JavaScript. The best place to learn new techniques is to view the source of a Web page you find interesting. Several Web sites also offer free JavaScripts. I'll be introducing some of these as we go along, but here are a few good examples to get you started:

http://www.js-planet.com

http://www.developer.earthweb.com/directories/pages/
dir.javascript.html

http://www.javascript.com

Another good place to get information is a JavaScript reference book. *The Book of JavaScript* is primarily a tutorial for learning basic JavaScript and making your Web site interactive. It's not a complete guide to the language, which includes too many details for even a 400-page introduction to cover. If you're planning to become a true JavaScript master, I suggest picking up *JavaScript: The Definitive Guide* by David Flanagan (O'Reilly and Associates, 1998) after making your way through this book. The last 500 or so pages of Flanagan's book not only list every JavaScript command, but also tell you in which browsers they work.

What Can JavaScript Do?

JavaScript can add interactivity to your Web pages in a number of ways. This book offers many examples of JavaScript's broad capabilities. The following are just two examples that illustrate what you can do with JavaScript.

The first example (Figure 1-1) is a flashing grid of colored squares (to get the full effect, visit http://hotwired.lycos.com/webmonkey/demo/96/35/ index4a.html or the bundled CD-ROM under chapter01/fig1-1.html) created by a fellow named Taylor. Flashy, isn't it? In this example, a JavaScript function changes the color of a randomly chosen square in the grid every second or so.

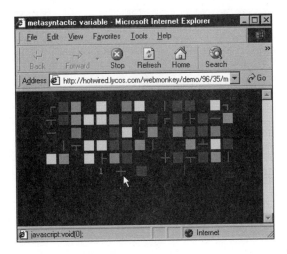

Figure 1-1: A demonstration of JavaScript's artful abilities

Mousing over one of the five icons below the squares (number, plus sign, square, letter, and horizontal line) tells the page to use that type of image for the new images appearing on the grid. For example, mousing over the number icon tells the JavaScript to start replacing the squares with 1s and 0s instead of different-colored squares. This page illustrates four important JavaScript features you'll learn about throughout the book: how to change images on a Web page, affect Web pages over time, add randomness to Web pages, and dynamically change what's happening on a Web page based on an action someone viewing the page takes.

Although Taylor's demo is beautiful, it's not the most useful application of JavaScript. Figure 1-2 (available on the CD-ROM in chapter1/figure1-2.html) shows you a *much* more useful page that calculates the weight of a fish based on its length. Enter the length and type of fish, and the JavaScript calculates the fish's weight. This fishy code demonstrates JavaScript's ability to read what a visitor has entered into a form, perform a mathematical calculation based on the input, and provide feedback by displaying the results in another part of the form. Maybe calculating a fish's weight isn't the most useful application of JavaScript either, but you can use the same skills to calculate a monthly payment on a loan (Chapter 7), score a quiz (Chapter 10), or verify that a visitor has provided a valid email address (Chapter 11).

These are just two examples of the many features JavaScript can add to your Web sites. Each chapter will cover at least one new application. If you want a preview of what you'll learn, read the first page or so of each chapter.

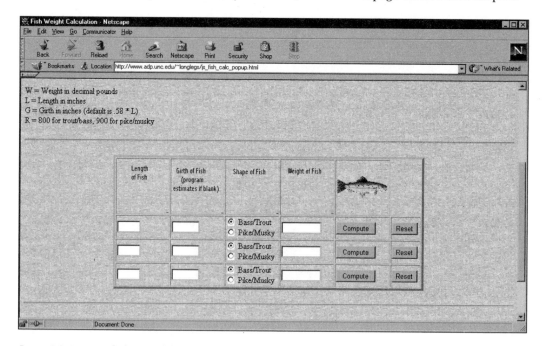

Figure 1-2: How much does my fish weigh?

What Are the Alternatives to JavaScript?

Several other programming languages can add interactivity to Web pages, but they all differ from JavaScript in important ways. The three main alternatives are CGI scripting, Java, and VBScript.

CGI Scripting

Before JavaScript, using CGI scripts was the only way to make Web pages do more than hyperlink to other Web pages. *CGI* (Common Gateway Interface— a language browsers and programs can use to communicate) scripts allow Web pages to send messages to computer programs on Web servers. For example, a Web browser can send information (perhaps the length and type of fish) to a CGI program that calculates the weight of fish. The program runs its calculations, formats the answer as an HTML page, and sends the answer back to the browser.

CGI scripts are very powerful, but because they reside on the Web server, they have some drawbacks. First, the connection between your Web browser and the Web server limits the speed of your Web page's interactivity. This may not sound like a big problem, but imagine the following scenario: You're filling out an order form with a dozen entry fields (such as name, address, and phone number—see Figure 1-3 on page 6), but you forget to include your phone number and address. When you press the Submit button to send the information across the Internet to the Web server, the Web server sees that you didn't fill out the form completely and sends a message back across the Internet requesting that you finish the job. This cycle could take quite a while over a slow connection. If you fill out the form incorrectly again, you have to wait through another cycle. People find this process tiresome, especially if they're customers who want their orders processed quickly.

With JavaScript, though, the programs you write run in the browser itself. This means the browser can make sure you've filled out the form correctly *before* sending the form's contents to the Web server. JavaScript reduces the time your information spends traveling between the browser and the server by waiting until you're really done before sending information.

Another drawback to CGI scripts is that the Web server running a CGI program can get bogged down if too many people use the program simultaneously. Serving up HTML pages is pretty easy for a Web server. However, some CGI programs take a long time to run on a machine, and each time someone tries to run the program, the server has to start up another copy of it. As more and more people try to run the program, the server slows down progressively. If 1,000 people run the program, the server might take so long to respond that some browsers give up, think the server is dead, and give visitors a "server busy" error. This problem doesn't exist in JavaScript because its programs run on each visitor's Web browser—not on the Web server.

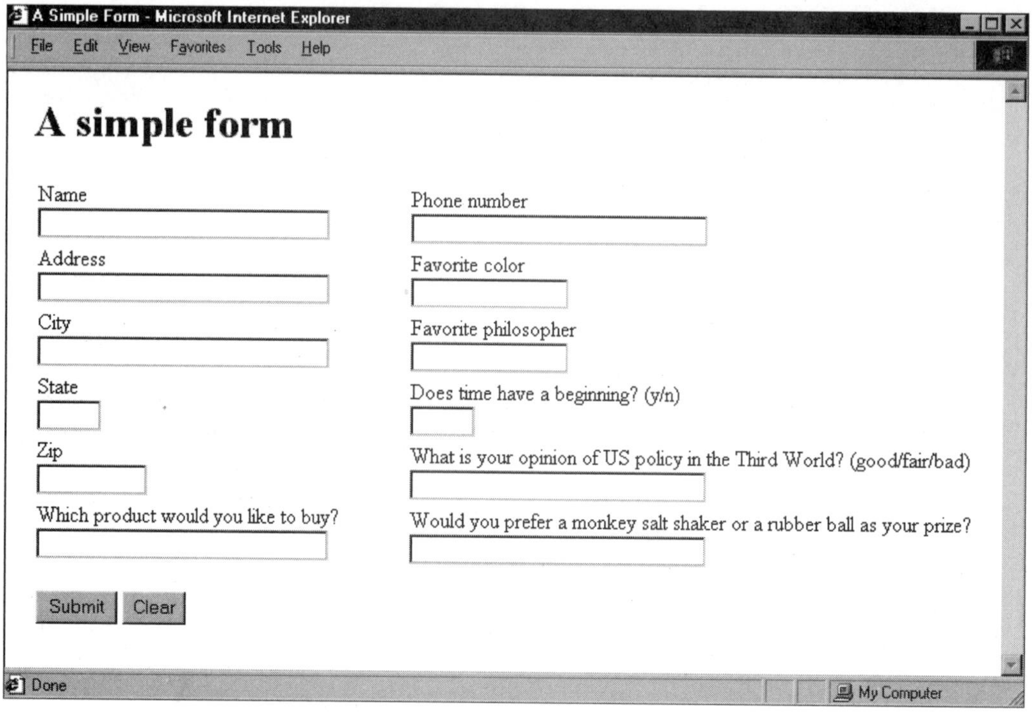

Figure 1-3: A simple order form

A third problem with CGI scripts is that not everyone has access to the parts of a Web server that can run CGI scripts. Since a CGI script can conceivably crash a Web server, engineers generally guard this area, only allowing fellow engineers access. JavaScript, on the other hand, goes right into the HTML of a Web page. If you can write a Web page, you can put JavaScript in the page without permission from recalcitrant engineers.

Java

Although JavaScript and Java have similar names, they aren't the same. Netscape initially created JavaScript to provide interactivity for Web pages, and Sun Microsystems wrote Java as a general programming language that works on all kinds of operating systems. As you'll see in Appendix A, though JavaScript can talk to Java programs, they're two totally separate languages.

VBScript

The language most similar to JavaScript is Microsoft's proprietary language, VBScript (VB stands for Visual Basic). Like JavaScript, VBScript runs on your Web browser and adds interactivity to Web pages. However, VBScript works only on computers running Microsoft Internet Explorer on Microsoft Windows, so unless you want to restrict your readership to people who use *that* browser on *that* operating system, you should go with JavaScript.

JavaScript's Limitations

Yes, JavaScript does have limitations—but they derive from its main purpose: to add interactivity to your Web pages.

JavaScript Can't Talk to Servers

One of JavaScript's drawbacks is also its main strength: It works entirely within the Web browser. As we've seen, this cuts down on the amount of time your browser spends communicating with a server. On the other hand, JavaScript can't handle some server tasks you may need to do.

The two primary tasks JavaScript can't handle are aggregating information from your users and communicating with other machines. If you want to write a survey that asks your visitors a couple of questions, stores their answers in a database, and sends an email thanks when they finish, you'll have to use a program on your server. As we'll see in Chapter 7, JavaScript *can* make the survey run more smoothly, but once a visitor has finished it, JavaScript can't store the information on the server—JavaScript works only on the browser and doesn't contact the server. In order to store the survey information, you need a CGI script or a Java applet, both of which fall outside the scope of this book.

Sending email with JavaScript is also a problem: Your JavaScript would have to contact a server to send the mail, and of course it can't do this. Again, you need a CGI script or Java applet for this job.

JavaScript Can't Create Graphics

Another of JavaScript's limitations is that it can't create its own graphics. Whereas more complicated languages can draw pictures, JavaScript can only manipulate existing pictures (that is, GIF or JPEG files). Luckily, because JavaScript can manipulate created images in so many ways, you shouldn't find this too limiting.

JavaScript Works Differently in Different Browsers

Perhaps the most annoying problem with JavaScript is that it works somewhat differently in various browsers. JavaScript first came out with Netscape 2.0 and has changed slightly with each new version of Netscape. Microsoft started including its own variation with Microsoft Internet Explorer 3.0 (MSIE) and added some features to its version of JavaScript when it introduced MSIE 4.0. Luckily, the core of JavaScript is identical in all the browsers; mostly the fancy stuff like Dynamic HTML (Chapter 13) is different. I've taken Netscape 3.0's JavaScript as the standard and I'll point out incompatibilities with other browsers as they come up throughout the book.

Getting Started

We're about ready to begin. You need a Web browser and a text editor. Any text editor will do: Notepad or Wordpad in Windows and SimpleText on a Macintosh are the simplest choices. Microsoft Word or Corel's WordPerfect will work as well. You can also use a text editor such as BBEdit and HomeSite—these are designed to work with HTML and JavaScript.

NOTE *Always save documents as text only and end their names with .html or .htm. Unless you tell Microsoft Word and WordPerfect otherwise, both programs write documents in formats Web browsers can't read. If you try to open a Web page you've written and the browser shows a lot of weird characters you didn't put in your document, go back and make sure you've saved it as text only.*

Some tools for building Web sites will actually write JavaScript for you—for example, Macromedia's DreamWeaver and GoLive's Cyberstudio 5.0. These tools work fine when you want to write common JavaScripts such as image rollovers and you know you'll never want to change them. Unfortunately, the JavaScript often ends up much longer than necessary, and you may find it difficult to understand and change to suit your needs. Unless you want a JavaScript that works *exactly* like one provided by the package you've purchased, you're often best off writing scripts by hand. However, these tools do a great job when you want to whip up a prototype. Once you've used the tool to figure out how you want your page to behave, you can go back and rewrite the script.

Where JavaScript Goes on Your Web Pages

Now let's get down to some JavaScript basics. Figure 1-4 shows you the thinnest possible skeleton of an HTML page with JavaScript. The numbered lines are JavaScript.

In Figure 1-4, you can see the JavaScript between the `<script language="JavaScript">` (❶) and `</script>` (❹) tags. With one exception, which Chapter 4 will cover, all JavaScript goes between these tags.

NOTE *You can't include any HTML between the open `<script>` and close `</script>` tags. While you're inside those tags, your browser assumes everything it sees is JavaScript. If it sees HTML in there, it gets confused and gives you an error message.*

The JavaScript tags can go in either the head or the body of your HTML page. It doesn't matter too much where you put them, although you're generally best off putting as much JavaScript in the head as possible. That way you don't have to look for it all over your Web pages.

```
  <html>
  <head>
  <title>JavaScript Skeleton</title>
❶ <script language="JavaScript">
❷ // JavaScript can go here!
❸ // But no HTML!
❹ </script>
  </head>
  <body>
❺ <script language="JavaScript">
❻ // JavaScript can go here too!
❼ // But no HTML!
❽ </script>
  </body>
  </html>
```

Figure 1-4: An HTML page with JavaScript

The lines that start with two slashes (❷, ❸, ❻, and ❼) are JavaScript comments. The browser ignores any text that appears after two slashes. Comments are extremely important because programming languages just aren't natural. The script you're writing may make perfect sense while you're writing it, but a few days later when you want to make a little modification, you might spend hours just figuring out what you wrote the first time. If you comment your code, you'll save yourself the hassle of trying to remember what you were thinking when you wrote that bizarre code at 2 a.m. in the midst of what seemed like an amazingly lucid caffeine haze.

Dealing with Older Browsers

There's a slight problem with the JavaScript skeleton in Figure 1-4 (other than the fact that it doesn't really have any JavaScript in it): Netscape didn't introduce the `<script>` tag until version 2.0, so any Netscape browser older than that won't recognize the tag.

When a browser sees an HTML tag it doesn't understand, it just ignores that tag. That's generally a good thing. However, a browser that doesn't understand JavaScript will write your lines of JavaScript to the browser as text. Figure 1-5 on page 10 shows what the JavaScript skeleton in Figure 1-4 would look like in an older browser.

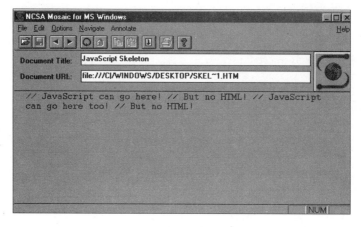

Figure 1-5: What Figure 1-4 would look like in an older browser

Hiding JavaScript from Older Browsers

For those who still use browsers like Microsoft Internet Explorer 2.0 or MacWeb 0.9, it's nice to add the code in ❶ and ❷ of Figure 1-6, which hides your JavaScript from them.

Figure 1-6: Hiding JavaScript from browsers that don't understand it

The important symbols are the `<!--` code at ❶ and the `// -->` comments at ❷. These weird lines work because older browsers see the `<!--` and `-->` code as marking an entire *block* of HTML comments, and just ignore everything between them. Luckily, browsers that understand JavaScript have different rules for HTML comments: They see everything from `<!--` to the end of that *line* as a comment, not the whole block between ❶ and ❷, so they won't ignore the JavaScript. The words in the tags ("hide me from older browsers" and "end hiding stuff") aren't important. You can make those whatever you want, or just leave them out entirely. It's the `<!--` and `// -->` tags that are important.

Frankly, this is a bit tough to understand. If you're having trouble wrapping your mind around why it works, don't worry—just remember to put the `<!--` tag on its own line right after `<script>` and the `// -->` tag on its own line right before `</script>`, and people with older browsers will thank you.

Your First JavaScript

It's time to run your first JavaScript program. I'll explain the code in Figure 1-7 in the next chapter, so for now just type the code into your text editor, save it as **my_first_program.html**, and then run it in your browser. If you don't want to type it all in, run the example from the CD-ROM under chapter01/fig1-7.html.

```
<html>
<head>
<title>JavaScript Skeleton</title>
</head>
<body>
<script language="JavaScript">
<!-- hide this from older browsers
// say hello world!
❶ alert("hello world!");
// end hiding comment -->
</script>
</body>
</html>
```

Figure 1-7: Your first JavaScript program

When a browser reads this Web page, the JavaScript at ❶ instructs the browser to put up a little window with the words hello world! in it. Figure 1-8 shows you what this looks like. Traditionally, this is the first script you write in any programming language. It gets you warmed up for the fun to come.

Figure 1-8: The "hello world!" script

Summary

Congratulations—you're now on your way to becoming a bona fide JavaScripter! This chapter has given you all the basic tools you need and has shown you how to get a very basic JavaScript program running. If you followed everything here, you now know:

- Some of the great things JavaScript can do.

- How JavaScript compares to CGI scripting, VBScript, and Java.

- JavaScript's main limitations.

- Where JavaScript goes on the page.

- How to write JavaScript older browsers won't misunderstand.

If you understood all that, you're ready to write some code!

Assignment

If you haven't tried typing Figure 1-7 into a text editor and running it in a Web browser, try it. You'll find next chapter's assignments hard to do if you can't get Figure 1-7 to work. If you're sure you've recreated Figure 1-7 exactly and it's not working, make sure you're saving the file as text-only. You may also find it helpful to peruse Chapter 14, which discusses ways to fix broken code. Although you may not understand everything in that chapter, you may find some helpful tips. It may also be wise to run the version of Figure 1-7 that is on your CD-ROM under chapter01/fig1-7.html. If that doesn't work, you may be using a browser that doesn't support JavaScript, or your browser may be set to reject JavaScript. If you're sure you're using a browser that supports JavaScript (Netscape 2.0 and higher versions, and Microsoft Internet Explorer 3.0 and higher), check your browser's options and make sure it's set to run JavaScript.

2

USING VARIABLES AND BUILT-IN FUNCTIONS TO UPDATE YOUR WEB PAGES AUTOMATICALLY

With JavaScript you can update the content on your pages automatically—every day, every hour, or every second. In this chapter, I'll focus on a simple script that automatically changes the date on your Web page.

Along the way you'll learn:

- How JavaScript uses variables to remember simple items like names and numbers.

- How JavaScript keeps track of more complicated items like dates.

- How to use JavaScript functions to write information to your Web page.

Before getting into the nuts and bolts of functions and variables, let's take a look at an example of a Web page that automatically updates itself. If you visit National Public Radio's Web site (http://www.npr.org/), you'll see that the time it displays changes every minute (Figure 2-1). How does NPR manage this? Does it have a team of volunteers who update the site every minute? On that budget? Forget about it.

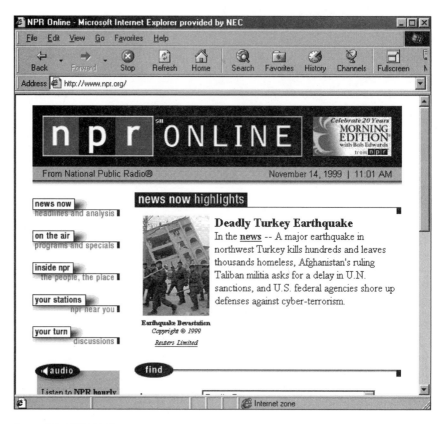

Figure 2-1: NPR's Web site

Instead of recruiting a merry band of Web volunteers, NPR uses JavaScript to determine the current time and write it to the Web page. The ability to write HTML to Web pages dynamically is one of JavaScript's most powerful features.

To understand how NPR updates the date and time on its page, you'll first have to learn about variables, strings, and functions. Your homework assignment at the end of this chapter will be to figure out how NPR updates the time.

Variables Store Information

Think back to those glorious days of algebra when you learned about variables and equations. For example, if x = 2, y = 3, and z = x + y, then z = 5. In algebra, variables like x, y, and z store or hold the place of numbers. In JavaScript, variables also store information.

Syntax

The *syntax* of variables (the rules for defining and using variables) is slightly different in JavaScript than it was in your algebra class. Figure 2-2 illustrates the syntax of variables in JavaScript with a silly script that figures out how many seconds there are in a day.

NOTE *Figure 2-2 does not write the results of the JavaScript to the Web page—I'll explain how to do that in Figure 2-3.*

```
<html>
<head>
<title>Seconds in a Day</title>

<script language = "JavaScript">
<!-- hide me from old browsers

❶ var seconds_per_minute = 60;
   var minutes_per_hour = 60;
   var hours_per_day = 24;

❷ var seconds_per_day = seconds_per_minute * minutes_per_hour * hours_per_day;

   // end hiding stuff -->
❸ </script>
</head>
<body>

<h1>Know how many seconds are in a day?</h1>
<h2>I do!</h2>

</body>
</html>
```

Figure 2-2: Defining and using variables

There's a lot going on here, so let's take it line by line. ❶ is a *statement* (a statement in JavaScript is like a sentence in English), and says to JavaScript, "Create a variable called seconds_per_minute, and set its value to 60." Notice that ❶ ends with a semicolon. Semicolons in JavaScript are like periods in English: They mark the end of a statement (for example, one that defines a variable, as above). As you see more and more statements, you'll get the hang of where to place semicolons.

The first word, var, introduces a variable for the first time—you don't need to use it after the first instance, no matter how many times you employ the variable in the script.

NOTE *Many people don't use* var *in their code. While most browsers let you get away without it, it's always a good idea to put* var *in front of a variable the first time you use it. (You'll see why when I talk about writing your own functions in Chapter 6).*

Naming Variables

Notice that, unlike algebra, the variable name in ❶ is pretty long—it's not just a single letter like x, y, or z. When using variables in JavaScript, you should give them names that reflect the value they hold. The variable in ❶ stores the number of seconds in a minute, so I've called it seconds_per_minute.

It's a good idea to name your variables descriptively; that makes it easier to understand your code later. Also, no matter what programming language you use, you'll spend about 50 percent of your coding time finding and getting rid of your mistakes. This is called *debugging*—and it's a lot easier to debug code when the variables have descriptive names.

Variable-Naming Rules

There are three rules for naming variables:

1. The initial character must be a letter, but subsequent characters may be numbers, underscores, or dashes.

2. No spaces are allowed.

3. Variables are case sensitive, so my_cat is different from My_Cat, which in turn is different from mY_cAt. To avoid any potential problems with capitalization, I use lowercase for all my variables, with underscores (_) instead of spaces.

Arithmetic with Variables

❷ in Figure 2-2 introduces a new variable called seconds_per_day, and sets it equal to the product of all the other variables using an asterisk (*), which means multiplication. A plus sign (+) for addition, a minus sign (-) for subtraction, and a slash (/) for division represent the other major arithmetic functions.

Moving On

When the browser finishes its calculations, it reaches the end of the JavaScript in the head (❸) and goes down to the body of the HTML. There it sees two lines of HTML announcing that the page knows how many seconds there are in a day.

```
<h1>Know how many seconds are in a day?</h1>
<h2>I do!</h2>
```

So now you have a page that knows how many seconds there are in a day. Big deal, right? Wouldn't it be better if we could at least tell our visitors what the answer is? Well, you can, and it's not very hard.

Write Here Right Now: Displaying Results

JavaScript uses the write()function to write stuff to a Web page. Figure 2-3 on page 18 shows how to use write() to let your visitors know how many seconds there are in a day. (The new code is in bold.)

Line-by-Line Analysis of Figure 2-3

❶ in Figure 2-3 writes the words there are to the Web page (only the words between the quote marks appear on the page). Don't worry about all the periods and what "window" and "document" really mean right now (I'll cover these topics in depth in Chapter 4, when we talk about image swaps). For now, just remember that if you want to write something to a Web page, use window.document.write("*whatever*");, placing the text you want written to the page between the quotes. If you don't use quotes around your text, as in

```
window.document.write(seconds_per_day);
```

then JavaScript interprets the text between the parentheses as a variable and writes whatever is stored in the variable (in this case, seconds_per_day) to the Web page (see Figure 2-4 on page 18). If you accidentally ask JavaScript to write out a variable you haven't defined, you'll get a JavaScript error.

```
<html>
<head>
<title>Seconds in a Day</title>

<script language = "JavaScript">
<!-- hide me from old browsers

var seconds_per_minute = 60;
var minutes_per_hour = 60;
var hours_per_day = 24;

var seconds_per_day = seconds_per_minute * minutes_per_hour * hours_per_day;

// end hiding stuff -->
</script>
</head>
<body>

<h1>My calculations show that . . .</h1>

<script language="JavaScript">
<!-- hide me

window.document.write("there are ");
window.document.write(seconds_per_day);
window.document.write(" seconds in a day.");

// show me -->
</script>

</body>
</html>
```

Figure 2-3: Use write() to write to a Web page

Figure 2-4: JavaScript's calculations

Be careful not to put quotes around variable names if you want JavaScript to know you're talking about a variable. Add quotes around the seconds_per_day variable, like this:

```
window.document.write("seconds_per_day");
```

and JavaScript writes the words seconds_per_day to the Web page. The way JavaScript knows the difference between variables and regular text is that regular text has quotes around it and variables don't.

Strings

Any series of characters between quotes is called a *string*. (You'll be seeing lots of strings throughout this book.) Strings are a basic type of information, like numbers—and like numbers, you can assign them to variables.

To assign a string to a variable, you'd write something like this:

```
var my_name = "thau!";
```

The word thau! is the string assigned to the variable my_name.

You can stick strings together with a plus (+) sign, as shown in the bolded section of Figure 2-5 on page 20. This figure illustrates how to write output to your page using strings.

The first new line in Figure 2-5,

```
var first_part = "there are ";
```

assigns the string "there are" to the variable first_part. The line

```
var last_part = " seconds in a day.";
```

sets the variable last_part to the string seconds in a day. ❶ glues together the values stored in first_part, seconds_per_day, and last_part. The end result is that the variable whole_thing includes the whole string you want to print to the page ("There are 86400 seconds in a day."). The window.document.write() line then writes whole_thing to the Web page.

NOTE *The methods shown in Figures 2-3 and 2-5 are both perfectly acceptable ways of writing "There are 86400 seconds in a day." However, there are times when storing strings in variables and then assembling them with the plus (+) sign is the best way to go. We'll see a case of this when we finally get to putting the date on a page.*

```
<html>
<head>
<title>Seconds in a Day</title>

<script language = "JavaScript">
<!-- hide me from old browsers

var seconds_per_minute = 60;
var minutes_per_hour = 60;
var hours_per_day = 24;

var seconds_per_day = seconds_per_minute * minutes_per_hour * hours_per_day;

// end hiding stuff -->
</script>
</head>
<body>

<h1>My calculations show that . . . </h1>

<script language="JavaScript">
<!-- hide me

var first_part = "there are ";
var last_part = " seconds in a day.";
❶ var whole_thing = first_part + seconds_per_day + last_part;

window.document.write(whole_thing);

// show me -->
</script>

</body>
</html>
```

Figure 2-5: Putting strings together

More About Functions

Whereas variables store information, functions process information.

All functions take the form *functionName*(). Sometimes there's something in the parentheses and sometimes there isn't. You've already seen one of JavaScript's many built-in functions: window.document.write(), which writes whatever lies between the parentheses to the Web page. Before diving into the date functions you'll need to write the date to your Web page, I want to talk about two interesting functions, just so you get the hang of how functions work.

The alert() Function

One handy function is alert(), which puts a string into a little announcement box (also called an *alert box*). Figure 2-6 demonstrates how to call an alert() and Figure 2-7 shows you what the alert box looks like.

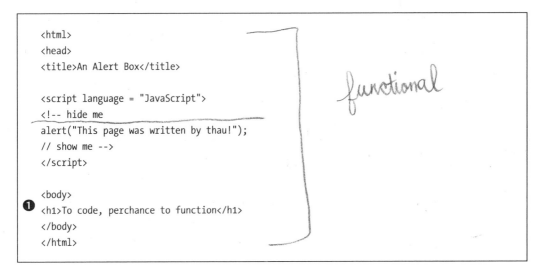

```
<html>
<head>
<title>An Alert Box</title>

<script language = "JavaScript">
<!-- hide me
alert("This page was written by thau!");
// show me -->
</script>

<body>
❶ <h1>To code, perchance to function</h1>
</body>
</html>
```

functional

Figure 2-6: Creating an alert box

Figure 2-7: The alert box

The first thing visitors see when they come to the page Figure 2-6 creates is an alert box announcing that I wrote the page (Figure 2-7).

While the alert box is on the screen, the browser stops doing any work. Clicking OK in the alert box makes it go away and allows the browser to finish drawing the Web page. In this case, that means writing the words "To code, perchance to function" to the page (❶).

The alert() function is useful when your JavaScript isn't working correctly. Let's say you typed in Figure 2-5, but when you run it, it says there are 0 seconds in a year instead of 86400. You can use alert() to find out how the different variables are set before multiplication occurs. The script in Figure 2-8 contains an error that causes the script to say there are undefined seconds in a year, as well as alert() function statements that tell you why this problem is occurring.

```
<html>
<head>
<title>Seconds in a Day</title>

<script language = "JavaScript">
<!-- hide me from old browsers

var seconds_per_minute = 60;
var minutes_per_hour = 60;
❶ var Hours_per_day = 24;
❷ alert("seconds per minute is: " + seconds_per_minute);
❸ alert("minutes per hour is: " + minutes_per_hour);
❹ alert("hours per day is: " + hours_per_day);
❺ var seconds_per_day = seconds_per_minute * minutes_per_hour * hours_per_day;



// end hiding stuff -->
</script>
</head>
<body>

<h1>My calculations show that . . . </h1>

<script language="JavaScript">
<!-- hide me

var first_part = "there are ";
var last_part = " seconds in a day.";
var whole_thing = first_part + seconds_per_day + last_part;

window.document.write(whole_thing);

// show me -->
</script>

</body>
</html>
```

Figure 2-8: Using alert to find out what's wrong

The problem with this script is in ❶. Notice the accidental capitalization of the first letter in Hours_per_day. This causes the script to misbehave, because ❺ is multiplying the variable hours_per_day with the other numbers—and because hours_per_day was not set, JavaScript thinks its value is either 0 or undefined, depending on your browser. Multiplying anything by 0 results in 0, so the script indicates that there are 0 seconds in a day. The same holds true for browsers that think Hours_per_day is undefined. Multiplying anything by something undefined results in the answer being undefined.

This script is short, making it easy to see the mistake. However, in longer scripts it's sometimes hard to figure out what's wrong. I've added ❷, ❸, and ❹ in this example to help diagnose the problem. Each of these lines puts a variable into an alert box. The alert on ❷ will say seconds_per_hour is: 60. The alert on ❹ will say hours_per_day is: 0. or, depending on your browser, the alert won't appear at all. Either way, you'll know there's a problem with the hours_per_day variable. If you can't figure out the mistake by reading the script, you'll find this type of information very valuable. Alerts are a very useful debugging tool.

The prompt() Function

Another helpful built-in function, the prompt() function asks your visitor for some information and then sets a variable equal to whatever your visitor types. Figure 2-9 on page 24 shows how you might use prompt() to write a form letter.

Notice that prompt()on ❶ has two strings inside the parentheses: "What's your name?" and "put your name here". If you run the code in Figure 2-9, you'll see a prompt box that resembles Figure 2-10 on page 24. Type your name and choose **OK**, and the page responds with Dear <put your name here>, Thank you for coming to my Web page.

The text above the box where your visitors will type their name ("What's your name?") is the first string in the prompt function; the text inside the box ("put your name here") is the second string. If you don't want anything inside the box, put two quotes ("") right next to each other in place of the second string to keep that space blank:

```
var the_name = prompt("What's your name?", "");
```

If you look at the JavaScript in the body (starting at ❷), you'll see how to use the variable the_name. First write <h1> to the page using normal HTML. Then launch into JavaScript and use **document.write(the_name)** to write whatever name the visitor typed into the prompt box for your page. If your visitor typed "yertle the turtle" into that box, "yertle the turtle" gets written to the page. Once the item in the_name is written, you close the JavaScript tag, write a comma and the **</h1>** tag using regular old HTML, and then continue with the form letter. Nifty, eh?

```
<html>
<head>
<title>A Form Letter</title>
<script language = "JavaScript">
<!-- hide me
```

❶ `var the_name = prompt("What's your name?", "put your name here");`

```
// show me -->
</script>
</head>
<body>
<h1>Dear
```

❷
```
<script language = "JavaScript">
<!-- hide me

document.write(the_name);

// show me -->
</script>

,</h1>

Thank you for coming to my Web page.

</body>
</html>
```

Figure 2-9: Use prompt() to write a form letter

Figure 2-10: Starting a form letter with a prompt box

The prompt() function is handy, since it enables your visitor to supply the variable information. In this case, after the user types a name into the prompt box in Figure 2-10 (thereby setting the variable the_name), your script can use the supplied information by calling that variable.

Parameters

The words inside the parentheses of functions are called *parameters*. The document.write() function requires one parameter: a string to write to your Web page. The prompt() function takes two parameters: a string to write above the box and a string to write inside the box.

Parameters are the only aspect of functions you can control. With a prompt() function, for example, you can't change the color of the box, how many buttons it has, or anything else. All you can do is change its parameters.

Writing the Date to Your Web Page

Now that you know about variables and functions, you can print the date to your Web page. To do so, you must first ask JavaScript to check the local time on your visitor's computer clock:

```
var now = new Date();
```

The first part of this line, var now =, should look familiar. It sets the variable now to some value. The second part, new Date(), is new: It creates an *object*.

Objects store data that require multiple bits of information, such as a particular moment in time. For example, in JavaScript you need an object to describe 2:30 p.m. on Tuesday, November 7, 2000, in San Francisco. That's because it requires many different bits of information: the time, day, month, date, and year, as well as some representation (in relation to Greenwich mean time) of the user's local time, and so on. As you can imagine, working with objects is a bit more complicated than working with just a number or a string.

Because dates are so rich in information, JavaScript has a built-in date object. When you want the user's current date and time, you use new Date() to tell JavaScript to create a date object with all the correct information.

NOTE *You must capitalize the letter D in "Date" to tell JavaScript you want to use the built-in date object. If you don't capitalize it, JavaScript won't know what kind of object you're trying to create, and you'll get an error message.*

Built-in Date Functions

Now that JavaScript has created your date object, let's extract information from it using JavaScript's built-in date functions. To extract the current year, use the date object's getYear() function:

```
var now = new Date();
var the_year = now.getYear();
```

Date and Time Methods

In the code above, the variable now is a date object and the function getYear() is the *method* of the date object. Date methods get information about the date from date objects. To apply the getYear() method to the date stored in the variable now, you would write:

```
now.getYear()
```

Table 2-1 lists commonly used date methods. (You can find a complete list of date methods in Appendix B.)

Table 2-1: Commonly used date and time methods

Name	Description
getDate()	Day of the month as an integer from 1 to 31
getDay()	Day of the week as an integer where 0 is Sunday and 1 is Monday
getHours()	The hour as an integer between 0 and 23
getMinutes()	The minutes as an integer between 0 and 59
getMonth()	The month as an integer between 0 and 11 where 0 is January and 11 is December
getSeconds()	The seconds as an integer between 0 and 59
getTime()	The current time in milliseconds where 0 is January 1, 1970, 00:00:00
getYear()	The year, but this format differs from browser to browser: Some versions of Netscape, like Netscape 4.0 for the Mac, always return the current year minus 1900. So if it's the year 2010, getYear() returns 110. Other versions of Netscape return the full four-digit year except if the year is in the 1900s, in which case they return just the last two digits. Netscape 2.0 can't deal with dates before 1970 at all. Any date before Jan. 1, 1970 is stored as Dec. 31, 1969. In Microsoft Internet Explorer, getYear() returns the full four-digit year if the year is greater than 1999 or earlier than 1900. If the year is between 1900 and 1999, it returns the last two digits. Don't you love it? All this weirdness occurred because the people who built the browsers didn't know how to deal with the year 2000.

NOTE *Notice that* getMonth() *returns a number between 0 and 11; if you want to show the month to your site's visitors, add 1 to the month after using* getMonth() *(see ➍ in Figure 2-11). JavaScript also suffers from the dreaded Y2K problem: Both Microsoft Internet Explorer and Netscape deal with years in strange ways. (You'd figure a language created in 1995 wouldn't have the Y2K problem, but the ways of software developers are strange.) I'll show you later how to fix this bug.*

Writing the Date: The Code

To get the day, month, and year, we use the getDate(), getMonth(), and getYear() methods.

Figure 2-11 on page 28 shows you the complete code for writing the month and day to a Web page.

If you run the code in Figure 2-11 on June 16, you'll see that it says "Today's date is: 6/16." Here are a few interesting things in this example.

Adjusting the month   ❶ through ❸ get the date from the computer's clock and then use the appropriate date methods to get the day and month. ❹ adds 1 to the month because getMonth() thinks January is month 0.

Getting the string right   ❺ builds the string we're going to print in the body of the page. Here's the wrong way to do it:

```
var the_whole_date = "the_month / the_day";
```

If you write your code this way, you'll get a line that says "The current date is the_month / the_day." Why? JavaScript doesn't look up variables if they're inside quotes. So place the variables outside the quote marks and glue everything together using plus (+) signs:

```
var the_whole_date = the_month + "/" + the_day;
```

JavaScript and HTML   Make sure to place your JavaScript and HTML in the proper order. In Figure 2-11, the HTML line Today's date is: precedes the JavaScript that actually writes the date, since the browser first writes that text and then executes the JavaScript. With JavaScript, as with HTML, browsers read from the top of the page down. I've put document.write() in the body so that the actual date information will come after the Today's date is: text. I've put the rest of the JavaScript at the head of the page to keep the body HTML cleaner.

document.write()   Notice that the code in Figure 2-11 uses document.write() instead of window.document.write(). In general, it's fine to drop the word window and the first dot before the word document. In future chapters I'll tell you when the word window must be added. Did you get all that? Good. Now let's look at NPR's slightly more complicated way of writing the date to a Web page.

How NPR Did It

Figure 2-12 on page 29 shows you how NPR writes the date to its page. See if you can figure out what is going on, and then look at my explanation. Because this script is a little long, I've excerpted only the code that deals with printing the date (this chunk of code won't run independently); I've also added comments to make it a bit clearer.

```
<html>
<head>
<title>Write the Date</title>
<script language="JavaScript">
<!-- hide me

// get the date information
//
❶ var today = new Date();
❷ var the_day = today.getDate();
❸ var the_month = today.getMonth();

// correct for the month starting from zero
//
❹ the_month = the_month + 1;

// create the string you want to print
//
❺ var the_whole_date = the_month + "/" + the_day;

// show me -->
</script>
</head>
<body>

Today's date is:

<script language="JavaScript">
<!-- hide me

// write the date
//
document.write(the_whole_date);

// show me -->
</script>

</body>
</html>
```

Figure 2-11: Getting today's day and month

```
    <SCRIPT language="JavaScript">

    // get the date information
    //
①  date = new Date();
②  month = new String;
③  day = new String;
④  year = new String;

⑤  month = date.getMonth()
⑥  day = date.getDate()
    // This is the y2k fixer function--don't worry about how this works,
    // but if you want it in your scripts, you can cut and paste it.
    //
⑦  function y2k(number) {
⑧   return (number < 1000) ? number + 1900 : number;
⑨  }

    // Get the year and fix the y2k bug using the fixer function.
    //
⑩  year = y2k(date.getYear())

    // Translate the number of the month to a word--so 0 becomes January.
    // Notice that I've cut months 3 to 10 to save space.  if you want to
    // run this example, you'll have to put those in place of the ellipsis, . . .
    //
⑪  if (month == "0")
        month = "January";
        else
    if (month == "1")
        month = "February";
        else
    if (month == "2")
        month = "March";
    ...


    if (month == "11")
        month = "December";

    // write the information
    //
⑫  document.write(month + " " + day + ", " + year);

    </script>
```

Figure 2-12: NPR's code

❶ should look familiar by now—it loads the current date into a variable called date.

❷ through ❹ are a little strange. They declare the variables that will hold the month, day, and year as strings. I'm not sure why NPR does this; the command new String causes an error in Netscape version 2. To declare the variables ahead of time, one should use var. I would have written:

```
var month, day, year;
```

This would declare the variables, but wouldn't tell JavaScript ahead of time that they're going to be strings.

❺ and ❻ use the date methods to get the month and day.

The rest of the script, up until the last line, may seem like mumbo-jumbo at this point, so I'll just tell you what the lines are doing without going into detail about how they work. ❼ through ❿ determine the year and take care of the Y2K problem I mentioned earlier. The script beginning with function y2k(number) creates a function that turns a number into the proper four-digit year. (I'll describe how this function works in Chapter 6.) To teach your script how to deal with Y2K issues, put the following lines in it:

```
function y2k(number) {
 return (number < 1000) ? number + 1900 : number;
}
```

Then, instead of using getYear() to get the year, write this to yield the appropriate four-digit number, regardless of the browser:

```
var year = y2k(date.getYear());
```

The part of the script beginning with if (⓫) turns the number from getMonth() into the name of the month. So instead of months 0, 1, and 2, we get January, February, and March. (I'll discuss this script more in Chapter 3.)

The last line (⓬) prints the month, day, and year to the Web page, inserting a space between the month and the day and a comma and space between the day and the year.

Voilà—you've written a date to the page.

Some Picky Notes About the NPR Script

A few little syntactical inconsistencies in NPR's code are worth pointing out, though none of them will cause big problems.

- The lack of comment tags (<!-- and // -->) will cause a problem with older browsers.

- It doesn't declare variables with var.

- Sometimes statements end with semicolons and sometimes they don't. (The JavaScript archaeologist in me believes that many hands have touched this script.) Although you can leave semicolons out, it's good practice to include them consistently at the end of your statements.

Summary

This chapter was chock full of JavaScript goodness. Here's a review of the most important points for you to understand:

- How to declare and use variables (use var the first time and use valid and descriptive variable names).

- How to write to Web pages with document.write().

- How to get the current date from JavaScript with the Date() object and its various methods.

If you got all that, you're well on your way to becoming a JavaScript superstar. Try the assignment below to stretch your JavaScript skills.

Assignment

Use the getHours(), getMinutes(), and getSeconds() methods of the Date() object to add the time to the script in Figure 2-10, then look at how NPR prints the time on its site. Though getHours() returns the hour as a number between 0 and 23, NPR prefers its time on a 12-hour clock. So instead of 19:40:33, the NPR site shows 7:40:33 p.m.

Once you've completed this exercise, look at NPR's JavaScript to see how it massages the hour into what NPR wants. You may not understand what's going on in the script right now, but you will by the end of the next chapter.

3

GIVE THE BROWSERS
WHAT THEY WANT

Much to the dismay of Web developers everywhere, different browsers implement JavaScript and HTML in slightly different ways. Wouldn't it be great if you could serve each browser exactly the content it could understand?

Fortunately, you can use JavaScript to find out which browser a visitor is using and, armed with this information, deliver content suitable for that specific browser.

This chapter covers the three topics you need to understand to deliver browser-specific pages:

- How to find out which browser your visitor is using.

- How to redirect the visitor to other pages automatically.

- How to send the visitor to the page you want, depending on which browser he or she is using.

Netboost.com: A Real-World Example of Browser Detection

Before we get into the details of browser detection and redirection, let's take a look at a real-world example.

Netboost (www.netboost.com), a company that sells software to high-end systems administrators, has a Web site (shown in Figure 3-1) that uses a lot of tricky JavaScript and Dynamic HTML (DHTML). Unfortunately, its DHTML works only in Microsoft Internet Explorer 4.0, so Netboost needs to redirect visitors who have other browsers to a page that does not contain the problematic code. Netboost uses JavaScript to determine which browser a visitor is using and then redirects the visitor to the appropriate page, if necessary.

If you visit Netboost using Netscape, the site redirects you to a Web page called neindex.html, specifically designed for Netscape browsers (Figure 3-2). If you have a version of MSIE older than 4.0, the site redirects you to a Web page called ie3index.html. Don't worry if you don't understand how this works—the rest of this chapter will explain the code that allows Netboost's site to work its magic.

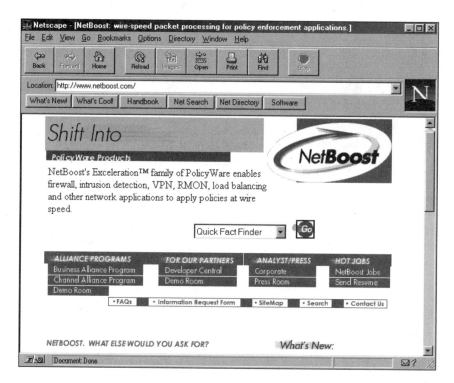

Figure 3-1: Netboost's home page

NOTE   *Redirecting visitors to different pages is only one way to deal with the differences between browsers. When we talk about image swapping in Chapter 4, we'll learn some other ways.*

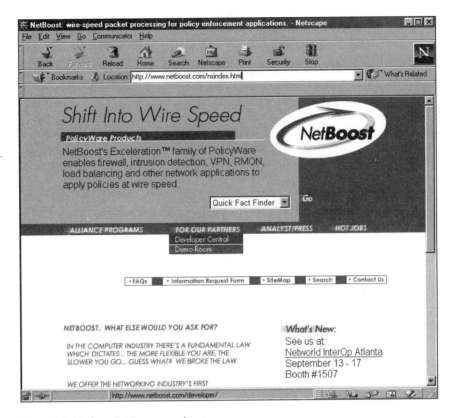

Figure 3-2: Netboost's Netscape redirect

The ability to send people to different pages according to what browser they're using depends on three things. First you have to figure out what browser they're using. Then you have to figure out where to redirect them. Finally, you have to know how to redirect them.

Let's first talk about figuring out what kind of browser a visitor is using.

Browser Detection

To determine the browser's identity, you need to know the company that made the browser and the version number.

The line

```
var browser_name = navigator.appName;
```

determines who made the browser. If the browser is a Netscape browser, browser_name equals the string "Netscape". If it's a Microsoft Internet Explorer browser, browser_name equals "Microsoft Internet Explorer". Every

JavaScript-enabled browser must have the variable navigator.appName. If you use Opera, navigator.appName equals "Opera".

Once you've figured out who built the browser, you have to determine its version. The key variable is navigator.appVersion. Unfortunately, navigator.appVersion isn't just a number, but a crazy string that varies from browser to browser. For example, Netscape 2.02 on a Macintosh sets navigator.appVersion to "2.02 (Macintosh; I; PPC)" (*PPC* stands for PowerPC and *I* stands for international version, which means the browser doesn't have U.S. trade secrets built into it). Microsoft Internet Explorer 4.0 running under Windows 95 has a navigator.appVersion that looks like this: "4.0 (compatible; MSIE 4.0; Windows 95)." It's ironic—the way to handle browser inconsistencies is itself inconsistent from browser to browser.

JavaScript can pick out the version numbers from those navigator.appVersion strings with the parseFloat() command, which looks at the string and grabs the first item that resembles a floating point number (a number that contains a decimal point). In the case of navigator.appVersion, that number is the browser version.[1] Thus the line

```
var browser_version = parseFloat(navigator.appVersion);
```

sets the variable browser_version to the version number of the visitor's browser.

Together, navigator.appName and navigator.appVersion tell you what browser you're using. Try the script in Figure 3-3 on your own browser.

```
<script language="JavaScript">
<!-- hide me from old browsers

var browser_name = navigator.appName;
var browser_version = parseFloat(navigator.appVersion);
document.write ("you're using " + browser_name + " version " +
 browser_version);

// show me -->
</script>
```

Figure 3-3: Finding the browser version number with parseFloat()

---

1 Annoyingly, there seems to be an exception to even this simple trick. The navigator.appVersion string for MSIE 5.0 is "4.0 (compatible; MSIE 5.0; Windows 95)." If you use the parseFloat() trick, your JavaScript will think that the 5.0 browser is a 4.0 browser. As far as I know, however, JavaScript is implemented the same way in MSIE 4.0 and MSIE 5.0. If you really want to distinguish MSIE 5.0 and 4.0, you'll have to use some of the fancy string-handling routines covered in Chapter 11.

Redirecting Visitors to Other Pages

Redirecting visitors to other pages is a simple process. To redirect someone to the No Starch Press Web site, for example, you'd write

```
window.location = "http://www.nostarch.com/";
```

When JavaScript sees a line like this, it loads the page with the specified URL into the browser.

NOTE *You're probably asking, "What's with all these periods in commands like* window.location *and* navigator.appName*?" This is a good question, and when I talk about image swaps in the next chapter, I'll also describe the dot notation. For now, just take my word for it—there is a method to the madness.*

if-then Statements

Now you know what browser your visitor is using and how to redirect him or her. Next, you need to find out how to tell JavaScript which page to send someone to. To redirect visitors to Web pages based on what browser they have, you tell JavaScript something like: "*If* the visitor is using Netscape, *then* send them to the Netscape-tailored page." In JavaScript, an *if-then* statement looks like this:

```
if (navigator.appName == "Netscape")
{
    // send them to the netscape page
    window.location = "netscape_page.html";
}
```

Here's the basic structure of an if-then statement:

```
if (some test)
{
 statement_1;
 statement_2;
 statement_3;

    ...

}
```

NOTE *JavaScript is unforgiving:* if *must be lowercase, and you must put parentheses around the test that follows it.*

The statement that appears between the parentheses is either true or false. If navigator.appName equals "Netscape," the statement between the parentheses is true, and the statements located between the curly brackets are executed. If navigator.appName doesn't equal "Netscape," the statement between the parentheses is false, and the statements between the curly brackets aren't executed.

Booleans

The statement in the parentheses after if is a *Boolean* statement—one that's either true or false. There are many types of Boolean statements. Table 3-1 lists the major ones you'll be using.

Table 3-1: Boolean statements

Test	Meaning	Example (all of these are true)
<	Less than	1 < 3
>	Greater than	3 > 1
==	The same as (equal)	"happy" == "happy", 3 == 3
!=	Different from (not equal)	"happy" != "crabby", 3 != 2
<=	Less than or equal to	2 <= 3, 2 <= 2
>=	Greater than or equal to	3 >= 1, 3 >=3

Use Two Equal Signs in if-then Statements

You must use two equal signs when you want JavaScript to see if two things are the same in an if-then statement. Accidentally using one equal sign inside an if-then statement is probably *the* major cause of mind-blowing programming errors. If you accidentally use only one equal sign, JavaScript thinks you mean to set the variable on the left of the equal sign to equal whatever is on the right of the equal sign, and it will act as if the test result is always true.

Here's an example of the trauma that this mistake can cause. Let's say you want to write a JavaScript that puts "Happy Birthday, Mom!" on your Web page when it's your mother's birthday. Say her birthday is August 6—you'd write something like Figure 3-4 (which contains the dreaded error).

If you try this script, you'll see that it *always* prints "Happy Birthday, Mom!" to the Web page, which is great for Mom, but probably not what you want. The script starts off correctly. When JavaScript sees

```
var month = today.getMonth();
```

it sets the variable month to whatever month it is. If you're running the script in March, it sets month to 2. The problem arises in the next line

```
if (month = 7)
```

```
<script language="JavaScript">
<!-- hide me from old browsers

var today = new Date();
var day = today.getDate();
var month = today.getMonth();

if (month = 7) // remember, January is month 0, so August is month 7
{
    if (day = 6)
    {
            document.write("<h1>Happy Birthday, Mom!</h1>");
    }
}

// show me -->
</script>
```

Figure 3-4: Mom's birthday—broken version

Here JavaScript sees one equal sign and thinks you want to set the variable month to the value 7. The script does what you're telling it to do, and then acts as if your test is true. Since the result is true, JavaScript moves to the curly brackets, where it finds another if-then statement that tells it to set the variable day to the value 6. It does this, then moves to the second set of curly brackets. There it sees that it's supposed to write <h1>Happy Birthday, Mom!</h1>, which it does—every time someone visits the page.

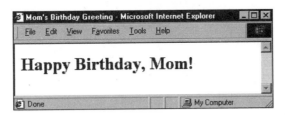

Figure 3-5: Mom's birthday greeting

NOTE *I remember the difference between one and two equal signs by thinking "is the same as" when I'm doing an if-then clause, and remembering that "is the same as" translates into two equal signs.*

Nesting

Figure 3-4 is the first example I've used of *nesting*—one if-then clause inside another. Although it sometimes makes sense to nest your if-then clauses, things get confusing if you start to get three or more levels deep. Try to write your code so it doesn't need more than two levels.

if-then-else Statements

There are a couple of fancier versions of the if-then statement. The first is the if-then-else statement:

```
if (navigator.appName == "Netscape")
{
    // send 'em to the Netscape-tailored page
    window.location = "netscape.html";
}
else
{
    // send 'em to the Microsoft Internet Explorer page
    window.location = "msie.html";
}
```

This reads nicely in English if you read "else" as "otherwise": "If they're using Netscape, send them to netscape.html; otherwise send them to msie.html."

if-then-else-if Statements

The above code assumes that there are only two browser manufacturers in the world, when there are actually several. We can solve this problem with an if-then-else-if statement that sends a visitor with a browser other than MSIE or Netscape to a page called unknown_browser.html.

```
if (navigator.appName == "Netscape")
{
    // send 'em to the Netscape-tailored page
    window.location = "netscape.html";
}
else if (navigator.appName == "Microsoft Internet Explorer")
{
    // send 'em to the Microsoft Internet Explorer page
    window.location = "msie.html";
}
else
```

```
{
    // send 'em to the default page
    window.location = "unknown_browser.html";
}
```

This code reads in English as: "If they're using Netscape, send them to netscape.html; if they're using Microsoft Internet Explorer, send them to msie.html. Otherwise send them to unknown_browser.html."

The *or* and *and* Operators

The if-then statements we've seen so far are pretty simple. You might, however, want to add more conditions to an if-then statement (for example, "If Joe is in high school *and* is not doing his homework, then tell him to get to work"). To add more conditions to an if-then statement, use the *or* and *and* operators.

or

Suppose you want to give different greetings to people who come to your site, depending on who they are. You could, as in Figure 3-6, use a prompt box to ask for a visitor's name (Figure 3-7), and then use an if-then statement to determine which greeting to give.

```
<script language="JavaScript">
<!-- hide me from old browsers

var the_name = prompt("what's your name?", "");
if (the_name == "thau")
{
    document.write("Welcome back, thau! Long time no see!");
} else {
    document.write("Greetings, " + the_name + ". Good to see you.");
}

// show -->
</script>
```

Figure 3-6: Asking for a visitor's name with the prompt box

Figure 3-7: The prompt box asking for a visitor's name

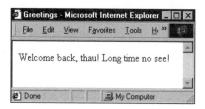

Figure 3-8: thau's greeting

This example greets thau with `Welcome back, thau! Long time no see!` (Figure 3-8) and everyone else with `Greetings, <name>. Good to see you.` If you wanted to greet others the same way you greet thau, you could use a series of if-then statements as in Figure 3-9.

```
if (the_name == "thau")
{
     document.write("Welcome back, thau! Long time no see!");
}
else if (the_name == "dave")
{
     document.write("Welcome back, dave! Long time no see!");
}
else if (the_name == "pugsly")
{
     document.write("Welcome back, pugsly! Long time no see!");
}
else if (the_name == "gomez")
{
     document.write("Welcome back, gomez! Long time no see!");
}
else
{
     document.write("Greetings, " + the_name + ". Good to see you.");
}
```

Figure 3-9: Personalized greetings with a series of if-then statements

This would work, but as you can see, there's a lot of waste here. We repeat basically the same document.write() line four times. What we really want to say is something like: "If the_name is thau, or dave, or pugsly, or gomez, give the 'Long time no see' greeting." Here's where the **or** operator comes in handy. Figure 3-10 shows **or** in use:

```
if ((the_name == "thau") || (the_name == "dave") ||
 (the_name == "pugsly") || (the_name == "gomez"))
{
    document.write("Welcome back, " + the_name + "! Long time no see!");
}
```

Figure 3-10: The or operator

Two vertical lines (||) represent or—you'll usually find these above the backslash (\) key.

NOTE *While each of the Boolean tests (for example,* the_name=="thau"*) has its own parentheses, these aren't strictly necessary. However, the set of parentheses around all four Boolean tests is required, and it's a good idea to include the other parentheses for legibility's sake.*

and

Another important operator is **and**, represented by two ampersands (&&). Figure 3-11 shows this operator in use.

```
var age = prompt("how old are you?", "");
var drinking = prompt("are you drinking alcohol (yes or no)?", "yes");

if ((age < 21) && (drinking == "yes"))
{
    document.write("beat it!");
}
else
{
    document.write("enjoy the show!");
}
```

Figure 3-11: The and operator

When bars have robot bouncers that run on JavaScript, this is the kind of code they'll be running. The example asks a person's age and whether he or she is drinking alcohol. If the person is under 21 and is drinking alcohol, the bouncer tells him or her to beat it. Otherwise, the visitor is perfectly legal and is welcome to stay.

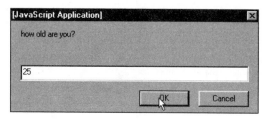
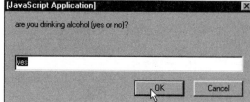

Figure 3-12: The bouncer's questions

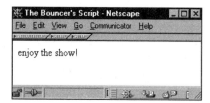

Figure 3-13: The bouncer's response

Putting It All Together

Now we know enough to understand how Netboost redirects visitors. Remember, its home page redirects users to one page if they're using Netscape and another page if they're using Microsoft Internet Explorer 3.0. Figure 3-14 on the opposite page shows Netboost's code.

Netboost has broken the code into two blocks of script tags. The first sets up the variables and the second does the redirection. Declaring variables at the top of your script is a good idea— if you want to change a variable later, you won't have to go hunting through a lot of HTML and JavaScript to find it.

Netboost does a few things differently from what I've covered in this chapter. In ❶, for example, Netboost uses parseInt() instead of parseFloat(). The parseInt() command does exactly what parseFloat() does, except that instead of pulling out the first floating point number it sees, it pulls out the first integer. If someone's using Netscape 4.5, parseInt() will say the version number is 4. That's fine if you only care whether the visitor has version 2, 3, or 4 and you don't need to distinguish 4.1 and 4.5. Since Netboost only needs to separate MSIE 4.0 and higher browsers from earlier versions of MSIE, both parseFloat() and parseInt() will do the trick.

```
    <script language="JavaScript">
    <!-- hide me from old browsers

    browserName = navigator.appName;
❶  browserVer = parseInt(navigator.appVersion);

    if (browserVer >=4) { version = "n4";

        } else {version = "n3"; }

❷  if (browserName == "Microsoft Internet Explorer" && version == "n3") {

        browser = "ie3";

❸  } else browser = "other";

    // stop hiding -->

    </script>

    <SCRIPT language="JavaScript">

    <!--

        if (browserName == "Netscape") {

❹  document.location.href = "neindex.html";

        } else if (browser == "ie3") {

❺  document.location.href = "ie3index.html";

        }

    // -->
    </script>
```

Figure 3-14: Netboost's redirection code

When and Where to Place Curly Brackets

Netboost formats its if-then statements a little differently than I have in this chapter. In ❷, for example, the Netboost coder puts the opening curly bracket right after the if-then clause, like this:

```
if (something == something_else) {
 blah_blah_blah;
}
```

Where you put the curly brackets is really a matter of taste. Many studies have tried to figure out which formatting style is most readable or which avoids bugs. When you get right down to it, just decide what you think looks good and go with that.

Note also that the browser="other" part in ❸ doesn't have curly brackets around it. This is legal; if the body of an if-then statement has only one line, it doesn't need curly brackets. However, it's always a good idea to put them in, because you might want to add a second line to that else clause. If you do so and forget to put the brackets around the two lines, your script won't work. With curly brackets, the Netboost script would look like this:

```
if (browserName == "Microsoft Internet Explorer" && version == "n3")
{
    browser = "ie3";
}
else
{
 browser = "other";
}
```

Netboost's Redirection

Netboost's redirection method in ❹ and ❺ is fine, except that it doesn't work in Netscape 2.0. Actually, that's precisely the point: Netboost doesn't want the redirection to work in Netscape 2.0. This method works, but it's kind of hacky. A coworker looking at the script might not know that document.location.href doesn't work with Netscape 2.0, and might spend hours wondering why the heck it won't redirect. It's better to use the window.location redirection I've covered in this chapter and an if-then clause to redirect Netscape 2.0 users. Be kind to others who must look at your JavaScript—code sensibly.

Figure 3-15 shows how I would rewrite Netboost's redirection script:

```
<script language = "JavaScript">
<!-- hide me from old browsers

var browser_name == navigator.appName;
var version = parseFloat(navigator.appVersion);


if (browser_name == "Netscape")
{
    window.location = "neindex.html";
}
else if (( browser_name == "Microsoft Internet Explorer") &&
(version >= 3) && (version < 4))
{
    window.location = "ie3index.html";
}

// end hide -->
</script>
```

Figure 3-15: My version of Netboost's redirection script

First, I use window.location instead of document.location.href to do the redirection. As mentioned earlier, not all browsers support document.location. href. The second difference between the scripts is that I've cut out two confusing variables in Netboost's script: version and browser. In that script, version is n4 if the visitor's browser is a 4.0 or higher version; otherwise it's n3. The code already has a variable called browserVer, containing the version number of the browser, so this other variable, which stores the same information, is redundant. The variable browser is also redundant, so I've cut that out as well. These changes result in a script that's shorter and a bit easier to understand.

Summary

Here are the things you should remember from this chapter:

- navigator.appName.

- navigator.appVersion.

- if-then statements.

- if-then-else statements.

- if-then-else-if statements.

- How to redirect your visitors to other Web pages.

Did you get all that? If so, here's an assignment for you.

Assignment

Write a Web page that asks for a visitor's name. If the visitor is someone you like, send him or her to your favorite page. If it's someone you don't know, send the visitor to a different page.

4

ROLLOVERS: EVERYONE'S FAVORITE JAVASCRIPT TRICK

You've seen rollovers a million times. You mouse over an image, and the image changes. You mouse off the image, and the image changes back to its original state. Rollovers are an easy way to make your site more interactive.

This chapter will show you how to create a good rollover by:

- Telling JavaScript to do an image swap when a visitor mouses over an image.

- Telling JavaScript which image to swap.

- Replacing the old image with a new one.

I'll also teach you a new way to detect what browser a visitor is using.

Let's take a look at rollovers in action.

The American Civil Liberties Union has a relatively straightforward and uncomplicated implementation of rollovers on its page at www.aclu.org (Figure 4-1). If you mouse over an image under "The Issues," a checkmark appears next to that image (Figure 4-2). Mouse over the left column, and those images change as well (see Figure 4-3 on page 52).

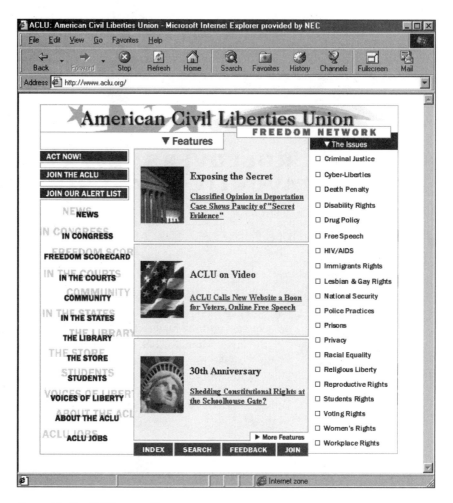

Figure 4-1: The ACLU page with no mouseovers

There are many different ways to script a rollover. Because rollovers don't work in 2.0 browsers, creating them also involves browser detection, so in this chapter you'll learn more ways to tailor JavaScripts to the visitor's browser.

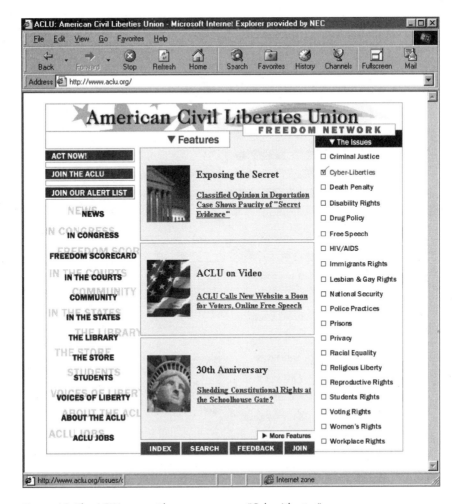

Figure 4-2: The ACLU page with a mouseover on "Cyber-Liberties"

Triggering Events

So far all the JavaScript we've seen gets triggered when a Web page loads into a browser. But JavaScript can also be *event-driven*.

Event-driven JavaScript waits for your visitor to take a particular action, such as mousing over an image, before it reacts. The key to coding event-driven JavaScript is to know the names of events and how to use them.

Event Types

With JavaScript's help, different parts of your Web page can detect different events. For example, a pull-down menu can know when it has changed (see Chapter 7); a window when it has closed (see Chapter 5); and a link when a visitor has clicked on it. In this chapter I'll focus on link events.

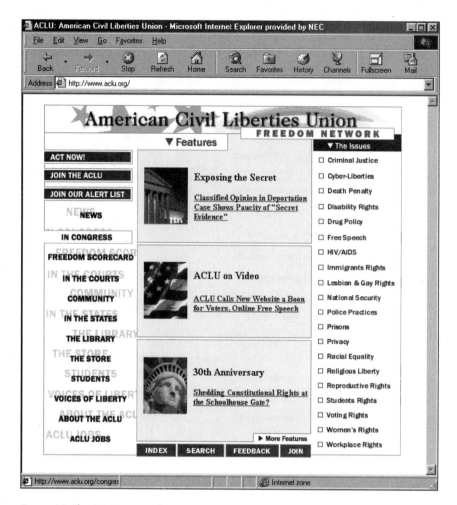

Figure 4-3: The ACLU page with a mouseover on "In Congress"

A link can detect three kinds of events: a click, a mouse rollover, and a mouse rolloff, all of which are captured the same way.

The onClick Event

Figure 4-4 shows the basic format of a link that calls an alert after a visitor clicks it.

Try putting the link with the onClick into one of your own Web pages. When you click on the link, an alert box should come up and say "off to the ACLU!" (Figure 4-5). When you click on OK in the box, the page should load the ACLU Web site.

Before JavaScript:

```
<a href="http://www.aclu.org">Visit the ACLU's Web site</a>
```

After JavaScript:

```
<a href="http://www.aclu.org"
  onClick="alert('off to the ACLU!');">Visit the ACLU's Web site</a>
```

Figure 4-4: A link that calls an alert

Figure 4-5: Event-driven "off to the ACLU!" alert box

Notice that, aside from the addition of onClick, this enhanced link is almost exactly like the normal link. The onClick code says, "When this link is clicked on, pop up an alert."

onMouseOver and onMouseOut

Links can capture two other events: onMouseOver and onMouseOut. Moving the mouse over a link triggers onMouseOver, as shown in Figure 4-6.

```
<a href="#" onMouseOver = "alert('hey! that tickles!');">elmo</a>
```

Figure 4-6: onMouseOver

In Netscape 3.0 and up, and MSIE 4.0 and up, moving the mouse off the link triggers onMouseOut. You can use onMouseOut, onMouseOver, and onClick in the same link, as in Figure 4-7.

Mousing over this link results in an alert box showing the words "hey! that tickles" (Figure 4-8). Pressing ENTER to get rid of the first alert and moving your mouse off the link results in another alert box that contains the words that's better! If you click on the link instead of moving your mouse off it, nothing will happen because of the "return false;" code in the onClick.

```
<a href="#"
onMouseOver = "alert('hey! that tickles!');"
onMouseOut = "alert('much better!');"
onClick = "return false;">
elmo
</a>
```

Figure 4-7: onMouseOut, onMouseOver, and onClick in the same link

Figure 4-8: An alert box produced by mousing over a link

Quotes in JavaScript

Inside the double quotes of the onClick (Figure 4-7) is a complete line of
JavaScript, semicolon and all. In previous chapters, we've placed all of our
JavaScript between open-script and close-script tags. The only exception to
this rule is when JavaScript is inside the quotes of an event. Your browser will
assume that the stuff inside these quotes is JavaScript, so you shouldn't put
<script> and </script> tags in there.

Also note that the quotes in the alert are single quotes ('). If these were
double quotes ("), JavaScript wouldn't be able to figure out which quotes go
with what. For example, if you wrote

```
onClick="alert("off to the ACLU!");"
```

JavaScript would think that the second double quote closed the first one,
which would confuse it and result in an error. Make sure that if you have
quotes inside quotes, one set is double and the other is single.

Apostrophes can also pose problems. For example, let's say you want the
alert in Figure 4-6 to say here's the ACLU page, you're gonna love it! You
would want the JavaScript to resemble this:

```
onClick="alert('here's the ACLU page, you're gonna love it!');"
```

Unfortunately, JavaScript reads the apostrophes in "here's" and "you're"
as single quotes inside single quotes and gets confused. If you really want
those apostrophes, *escape* them with a back slash (\), like this:

```
onClick="alert('here\'s the ACLU page, you\'re gonna love it!');"
```

Putting a back slash before a special character, such as a quote, tells JavaScript to print the item rather than interpret it.

Clicking the Link to Nowhere

When you click on OK in the alert box in Figure 4-6, the link takes you to the ACLU page. You can also use a link to trigger an action; Figure 4-9, for instance, uses an event to customize a page's background color.

```
<a href="#"
onClick="var the_color = prompt('red or blue?','');
window.document.bgColor=the_color;
return false;">
change background</a>
```

Figure 4-9: Customizing background color

When you click this link, a prompt box asks if you want to change the background to red or blue. When you type your response, the background changes to that color. In fact, you can type whatever you want into that prompt box and your browser will try to guess the color you mean. (You can even do a kind of personality exam by typing your name into the prompt and seeing what color your browser thinks you are. When I type thau into the prompt, rather than red or blue, the background turns pea green.) This example contains three new facts about JavaScript you should know. First, notice that the onClick triggers three separate JavaScript statements. You can put as many lines of JavaScript as you want between the onClick's quotes, although if you put too much in there the HTML starts to look messy.

Second, notice that you can change the background color of a page by setting **window.document.bgColor** to the color you desire. To make the background of a page red, you'd type:

```
window.document.bgColor = 'red';
```

In the example, we're setting the background color to whatever color the user enters into the prompt box.

Finally, I've included some code to prevent the browser from going to another page after a visitor clicks on the link. First, in the link's href I've put a pound (#) sign (HTML for "this page"). If you leave the href blank, you'll get weird behavior in Microsoft Internet Explorer 4.0 and higher versions. Second, I've put the line return false; at the end of the onClick to tell the browser not to follow the link.

NOTE *Unfortunately,* `return false;` *doesn't work in Netscape 2.0, so put the pound sign in the* `href` *to cancel the link for all browsers.*

Swapping Images

Using JavaScript, you can change or swap images on your Web pages, making buttons light up, images animate, and features explain themselves.

Before you tell JavaScript to swap an image, you have to tell it what image to swap by naming the image. Figure 4-10 shows you how.

Before JavaScript:

```
<img src="happy_face.gif">
```

After JavaScript:

```
<img src="happy_face.gif" name="my_image">
```

Figure 4-10: Naming an image

In this example, I've put an image of a happy face on the page and named it `my_image`.

NOTE *You can call an image whatever you like, but the name can't have spaces in it.*

Once you've named an image, it's easy to tell JavaScript to swap it with a new one. Let's say you have an image named `my_image`. To create an image swap, tell JavaScript you want to change the `src` of that image to another GIF:

```
window.document.my_image.src = "another.gif";
```

Figure 4-11 shows the code for a very basic page with an image and a link; click the link and the image changes to `happy_face.gif` (Figure 4-12).

Working with Multiple Images

If you have more than one image on a page, you should give each one a different name. Figure 4-13 has two images and two links. The first link tells JavaScript to swap the image called `my_first_image` (the sad face) with `happy_face.gif`. The second link tells JavaScript to swap the image called `my_second_image` (a circle) with `square.gif`.

NOTE *When using more than one image, you must name your images differently. If you accidentally give two images the same name, the swap won't work.*

```
<html><head><title>Simple Image Swap</title></head>
<body>
<img src="sad_face.gif" name="my_image">
<br>
<a href="#"
onClick="window.document.my_image.src='happy_face.gif';
return false;">make my day!</a>
</body>
</html>
```

Figure 4-11: Basic image swap

Figure 4-12: Swapping a sad face for a happy one

```
<html><head><title>Two Image Swaps</title></head>
<body>
<img src="sad_face.gif" name="my_first_image"><br>
<img src="circle.gif" name="my_second_image">
<br>
<a href="#"
 onClick="window.document.my_first_image.src='happy_face.gif';
 return false;">make my day!</a>
<br>
<a href="#"
 onClick="window.document.my_second_image.src='square.gif';
 return false;">square the circle!</a>
</body>
</html>
```

Figure 4-13: JavaScript for swapping two images

Figure 4-14: Swapping two images

NOTE *Image swapping doesn't work in browsers before Internet Explorer 4.0 or Netscape 3.0. Furthermore, if you're trying to replace a small image with a bigger one, or a big image with a smaller one, browsers below Netscape 4.61 and Internet Explorer 4.0 will squash or stretch the new image to fit the space the old one occupied. Later versions of these browsers adjust the page to fit the bigger or smaller image.*

What's with All the Dots?

You may wonder why JavaScript refers to my_image as window.document.my_image, and not just as my_image. You may also wonder why you would use window.document.my_image.src when you want to change the src of that image. In short, what's with all the dots?

The answer has to do with how your browser looks at your Web page.

Figure 4-15 shows the hierarchical organization of a Web page as JavaScript understands it—through the document object model (DOM). At the top of the DOM is the window that contains the Web page you're viewing. That window contains the navigator, document, and location objects. Each of these objects has a lot of information in it, and by changing one you can change what happens on your Web page.

The dots in a line of JavaScript separate objects; when JavaScript sees a series of objects separated by dots, it goes to the last object in the series. So, for example, the phrase window.location means "find the location object inside the current window." Similarly, the line window.document tells JavaScript to find the document object in the current window. The current window is the one in which the JavaScript is located.

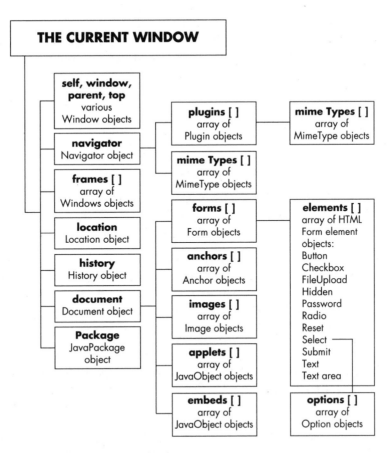

Figure 4-15: DOM's hierarchical organization

The Document Object

The document object lists all the images, links, forms, and other stuff on a Web page. To code an image swap, we must tell JavaScript to find the document object in the window, then locate the image object we would like to change in the document object's list, and finally change the image's src. In JavaScript terms (where happy_face.gif is the image we're swapping in), this is how it looks:

```
window.document.my_image.src = "happy_face.gif";
```

Object Properties

The object's properties are the bits of information that describe the object, such as its height, width, and src (the name of the file that the image displays). Some properties, like the src of an image, can be changed, and others can't. As we've seen, changing the src property of an image object changes which file is displayed:

```
window.document.my_image.src = "happy_face.gif";
```

Other properties, like the image's height and width, are read-only and cannot be changed.

NOTE *Each JavaScript object has its own set of properties. See Appendix B for a list of the various objects and their properties.*

You Can't Put Events Inside Image Tags

Now that we know how to tell JavaScript how to do an image swap and how to trigger JavaScript based on a user event with onClick, onMouseOver, and onMouseOut, we should be able to do the rollover. But there's a little trick you have to know first.

For some reason, most browsers won't let you put events such as onMouseOver and onMouseOut directly inside image tags. Instead, you have to wrap your image tags in an invisible link and put onMouseOver and onMouseOut inside that link, like so:

```
<a href="#"><img src="whatever.gif" border="0"></a>
```

The border="0" inside the image tag keeps the link from wrapping the image with a blue border. (Try it with border="10" to see what happens.)

Once you've wrapped your image in a link, you can put the onMouseOut and onMouseOver information in the link. Figure 4-16 shows a rollover with happy.gif and sad.gif.

```
<html><head><title>Simple Rollover</title></head>
body>
<a href="#"
    onMouseOver="window.document.my_first_image.src='happy_face.gif';"
    onMouseOut="window.document.my_first_image.src='sad_face.gif';"
    onClick="return false;">
<img src="sad_face.gif" name="my_first_image" border="0">
</a>
</body>
</html>
```

Figure 4-16: Simple rollover script

When first loaded, the image shows the sad_face.gif because that's what the image tag calls.

```
<img src="sad_face.gif" name="my_first_image" border="0">
```

Then, when the mouse moves over the image, the link around it captures the onMouseOver, and the image swaps to happy_face.gif, like so:

```
onMouseOver="window.document.my_first_image.src='happy_face.gif';"
```

When the mouse moves off the image again, the link captures the onMouseOut event, which causes JavaScript to swap sad_face.gif back into the image:

```
onMouseOut="window.document.my_first_image.src='sad_face.gif';"
```

Image Swap Gotchas

That's pretty much all there is to your basic image swap. As usual, there are a couple of gotchas that make the process a little more difficult. One easy problem to solve is that not all browsers can do image swaps, so we'll have to do a little browser detection to keep old browsers from breaking down.

A harder problem is that when you do an image swap as I've described, the image that's swapped in only downloads when your visitor mouses over the image. If your network connection is slow or the image is big, there's a delay between the mouseover and the image swap.

Solving the Hard Gotcha: Preloading Your Images

The way around this potential download delay is to *preload* your images—grabbing them all before they're needed and saving them in the browser's cache. When the mouse moves over a rollover image, the browser first looks to see if the swap image is in its cache. If the image is there, the browser doesn't need to download the image, and the swap occurs quickly.

There are hundreds of image preloading scripts, and they're all basically the same. Rather than write your own, you can download one of the free ones and paste it into your page (Webmonkey has a good one at http://www.hotwired.com/webmonkey/reference/javascript_code_library/wm_pl_img/). Let's go over the basics of how preloads work so you'll recognize them when you see them.

Preload Basics

There are two parts to a preload. First, you create a new image object. The line

```
var new_image = new Image();
```

creates a new image object that has no information. It doesn't have a GIF or JPG associated with it, nor does it have a height or width. Once you've created this new object,

```
new_image.src = "my_good_image.gif";
```

forces the browser to download an image into its cache by setting the image object's src. When the image is in the browser's cache, it can be swapped for another image without any download delays. Figure 4-17 incorporates a preload with the rollover we saw in the last example.

```
<html><head><title>Preloaded Rollover</title>
<script language="JavaScript">
<!-- hide me from old browsers

var some_image = new Image();
some_image.src = "happy_face.gif";

// end hide -->
</script>
</head>
<body>
<a href="#"
    onMouseOver="window.document.my_first_image.src='happy_face.gif';"
    onMouseOut='window.document.my_first_image.src='sad_face.gif';"
    onClick="return false;'>
<img src="sad_face.gif" name="my_first_image" border="0">
</a>
</body>
</html>
```

Figure 4-17: Image preload and rollover

Solving the Easy Gotcha: Browser Detection

It's sad, but true: Netscape 2.0 and down and most versions of Microsoft Internet Explorer 3.0 and down can't do image swaps. To keep older browsers from giving JavaScript errors, we have to make sure the visitor's browser can handle the swaps in our pages. There are two ways to do this. First, we could use the browser detection code that we learned in the last chapter (page 35). Figure 4-18 incorporates that code into our image-swapping example.

```
<html><head><title>Browser-Detecting Preloaded Rollover</title>
<script language="JavaScript">
<!-- hide me from old browsers

var browser_name == navigator.appName;
var version = parseFloat(navigator.appVersion);

❶ var swappable = false;          // this will be set to true if
                                 //the browser can handle image swaps

  if ((browser_name == "Netscape") && (version >= 3.0))
  {
❷  swappable = true;
  }

  if ((browser_name == "Microsoft Internet Explorer") &&
  (version >= 4.0))
  {
❸  swappable = true;
  }

❹ if (swappable)
  {
   var some_image = new Image();
   some_image.src = "happy_face.gif";
  }

                              // end hide -->
</script>
</head>
<body>
```

Figure 4-18: Browser detection and image swaps (continued next page)

```
<a href="#"
onMouseOver="if (swappable)
 {window.document.my_first_image.src='happy_face.gif';}"

onMouseOut="if (swappable)
 {window.document.my_first_image.src='sad_face.gif';}"

onClick="return false;">
<img src="sad_face.gif" name="my_first_image" border="0">
</a>

</body>
</html>
```

Figure 4-18 (continued): Browser detection and image swaps

Notice the Boolean code in ❹. Booleans (see page 38) are useful if you want to do some shorthand in your if-then statements. For example, the line

```
if (swappable == true)
```

can be shortened to

```
if (swappable)
```

Similarly, you can replace

```
if (swappable == false)
```

with

```
if  (!swappable)
```

This reads as "if not swappable." Notice the exclamation point—that's the "not" in "not swappable."

This shorthand only works if the variable has been assigned a value of true or false (❶, ❷, and ❸—note that there are no quotes). The example starts by setting the variable called *swappable* to false (❶).

After that, I do the browser detection, as we learned in the last chapter. If the browser is Netscape 3.0 or higher, I change the swappable variable from false to true. You can read this statement in English as: "If the browser is Netscape and the version is 3.0 or higher, it can do image swaps." The next set of lines is the same. It can be read as: "If the browser is Microsoft Internet Explorer and the version is 4.0 or higher, it can do image swaps."

A Closer Look at the Rollover

Now that we've finished with browser detection, it's time to look at the actual rollover. The interesting point here is that the onMouseOut and onMouseOver statements contain entire if-then clauses. Let's look at the onMouseOver:

```
onMouseOver="if (swappable)
 {window.document.my_first_image.src='happy_face.gif';}"
```

(Remember, everything between the quotes of the onMouseOver executes as if it were between <script> and </script> tags.) This if-then statement says, "If the image is swappable, then do the image swap." Be sure to include all the semicolons and curly brackets you would use in any if-then statement. Also, note the use of shorthand—the line could have been written thus:

```
onMouseOver="if (swappable == true)
 {window.document.my_first_image.src='happy_face.gif';}"
```

Another Way to Check for Image Swappability

Figure 4-18 works fine for people who visit your pages using Netscape or Microsoft Internet Explorer. However, anyone visiting your page with a different kind of browser that does image swaps is out of luck. Opera, for example, is a fairly popular browser that understands JavaScript and can do image swaps. Unfortunately, Figure 4-18 treats Opera as though it can't do swaps.

Here's a better way to check whether a browser can swap images:

```
if (window.document.images)
{
     do the image swap
}
```

This works because browsers that can do image swaps have window. document.images built into them, while browsers that can't do image swaps don't know what window.document.images means. If you look for window.document. images in a browser that doesn't have it, that browser will return false. If you look for window.document.images in a browser that does have it, the browser will return true. This is a better solution than the one mentioned earlier because it works for any browser, even obscure ones. It's also quicker to implement than the previous example, as you can see by looking at Figure 4-19.

```
<html><head><title>Nicer Browser-Detecting Preloaded Rollover</title>
<script language="JavaScript">
<!-- hide me from old browsers

if (window.document.images)
{
 var some_image = new Image();
 some_image.src = "happy_face.gif";
}

// end hide -->
</script>
</head>
<body>

<a href="#"
 onMouseOver="if (window.document.images)
  {window.document.my_first_image.src='happy_face.gif';}"

    onMouseOut="if (window.document.images)
  {window.document.my_first_image.src='sad_face.gif';}"

 onClick="return false;">
<img src="sad_face.gif" name="my_first_image" border="0">
</a>

</body>
</html>
```

Figure 4-19: An alternative solution for browser detection and image swapping

Real-World Example: How the ACLU Swaps Images

Since there are too many images on the ACLU's page to include here, Figure 4-20 just shows the code for swapping the first two images on the page.

As you can tell, there are as many ways to code JavaScript as there are JavaScripters. The ACLU's method of browser detection and image preloading is slightly different from what I've taught you so far.

```
<HTML><HEAD><TITLE>ACLU: American Civil Liberties Union</TITLE>
<SCRIPT language=javascript>

    if (navigator.appVersion.substring(0,1) >= 3) {
            hpbtact1=new Image(158, 25);
            hpbtact1.src="/graphics/hpbt-act1.gif";
            hpbtact2=new Image(158, 25);
            hpbtact2.src="/graphics/hpbt-act2.gif"; }
</SCRIPT>
</HEAD>
<BODY aLink=#0033cc bgColor=#ffffff link=#0033cc vLink=#0033cc>

<A
    href="http://www.aclu.org/congress/issues.html"
    onmouseout="if (navigator.appVersion.substring(0,1) >= 3)
hpbtact.src=hpbtact1.src"
    onmouseover="if (navigator.appVersion.substring(0,1) >= 3)
hpbtact.src=hpbtact2.src">
<IMG  alt="Act Now!" border=0 height=25 name=hpbtact
    src="ACLU American Civil Liberties Union_files/hpbt-act1.gif"
    width=158>
</A>
<A
    href="http://www.aclu.org/really_long.html"
    onmouseout="if (navigator.appVersion.substring(0,1) >= 3)
hpbtjoin.src=hpbtjoin1.src"
    onmouseover="if (navigator.appVersion.substring(0,1) >= 3)
hpbtjoin.src=hpbtjoin2.src">
<IMG  alt="Join the ACLU" border=0 height=29 name=hpbtjoin
    src="ACLU American Civil Liberties Union_files/hpbt-join1.gif"
    width=158></A>

</BODY></HTML>
```

Figure 4-20: The ACLU's image-swapping code

ACLU's Browser Detection

The great thing about using real-world examples is that you see more than one way to write a piece of code. Let's first look at how the ACLU page detects browsers:

```
if (navigator.appVersion.substring(0,1) >= 3)
```

This technique uses a function called *substring* to look at what's in `navigator.appVersion`. Substring takes two parameters. The first tells substring where in the string to start (0 is the first character), and the second, how many characters to consider. So the line says, "Look at the first character of `navigator.appVersion` and see if it's greater than or equal to 3."

We'll see more of substrings and other string-handling tools in Chapter 10, which focuses on string handling. For now it's enough to know that the line is examining the first character of `navigator.appVersion`. This method is an alternative to what we've used in the past, `parseFloat(navigator.appVersion)`, and it's perfectly fine. The problem with the ACLU's code, however, is that it will think Microsoft Internet Explorer 3.0 can do image swaps, which is incorrect. Actually, there might be a whole bunch of version 3.0 or higher browsers that can't do image swaps. To avoid worrying about which browsers support image swaps and which ones don't, it's best to use the `if(window.document.images)` style of browser detection.

The ACLU Site's Preload

Here's the ACLU page's preload:

```
hpbtact1=new Image(158, 25);
hpbtact1.src="/graphics/hpbt-act1.gif";
```

Notice that the script doesn't use var to introduce new variables. That won't pose a problem on most browsers, but it's better practice to use var when you introduce variables the first time. Also notice the parameters in the call to new Image(). Those numbers represent the height and width of the image. It's not necessary to include that information when creating a new image, but it doesn't hurt.

The ACLU Site's Image Swap

Here's how the ACLU page does its image swap:

```
<A
     href="http://www.aclu.org/congress/issues.html"
     onmouseout="if (navigator.appVersion.substring(0,1) >= 3)
hpbtact.src=hpbtact1.src"
     onmouseover="if (navigator.appVersion.substring(0,1) >= 3)
hpbtact.src=hpbtact2.src">
<IMG  alt="Act Now!" border=0 height=25 name=hpbtact
     src="ACLU American Civil Liberties Union_files/hpbt-act1.gif"
     width=158>
</A>
```

Notice that the ACLU puts a URL in its `href`, whereas we used a pound sign (#) in our examples (Figures 4-16 to 4-19). The ACLU wants you to go to http://www.aclu.org/congress/issues.html when you click on the image. Note also that the link does not include the term `onClick="return false";`. If it did, clicking on that link wouldn't take the visitor to the specified URL.

Now check out the `onmouseout` part:

```
onmouseout="if (navigator.appVersion.substring(0,1) >= 3)
  hpbtact.src=hpbtact1.src"
```

Notice the use of `onmouseout` instead of `onMouseOut`. In terms of adhering to the HTML specification as described by the World Wide Web Consortium (www.w3.org), it's probably better to follow the ACLU's lead and write everything in lowercase. Though `onMouseOut` is more traditional and easier to read, it's not as correct technically. The majority of HTML currently on the Web does not adhere strictly to the W3's specifications, so a little violation here and there for the sake of legibility isn't a crime.

Also notice the absence of curly brackets and semicolons in the if-then statement. As I noted in the last chapter (page 46), you can leave that stuff out when your if-then statement consists of only one line. I like to put the curly brackets and semicolons in anyway, because if I want to put a second line in there later, I won't have to remember to add the curly brackets.

Finally, notice the way this code actually swaps the image. Instead of following what I've written in earlier examples, `window.document.hpbtact.src = "happy.gif"`, it follows the format `hpbtact.src=hpbtact1.src`.

The first difference is that the ACLU's line drops the `window.document` in front of the image's name. That actually works fine for image swaps as long as the image is in the same window as the JavaScript. However, if you want to use JavaScript to swap images from other windows (see Chapter 5), you can't omit that piece of code.

NOTE *You can use a similar shorthand by substituting* `if(document.images)` *for* `if (window.document.images)`. *In general, the word* `window` *is assumed, so you can usually drop it. The word* `document`, *however, is sometimes necessary, so it's best to leave it.*

The second point worth noticing is that the ACLU code doesn't set the `src` of the image to a string, as my previous examples did. Instead, it sets `hpbtact.src` to the `src` of one of the preloaded images:

```
hpbtact1=new Image(158, 25);
hpbtact1.src="/graphics/hpbt-act1.gif";
```

(Look in the preload section of the ACLU script and you'll see it.) This is a tidy substitution. If the site administrator decides to use a different GIF, he or she need only change the name in the preload part—there's no need to change the GIF's name in the swap part.

Summary

In this chapter you've learned about:

- Events, such as onMouseOver and onMouseOut.

- How to nullify a link with return false inside onClick.

- How to change the background color of a page.

- How to swap images.

- How to preload images so they'll swap in more quickly.

- A new form of browser detection: if (document.images).

- What all those dots are about.

Now that you know the basics of image swapping, you can perform lots of tricks. You can make an image vanish by swapping in one that's the same color as the page background. You can make images composed of explanatory text and place them next to the feature they describe. There's no end to the fun you can have with image swaps.

As always, we'll be revisiting many of these points in later chapters, so you'll become more and more familiar with them. To make sure you understand how they work, try the following assignment.

Assignment

Figures 4-21 and 4-22 show you a page on the World Wildlife Foundation's Web site. Notice that mousing over the text on the left side of the screen turns the text blue, and also makes some explanatory text appear under the "Saving the Amazon" banner. Both of these bits of text are actually images, swapped using the techniques we've learned in this chapter. Your assignment is to write a similar page where mousing over one image causes two images to change.

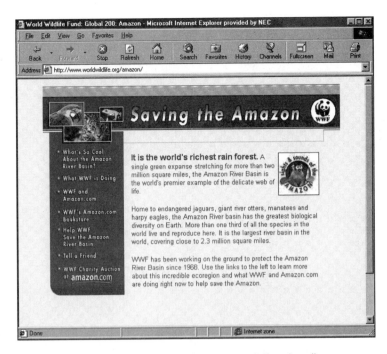

Figure 4-21: The World Wildlife Foundation's page before the rollover

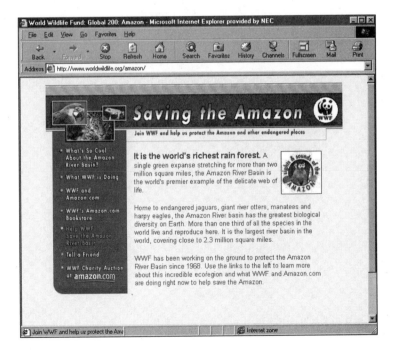

Figure 4-22: The page after the rollover

5

OPENING AND
MANIPULATING WINDOWS

JavaScript gives you the ability to open multiple windows in your browser and control what's inside them. JavaScript can also change where windows are located on your visitor's screen. You can use the windows you open to present a slide show or some help information, or to build a remote-control device for your site. In this chapter, you'll learn how to:

- Open new windows with JavaScript.

- Make those windows look the way you'd like.

- Position the windows on your visitor's screen.

- Swap images inside windows you've opened (in the homework assignment at the end).

Windows Examples from the Real World

Few sites utilize windows to their fullest extent. Some sites, like the community site Tripod, use windows for what's called pop-up advertising. If you look at any member page on Tripod (http://book_of_javascript.tripod.com/, for example), or open the Tripod page on the CD-ROM (sites/tripod.html), a little window showing an ad appears on your screen. Figure 5-1 shows you what this looks like. Although these pop-up ads are a little annoying, they are a good way to separate advertisements from the content of a page.

Figure 5-1: A Tripod page with an advertisement window

Another good example of using JavaScript's windows functions is Salon's bug-eating pictorial. Rather than just popping up when you load the page, as on the Tripod site, the pictorial window opens when you click on a link. Open the Salon page on the CD-ROM (sites/salon/frame.html), then choose to see the pictorial. You'll see the pictorial window appear, as in Figure 5-2.

A third site that uses JavaScript windows in an interesting way is ParentsPlace, which employs windows to provide readers with extra information about terms they may find unfamiliar. For example, if you're trying to take the survey at http://www.parentsplace.com/pregnancy/birthplan but

Figure 5-2: The Salon page and pictorial window

don't know the term *fetal monitoring*, just select it, and a little help window appears, offering a definition. Click on the close button inside the window and it disappears. Figure 5-3 shows you what this looks like. You'll find the ParentsPlace page on the companion CD-ROM (sites/parentsplace/index.html).

NOTE *Some browsers will only run the Parent's Place code if the Web page resides on a Web server. If you try running the Parent's Place page on the CD-ROM and it doesn't work, please visit the Parent's Place site and try from there.*

Each of these examples is interesting, but JavaScript can do even more with windows. This chapter will show you how to do the tricks I mentioned above, as well as a few fancier ones that will make your site even spiffier than these professional examples.

Opening Windows

Since windows are objects, you can manipulate them the same way you would any object (see Chapter 2 for a discussion of objects and methods):

```
window_name.method_name();
```

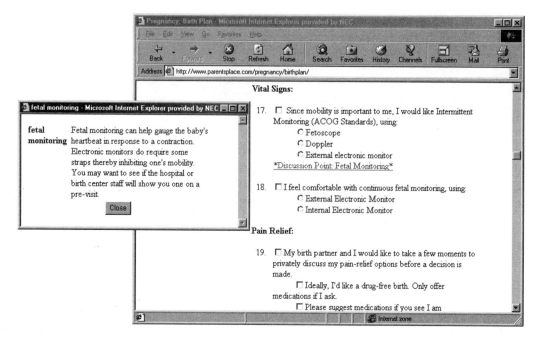

Figure 5-3: ParentsPlace's use of windows to display additional information

The open() method opens a window that has the characteristics specified inside parentheses:

```
var window_name = window.open("some_url", "window_name", "feature1,feature2,feature3,…");
```

In the above example, I've set up a variable called window_name to refer to the window we're opening. When I want to use JavaScript to change or manipulate what's inside the window, I'll refer to this window as window_name (window_name is just a variable—you could use the word fido in its place if you so desired).

Manipulating the Appearance of New Windows through open() Parameters

The three parameters of the window.open() command control the new window's characteristics:

The URL Parameter

The first parameter is the URL of the page in which you want the window to open. If you'd like to open a window with the *New York Times* Web site, inside the script tags you'd write:

```
var window_name = window.open("http://www.nytimes.com/", "window_name" ");
```

The HTML Name Parameter

The HTML name of the window (the second parameter inside the parentheses) is only useful if you want to use the target element of HTML links. For example, if you open a window using window.open() and name the window my_window, you can then use an HTML link to load a page into your new window. Clicking on this link loads the Webmonkey site into my_window:

```
<a href="http://www.webmonkey.com/" target="my_window">Put Webmonkey into my new window!</a>
```

You can also use the target element of the link tag to open windows without using JavaScript. For example, if a visitor clicks on a link like the one above and you *haven't* opened a window named my_window with JavaScript, your browser opens a new window and loads the link. The downside to opening a window without using JavaScript is that you have no control over what the window looks like and you can't change it once you've opened it.

The Features Parameter

The third parameter in the window.open() command is a list of features that lets you control what the new window will look like. This is where things start to get fun. Figure 5-4 illustrates the parts of each browser window JavaScript allows you to control.

The features parameter lets you open a new window with all, some, or none of these features. If you leave out the third parameter (that is, you list just the first two parameters and nothing more—not even empty quotes), the window you open will have all the features you see in Figure 5-4 and will be the same size as the previous window. However, if you list any of the features in the third parameter, only the listed features appear in the window you open. So if you open a window with the command

```
var salon_window = window.open("http://www.salon.com/", "salon", "resizable");
```

you'll get a resizable window with the Salon site in it. This window will be the same size as the window from which you opened it, but will lack the menu bar, status bar, scroll bars, and other features. Figure 5-5 shows what that looks like.

If you want more than one feature, you can list them inside the quotes, separated by commas. *Make sure to leave all spaces out of this string.* For some reason, spaces inside a feature string cause some browsers to draw your windows incorrectly. Here's an example of a window with two features (height and width):

```
var pictures=window.open("http://www.salon.com/wlust/pass/1999/02/bugs/frame.html",
"pictures", "width=605,height=350" );
```

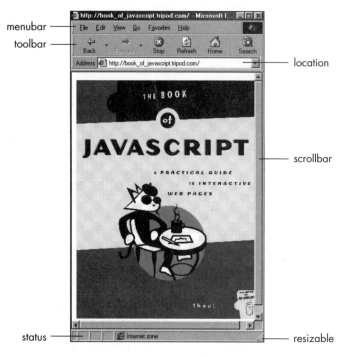

Figure 5-4: Browser window features you can control with JavaScript

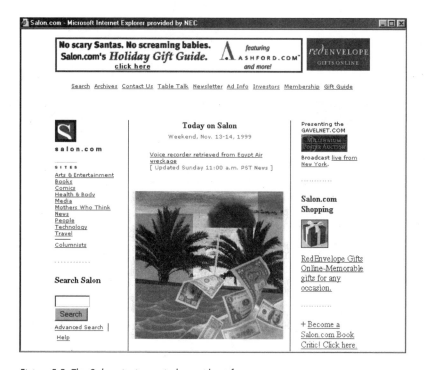

Figure 5-5: The Salon site in a window without features

Figure 5-6 shows you what a window looks like when height and width are specified.

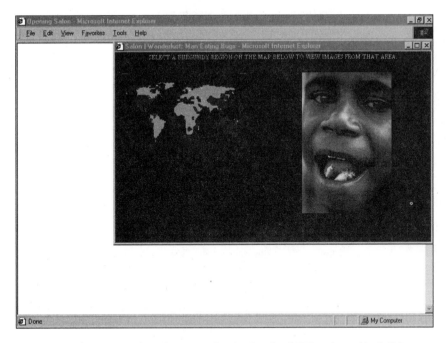

Figure 5-6: Salon's pictorial window opened with a height of 350 and a width of 605

Table 5-1 on page 80 lists all the different features you can play with. Try experimenting with different ones to see what they do. Except for the features that deal with pixels (for example, height), all you have to do is type the feature name inside the third parameter's quotes.

Some Browsers Open Windows Differently

The process of opening windows differs slightly in Netscape 2 and on a Macintosh.

JavaScript windows on Macintosh computers are always resizable, so even if you leave that feature out of the string, the window remains resizable. Another difference is that Macs don't have the menu bar feature.

In Netscape 2, you have to open a window twice to load the URL into it. Also, if you have any features in the third parameter, you must leave the second parameter blank. A very common work-around, illustrated in Figure 5-7 on page 8080, can solve these problems. This script fragment checks to see if the browser in use is Netscape 2. If it is, the script opens the window a second time to make sure the URL loads.

Table 5-1: JavaScript window features

Feature	Effect
directories	Adds buttons such as What's New and What's Cool in the Netscape browser.
height=X	Adjusts the height of the window to X pixels.
left=X	Places the new window's left border X pixels from the left edge of the screen in Internet Explorer 4 and up.
location	Adds the bar where you enter URLs.
menubar	Adds the menu bar.
resizable	Controls whether you can resize the window; all Mac windows are resizable even if you leave this feature out.
scrollbars	Adds scroll bars if the contents of the page are bigger than the window.
screenX=X	Places the window's left border X pixels from the left edge of the screen in Netscape 4 and up.
screenY=X	Places the window's top border X pixels from the top edge of the screen in Netscape 4 and up.
status	Adds the status bar to the bottom of the window.
toolbar	The bar with the back, forward, and stop buttons.
top=X	Places the window's top border X pixels from the top edge of the screen in Internet Explorer 4 and up.
width=X	Adjusts the window width to X pixels.

```
var my_window = window.open("http://www.wired.com/", "", "height=200,width=200");
if ((navigator.appName == "Netscape") && (parseInt(navigator.appVersion) == 2))
{
    my_window = window.open("http://www.wired.com/", "", "height=200,width=200");
}
```

Figure 5-7: A work-around for Netscape 2's window problems

Closing Windows

If you've opened a window called my_window and want to close it later in the script, try the close() method:

```
my_window.close();
```

You'll recall from Chapter 4 that the word window refers to the window containing the JavaScript. This means you can also use JavaScript to close the window that's actually running the JavaScript, like this:

```
window.close();
```

This is exactly what ParentsPlace does on its site. If you view the source code on the page that loads into one of the help windows, you'll see it has a button toward the bottom, labeled "close." If that button were a link, the script would look like this:

```
<a href="#" onClick="window.close(); return false;">Close me!</a>
```

Figure 5-8 shows what the bottom code of the ParentsPlace help page looks like.

```
<FORM><INPUT TYPE="BUTTON" VALUE="Close" onClick="self.close()">
```

Figure 5-8: How ParentsPlace closes its help windows

The primary difference between ParentsPlace's code and the simple link I described is that ParentsPlace uses a button instead of a link. The button is a form element that takes an onClick, just as a link does. Another difference is that instead of using the word window before close(), ParentsPlace uses the word self. These words are interchangeable, although I seldom see self in use.

Using the Right Name: How Windows See Each Other

Every window is a bit egocentric and thinks of itself as window. Let's say you open a Web page titled "The Original Window." Now let's say that window opens the window new_window.html (titled "The New Window") using JavaScript, like this:

```
var new_window = window.open("new_window.html","new_window","height=100,width=100");
```

These two windows see each other in different ways. The original window thinks the new window is called new_window. The new window, however, thinks of itself as window. This means if you want to close the *new* window using JavaScript inside the *original* window, you'd write this code:

```
new_window.close();
```

But to close the new window using JavaScript inside the *new* window, you'd write the following in new_window.html:

```
window.close();
```

This window centrism is one of the aspects of object-oriented programming that makes it interesting. It's like dealing with distinct individuals who have different perspectives on the world.

NOTE *Unless an event triggers them (as in Figure 5-8), the lines* new_window.close() *and* window.close() *close the corresponding window (*new_window *and* window *respectively) immediately after the window opens.*

Before doing slideshow.focus()   After doing slideshow.focus()

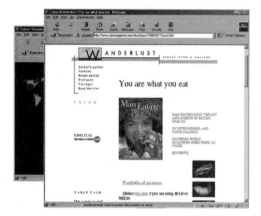

Figure 5-9: The focus() command in action

Moving Windows to the Front and Back of the Screen

Once you've opened a window, you can do much more than just close it. You can move it to the front of the screen (on top of the other windows) or to the back of the screen (behind all the other windows). The focus() method brings a window forward, and blur() puts the window in back. The focus() method is especially useful when you have a window you always want to appear at the front of a screen. For example, if Salon wanted its pictorial window to appear over the intro page, it could make all the links using this technique:

```
<a href="#" onClick = "pictures =
window.open('http://www.salon.com/wlust/pass/1999/02/bugs/frame.html', 'pictures',
'width=605,height=350' );pictures.focus(); return false;">Portfolio of pictures</a>
```

This line opens the pictorial window and brings it up to the front.

NOTE *Notice that I didn't put the word* var *before the* pictures *variable when I called* window.open(). *If you use* var *inside a link, JavaScript will forget the name of the window once it executes the rest of the JavaScript commands in the* onClick. *The reason for this will be clearer after you read Chapter 6.*

The unfortunate hitch with focus() and blur() is that they don't work in Netscape 2 or Microsoft Internet Explorer 3, so you'll have to do some browser detection if you don't want your page to give error messages.

Window Properties

So far we've seen four methods for the window object: open() , close(), focus(), and blur(). It has a few other properties that come in handy from time to time.

The status Property

One of the most useful (and most abused) of these properties is the window's status. This appears in the window's status bar (see Figure 5-4). One common status is the URL of a link you are mousing over.

You can use the status property to change what appears in the status bar. You may have noticed that some people put a kind of marquee in this area, scrolling across the bottom with messages like "Buy our stuff! Buy our stuff!" I don't want to encourage status bar abuse, so I'm not going to teach you exactly how to do that; but you *could* use these JavaScript techniques to create a similar effect. To change what appears in the status bar of a window, use a body tag like this:

```
<body onLoad="window.status = 'hi there!';">
```

This tag tells JavaScript to change the contents of the window's status bar after the page has been fully loaded into the browser.

You might want to use the status property to inform visitors about the site they'll see if they click on a link. For example, if you have a link to a very graphics-intensive site, the words "Warning, this site has a lot of graphics" could appear in the status bar when the visitor mouses over the link. You can set this up with an onMouseOver:

```
<a href="http://www.animationexpress.com/" onMouseOver="window.status='Warning, this site has
a lot of graphics'; return true;">Animation Express</a>
```

Notice the return true after the window.status command. This is similar to the return false I put at the end of my onClicks (see Chapter 4), and it does almost the same thing. When the user enacts an onMouseOver, return true prevents the URL from appearing in the status bar. If you don't put it there, the words "Warning, this site has a lot of graphics" flash in the status bar; then the link's URL quickly replaces them before the warning can be seen.

You might be asking, "Why is it return false in the case of onClick and return true in the case of onMouseOver?" That's a good question, and unfortunately there's no good answer—that's just how it is. The best you can do is memorize which goes with which.

The opener Property

When one window opens a new window, the new window stores a pointer to its parent (the original window) in the opener property. An opened window can access its parent through this pointer and then manipulate the parent. For example, if you want a link in the new window to change the contents of the status bar in the original window, you'd include the following code inside a link in the new window:

```
<a href="#" onClick="var my_parent = window.opener; my_parent.status='howdy'; return
 false;">put howdy into the status bar of the original window</a>
```

The first statement inside the onClick says, "Find the window that opened me, and set the variable my_parent to point to that window." The second statement changes the status property of that window to "howdy." Alternatively, you could combine the lines:

```
<a href="#" onClick="window.opener.status = 'howdy'; return false;"> put howdy into the status
 bar of the original window</a>
```

Using the opener Property in a Remote Control

The opener property is very useful if you want to have a remote control that affects the contents of the original window. The remote_control file on the CD-ROM (chapter05/fig5-10.html) offers an example of this. Figure 5-10 shows the code that triggers the remote control.

```
<html>
<head>
<title>The Controlled Window</title>
<script language = "JavaScript">
<!-- hide me from older browsers
// open the control panel window
var control_window = window.open("the_remote.html","control_window","width=100,height=100");
// show me -->
</script>
</head>
<body>
Use the remote control to send various Web pages to this window.
</body>
</html>
```

Figure 5-10: The code for the window that calls the remote control

This code opens a little window and loads the Web page called the_remote.html (Figure 5-11). Figure 5-12 shows you the code for the_remote.html.

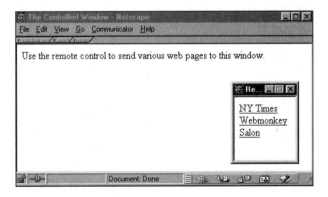

Figure 5-11: The page that calls the remote control, and the remote control itself

The code between ❶ and ❷ of Figure 5-12 on page 86 determines whether a visitor's browser can handle window.focus(). Remember that Netscape 2.0 and Internet Explorer 3.0 can do neither window.focus() nor window.blur(). If the browser can do window.focus(), the variable can_focus is set to true. Otherwise, can_focus is false.

Once we've determined whether the browser can do window.focus() we close off the JavaScript tag and enter the body of the page.

❸ is a typical link using an onClick. When a visitor clicks on the *New York Times* link, JavaScript looks up window.opener (the window that opened the remote control) and then changes its location to http://www.nytimes.com/. Then, if can_focus is true, JavaScript brings the remote-control window to the front of the screen. Notice that because this JavaScript is running inside the remote-control window, we can bring that window forward with window.focus().

```
<html>
<head>
<title>Remote Control</title>
<script language="JavaScript">
<!-- hide me from older browsers
// the code in this script section sets can_focus to true if the
// visitor is using a browser that can do window.focus()
//

// first, set some variables
//
var can_focus = false; // this will be made true if the
                       //browser can do window.focus()
var version = parseInt(navigator.appVersion);
var app_name = navigator.appName;

// now set can_focus to true if the browser can do window.focus()
//
if ((app_name == "Netscape") && (version > 2))
{
    can_focus = true;
}
else if ((app_name == "Microsoft Internet Explorer") && (version > 3))
{
    can_focus = true;
}

// show me -->
</script>
</head>
<body>
<a href="#" onClick="window.opener.location='http://www.nytimes.com/';
 if (can_focus) {window.focus();}">NY Times</a><br>
<a href="#" onClick="window.opener.location='http://www.webmonkey.com/';
 if (can_focus) {window.focus();}">Webmonkey</a><br>
<a href="#" onClick="window.opener.location='http://www.salon.com/';
 if (can_focus) {window.focus();}">Salon</a><br>
</body>
</html>
```

Figure 5-12: The remote control code

Advanced Window Tricks

Everything I've covered so far, except for `window.focus()` and `window.blur()`, works in all JavaScript-compatible browsers. However, Netscape 4.0 and Internet Explorer 4.0 introduced a couple of interesting capabilities. Most of these new window features fall into two categories: methods of resizing the window and methods of moving a window around the user's desktop.

Resizing Windows

The 4.0 browsers provide two different ways to resize a window. The `window.resizeTo()` method resizes a window to a given width and height. To change a small window into one that's 500 pixels wide and 200 pixels high, you'd use the following script:

```
window.resizeTo(500,200);
```

Alternatively, you can change the size of a window by a specific amount using `window.resizeBy()`. The `window.resizeBy()` method takes two numbers: how much the width of the window should change and how much the height should change. The code

```
window.resizeBy(10, -5);
```

makes a browser 10 pixels wider and 5 pixels shorter.

Moving Windows

The `window.moveTo()` method moves a window to an absolute position on the screen. If you want the window in the upper left corner of the user's screen, you'd type:

```
window.moveTo(0,0);
```

The first number is the number of pixels from the left border of the screen you want the window's upper left corner to appear, and the second number is the number of pixels from the top of the screen.

An alternative to `window.moveTo()` is `window.moveBy()`. If you want to move a window 5 pixels to the right and 10 pixels down from its current position, you'd type:

```
window.moveBy(5,10);
```

The first number is the number of pixels to the right you want to move the window, and the second number is the number of pixels down. If you want to move the window 10 pixels up and 5 to the left, just use negative numbers:

```
window.moveBy(-5,-10);
```

Don't Move the Window Off the Visitor's Screen

Be careful not to move a window entirely off a user's screen. To ensure against this possibility, you have to know the size of the user's screen. The two properties that indicate this are:

```
window.screen.availHeight
window.screen.availWidth
```

Figure 5-13 shows how you can use `window.screen.availHeight` and `window.screen.availWidth` to move a window to the center of the screen. This script centers the window on any screen, regardless of its size.

❶ through ❸ resize the window to 200 by 200 pixels. Once that's done, the script uses `window.screen.availHeight` and `window.screen.availWidth` to figure out how high and wide the screen is. After determining those values, the script does some calculations to figure out where the upper left corner of the window should go. Let's look at the formula to calculate the left-hand position of the window:

```
var left_point = parseInt(width / 2)  - parseInt(window_width / 2);
```

The first part of this formula determines the screen's midpoint by dividing the width of the screen by two (remember, we've defined the variable width in ❹). The `parseInt()` command ensures that the resulting number is an integer. Knowing the screen's midpoint isn't enough to center the window, however, because `window.moveTo()` sets the left border of the window you're moving. If you move the left border of the window into the center of the screen, the window will be too far to the right. To get the window to the center of the screen, we have to move it over to the left. The second part of the formula, subtracting `parseInt(window_width / 2)`, figures out how far to move the window to the left: half the window's width (see Figure 5-14 on page 90).

```
<html>
<head>
<title>Center Window</title>
<script language="JavaScript">
<!-- hide me from older browsers

// set some variables
❶ var window_height = 200;
❷ var window_width = 200;

// make the window smallish
❸ window.resizeTo(window_height, window_width);

// find out how big the screen is
var height = window.screen.availHeight;
❹ var width = window.screen.availWidth;

// get the left position
// it'll be half of the screen, minus
// half of the window width
var left_point = parseInt(width / 2) - parseInt(window_width / 2);

// get the top position
// similar calculation as for the left position
❺ var top_point = parseInt(height/2) - parseInt(window_height / 2);

// now, move the window
//
❻ window.moveTo(left_point, top_point);

// show me -->
</script>
</head>
<body>
<h1>Hi!</h1>
</body>
</html>
```

Figure 5-13: Code for moving a window to the center of the screen

If you move the window to the middle of the screen, it won't be centered. You have to move it a bit to the left.

screen

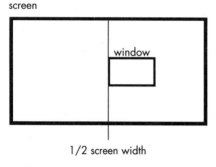

1/2 screen width

To center the window, move it over 1/2 of its width to the left. In other words, the left border is: 1/2 screen width – 1/2 window width

screen

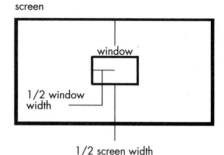

1/2 screen width

Figure 5-14: Calculating how to center a window

❺ performs a similar calculation to determine where to set the top of the window. Once we've determined the window's correct top and left position, we use the window.moveTo() command to move it (**❻**).

Summary

In this chapter you've learned:

- How to open new windows with window.open().

- What the various parts of the browser window are called.

- How to select and manipulate different features in windows.

- How to open windows in Netscape 2.0.

- How to close the windows you've opened with window_name.close().

- How to move windows to the front of the screen with window.focus().

- How to send them to the back of the screen with window.blur().

- How to change the message in the window's status bar by setting window.status.

- How a window you've opened can affect the previous window with window.opener.

- How to resize windows in 4.0 browsers with window.resizeTo() and window.resizeBy().

- How to move windows in 4.0 browsers with window.moveTo() and window.moveBy().

Congratulations! Now that you know how to swap images and mess with windows, you can handle about 75 percent of what most Web professionals do with JavaScript. The next couple of chapters will cover some details of JavaScript as a programming language, and then we'll be ready for some *really* fancy stuff.

Assignment

We've learned how to change the contents of the status bar of a window we've opened using JavaScript:

```
var my_window = window.open("http://www.nostarch.com","my_window");
my_window.status = "I'm in the new window's status bar!";
```

We can use a similar technique to swap an image in a window we've opened using JavaScript. Remember, the code to swap an image looks like this, where the_image is the name of an image on the page:

```
window.document.the_image.src = "new_image.gif"
```

To swap an image in another window, just replace window in the script with the name of the window containing the image.

Your homework assignment is to write a page (let's call it the main page) that contains two links. Write some JavaScript so that when the main page opens, it also opens a little window containing an image. When clicked on, the two links on the main page swap different images into the little window. Figures 5-15 below and 5-16 on the next page demonstrate what I mean.

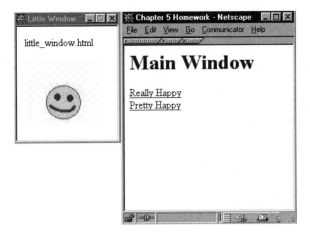

Figure 5-15: After opening the main window

Figure 5-16: After clicking on the Really Happy link

This assignment is a bit tricky, but give it your best shot before looking at the solution.

6

GETTING FUNCTIONAL: WRITING YOUR OWN JAVASCRIPT FUNCTIONS

In this chapter we're going to focus on a new programming concept—writing your own functions. Knowing how to write your own functions will improve almost any JavaScript you create. In fact, you'll see how you can use them to enhance several of the JavaScript tricks you've already learned.

In this chapter, you'll learn how to:

- Write your own functions.

- Use home-made functions to improve your code.

- Write functions you can cut and paste into whatever pages you want.

We'll be using home-made functions in every chapter from now on, so pay extra-close attention to what's going on in this chapter. You'll be glad you did.

Functions as Shortcuts

Functions aren't anything new. You've already seen a number of functions that come built into JavaScript. The alert() function, for example, takes whatever text you put inside the parentheses and displays an alert box with that text.

In its simplest form, a *function* is just a shorthand name for a bunch of lines of JavaScript. When you call the alert() function, JavaScript understands it as a command to carry out some task, such as opening a little window with an OK button and a close button, and putting some text in the window.

The functions you create act as shorthand as well. Let's say you want to write a link that opens a small window and then centers that window on the screen if the visitor is using Netscape 4.0 or above.

You *could* write a link resembling Figure 6-1 (most of the code in it is similar to Figure 5-13).

```
<a href="#"
    onClick = "if ((parseInt(navigator.appVersion > 3) && (navigator.appName == 'Netscape')) {
        var the_window =

window.open('http://www.nostarch.com/','the_window','height=200,width=200');
        var screen_height = window.screen.availHeight;
        var screen_width = window.screen.availWidth;
        var left_point = parseInt(screen_width / 2) - 100;
        var top_point = parseInt(screen_height/2) - 100;
        the_window.moveTo(left_point, top_point);
} return false;">click on me to open a small centered window</a>
```

Figure 6-1: A link that opens a small window and centers it in Netscape 4 and above

However, it is not a good idea to write a link in this way: There's too much JavaScript in the HTML. Excessive JavaScript makes HTML hard to follow, even for people who know JavaScript. Furthermore, if you want two or three links on your page, your HTML becomes even uglier and your page's download time increases. Even more problematic, if you want to change the code to affect window size or centering, you have to make the change everywhere you put the link.

The solution to these problems is to give all the JavaScript in Figure 6-1 a name, then simply call that name when you want to open and center a window. That's exactly what home-made functions are for: They allow you to call a set of JavaScript lines (the function) with just a name.

Basic Structure of JavaScript Functions

Figure 6-2 shows you the skeleton of a home-made function.

```
function functionName()
{
    a line of JavaScript;
    another line of JavaScript;
    more lines of JavaScript;
}
```

Figure 6-2: The basic structure of a home-made function

Functions start with the word function. When JavaScript sees that word, it knows you're about to define a bunch of JavaScript as a function.

Naming Your Functions

Next comes the function's name. The rules for naming a function are similar to those for naming a variable. The first character must be a letter; the rest of the characters can include letters, numbers, dashes, and underscores. No other characters will work, including spaces. Like variables, function names are case sensitive, so a function called feedTheCat() is different from a function called FeedTheCat().

Make sure you don't give a function and a variable the same name. If you have a variable called my_cat and a function called my_cat, JavaScript will forget either what the function's supposed to do or what value you've stored in the my_cat variable. This weird fact, coupled with the case sensitivity of function names, means that it makes sense to have a different convention for naming functions than for naming variables. The convention I use for variables is lowercase letters with underscores, and for functions I use what's called *in-caps* notation. Names following an in-caps notation are strings of words without spaces, in which every word except the first is initial-capitalized as in myCat(), openAndCenterTheWindow(), and printDate(). In-caps is a pretty common convention, and should serve you well.

Parentheses and Curly Brackets

A pair of parentheses follows the function's name. For now, you won't be entering anything between them, but they're still necessary.

After the parentheses you need a pair of curly brackets containing the JavaScript which will run when the function is called.

An Example of a Simple Function

Figure 6-3 shows you how the window centering code in Figure 5-13 on page 89 would look rewritten as a Web page containing a function.

Notice that the link calling the function (❶) has the same form as a link that calls a built-in JavaScript function—the function name appears inside an onClick.

```
<html>
<head>
<title>Getting Centered</title>
<script language = "JavaScript">
<!- hide me from old browsers
function openAndCenterWindow()
{
    if ((parseInt(navigator.appVersion) > 3) && (navigator.appName == "Netscape")) {
        var the_window =
            window.open('http://www.nostarch.com/','the_window','height=200,width=200');

        var screen_height = window.screen.availHeight;
        var screen_width = window.screen.availWidth;
        var left_point = parseInt(screen_width / 2) - 100;
        var top_point = parseInt(screen_height/2) - 100;
        the_window.moveTo(left_point, top_point);
    }
}
// show me ->
</script>
</head>
<body>
❶ <a href="#" onClick="openAndCenterWindow(); return false;">click on me to open a small
centered window</a>
</body>
</html>
```

Figure 6-3: Opening and centering a window using a function

Next, notice that I've put the JavaScript declaring the function in the head of the page. You can declare functions in either the head or the body, but I like to declare my functions in the head because that way I don't have to search for them all over the HTML page.

Finally, it's important to remember that the browser reads the page from the top down. When it sees the word function, it remembers the function name and the lines of JavaScript you've associated with that name. However, the JavaScript between the curly braces doesn't actually execute until the onClick in the link calls the function. When we start putting more than one function on a Web page, you'll see why it's important to keep this in mind.

Simple Functions in the Real World

We've already seen an example of a page that uses a home-made function like the one in Figure 6-3—in the last chapter, when we discussed how Tripod serves pop-up ads on users' home pages (see Figure 5-1). Figure 6-4 shows you the JavaScript that Tripod uses to open its ad windows.

```
<SCRIPT language=JavaScript>
<!--
function TripodShowPopup()
{
    // open the popup window. stick a timestamp to foil caching.
❶   var now = new Date();
❷   var popupURL = "/adm/popup/roadmap.shtml?"+now.getTime();
❸   var popup = window.open(popupURL,"TripodPopup",'width=593,height=125');
❹   if ( navigator.appName.substring(0,8) == "Netscape" )
    {
            popup.location = popupURL;
    }
}

❺ TripodShowPopup();

// -->

</SCRIPT>
```

Figure 6-4: Tripod's pop-up ad window

If you look at the source code of the page at http://book_of_javascript.tripod.com/, you'll see this code right at the top. Let's look at the function line by line.

Analysis of Tripod's Pop-up Ad Code

❶ loads the current date and time into the variable called now (see Chapter 2 for a discussion on dates).

❷ provides the URL of the ad Tripod wants to appear in the pop-up window. The URL is a bit unusual; instead of ending in .html, it ends in .shtml. Pages that end in .shtml generally invoke some kind of Perl script or C program on the server to generate a page. This one decides what ad to put into the window. Notice that Tripod appends time information at the end of the URL using now.getTime(). As we learned in Chapter 2, getTime() returns the number of milliseconds between the current date and January 1, 1970. Tripod adds this information to the URL to trick your browser into thinking it's never seen this page before. If the browser thinks it has seen the page before, it will read the page from its cache instead of from the site. This is bad for Tripod, because it only makes money if the browser reads the ad from its site. Since getTime() calculates the time since January 1, 1970, it'll never be the same number twice, so the URL that ❷ generates will always be different from any the browser has seen. This is a bit outside the scope of this book, but it is a great example of how JavaScript and server-side scripts can work together.

❸ opens the little window with the URL provided in ❷. The if-then clause starting at ❹ takes care of the weird problem Netscape 2 has with opening windows: Sometimes you have to make sure the URL actually does load into the window (see page 79). This clause is the last part of the function.

❺ makes sure the function gets called when the page reads in. We've seen functions called within a link, like this:

```
<a href="#" onClick = "TripodShowPopup(); return false;">show me an ad!</a>
```

If you want to call a function within JavaScript without requiring that the user click on a link, you can just call it by name, as Tripod has done in ❺.

Writing Flexible Functions

Let's go back to the example in Figure 6-3, in which the function openAndCenterWindow() opened and centered a window containing No Starch Press's home page. What if you wanted another link to open and center a different window with a different URL in it—Webmonkey's, for example? One approach would be to write a second function that looks just like the first one, the only difference being that you'd replace the line

```
var the_window = window.open('http://www.nostarch.com/','the_window','height=200,width=200');
```

with the line

```
var the_window = window.open('http://www.webmonkey.com/','the_window','height=200,width=200');
```

This would work fine, but it's not a good idea to have two functions that do almost the same exact thing. First of all, it's wasteful. If you could write one function that works regardless of the URL, you'd save both typing and download time. Even more important, if you want to change how you're doing the centering, you'll have to change two functions instead of just one.

Parameters

Luckily, there's a way to make your function more flexible. The trick is to add a parameter. Remember, the function alert() takes one parameter—the words you want to appear in the alert. You can write the openAndCenterWindow() function to take a parameter, too. In this case, the parameter would be the URL of the Web page you want to appear in the window.

Figure 6-5 shows how to add a parameter to your function and how to call the function with this parameter.

```
<html>
<head>
<title>Getting Centered Functionally</title>
<script language = "JavaScript">
<!- hide me from old browsers
function openAndCenterWindow(the_url)
{
    if ((parseInt(navigator.appVersion) > 3) && (navigator.appName == "Netscape"))
    {
        var the_window =
            window.open(the_url,'the_window','height=200,width=200');
        var screen_height = window.screen.availHeight;
        var screen_width = window.screen.availWidth;
        var left_point = parseInt(screen_width / 2) - 100;
        var top_point = parseInt(screen_height/2) - 100;
        the_window.moveTo(left_point, top_point);
    }
}
// show me -->
</script>
</head>
<body>
<a href="#" onClick="openAndCenterWindow('http://www.webmonkey.com/'); return false;">click
on me to put Webmonkey in  a small centered window</a>
<a href="#" onClick="openAndCenterWindow('http://www.nostarch.com/'); return false;">click
on me to put No Starch Press in  a small centered window</a>

</body>
</html>
```

Figure 6-5: Opening and centering a window with a parameter

Analysis of Figure 6-5

The lines

```
<a href="#" onClick="openAndCenterWindow('http://www.webmonkey.com/'); return false;">click on
  me to put Webmonkey in a small centered window</a>
```

call the function with the URL for Webmonkey in parentheses (see the result in Figure 6-6). Here Webmonkey's URL acts just like the words that go into the alert() function, except instead of any random string, it's a URL. Similarly, the lines

```
<a href="#" onClick="openAndCenterWindow('http://www.nostarch.com/'); return false;">click on
me to put No Starch Press in a small centered window</a>
```

call the function with the URL for No Starch Press.

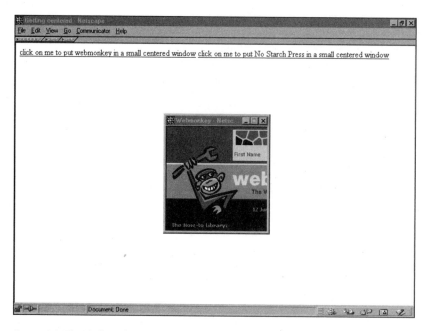

Figure 6-6: The Webmonkey site, opened and centered

Now let's look at the function itself. Only two lines differ from those in Figure 6-3. The first line of the function now looks like this:

```
function openAndCenterWindow(the_url)
```

Notice that a word appears inside the parentheses now. This term is a variable, storing whatever you use to call the function. So if the line

```
openAndCenterWindow("happy happy!");
```

calls the function, the variable the_url holds the value happy happy!. When we call the function in Figure 6-5 as follows, the variable the_url holds the value http://www.nostarch.com/:

```
<a href="#" onClick="openAndCenterWindow('http://www.nostarch.com/'); return false;'>click on
me to put No Starch Press in a small centered window</a>
```

The second line in the function that differs from Figure 6-3 is the one that opens the window (❷). In Figure 6-3 we opened the window with a Web page:

```
var the_window =
        window.open('http://www.nostarch.com/', 'the_window',
           'height=200,width=200');
```

In Figure 6-5 we open the window with the variable that was set when the function was called:

```
var the_window =
        window.open(the_url, '', 'height=200,width=200');
```

JavaScript sees the variable the_url and knows it's a variable because no quotes surround it. If the function has http://www.nostarch.com/ inside the parentheses, like this:

```
openAndCenterWindow('http://www.nostarch.com/');
```

the variable the_url has the value http://www.nostarch.com/ so the window opens with the No Starch Press Web site. Figure 6-7 shows you graphically what's going on here.

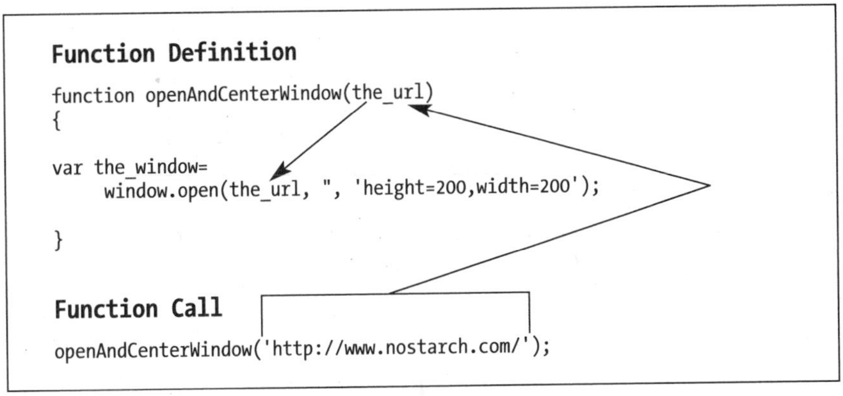

```
Function Definition
function openAndCenterWindow(the_url)
{

var the_window=
       window.open(the_url, ", 'height=200,width=200');

}

Function Call
openAndCenterWindow('http://www.nostarch.com/');
```

Figure 6-7: Passing variables

Using More Than One Parameter

Sometimes you want to change more than one thing each time you call a function. The built-in JavaScript function prompt(), for example, can change two sets of words: the words that appear above the text box and those that appear within it. When we call prompt() below, we pass in two parameters, separated by a comma:

```
var the_answer = prompt("What's your favorite color?","yellow?");
```

The method window.open() provides an example of three parameters: the URL you want to open inside the window, the name of the window, and the window's features.

The functions you write can also take more than one parameter. Let's say you want to write a function to display a Web page in a square window. You might write a function that finds the name of the page and the length of one of the sides of a window. Figure 6-8 shows you what this would look like.

```
<html>
<head>
<title>Square Windows</title>
<script language="JavaScript">
<!-- hide me
❶ function openSquareWindow(the_url, the_length)
{
    var the_features = "width=" + the_length + ",height=" + the_length;
    var the_window = window.open(the_url, "", the_features);
}
// show me -->
</script>
</head>
<body>
❷ <a href="#" onClick="openSquareWindow('http://www.webmonkey.com/', 400); return false;">open
Webmonkey in a big square window</a><br>
<a href="#" onClick="openSquareWindow('http://www.nostarch.com/', 100); return false;">open
No Starch Press in a small square window</a><br>
</body>
</html>
```

Figure 6-8: Writing functions that take more than one parameter

Notice that in ❶ two variables now appear between the parentheses following the function name: the_url and the_length. In ❷ we're calling the function as we would call `prompt()`, with two parameters separated by a comma. Calling the function sets the first variable in the function definition to the first parameter, so in the case of ❷, the_url is set to `http://www.webmonkey.com/`. Similarly, the second variable in the function definition is set to the second parameter in the function call. If we call the function as in ❷, the_length is set to 400. Figure 6-9 depicts the results of calling functions with two parameters.

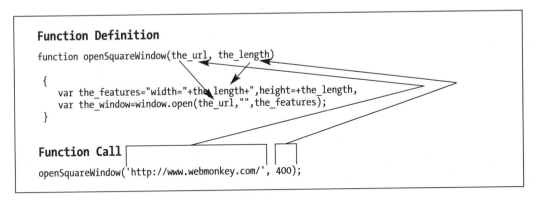

Figure 6-9: Calling functions with two parameters

A Real-World Example of a Function with Parameters

The ParentsPlace survey we looked at in the last chapter (see Figure 5-3) has six different help windows. Each help window looks exactly like the others except for the word it defines and the definition. The people who wrote the survey could have written six different HTML pages, one for each definition. When a user clicked on a help link, JavaScript would open the help window, then read in the appropriate HTML page.

This would work fine, but it means creating a bunch of little HTML pages. If you had 100 different help links to create, you'd be facing a tough task. Furthermore, if ParentsPlace wanted to change the format of its help pages, it would have to change each HTML page individually.

The creators of the ParentsPlace site did not write a bunch of separate HTML pages; instead, they wrote a JavaScript function that creates an HTML page for each word and definition. If they need to change how the help pages look, they simply change the JavaScript function, as opposed to altering umpteen HTML pages. And they don't have to create a new HTML page whenever they want an additional help page—they just call the function. Figure 6-10 shows an abbreviated listing of how ParentsPlace has set this up and the result is shown in Figure 6-11. If you want to see the full source code, look at the parentsplace.html file in the Sites folder on the accompanying CD-ROM.

```
      <html>
      <head>
      <title>Abbreviated Listing of ParentsPlace Help Page Generator</title>
      <script language="JavaScript">
      <!-- hide me from older browsers
❶  newWindow = new Object;
❷  newWindow.closed = true;
❸  function newWindowopener(word, def)
      {
❹  if (!newWindow.closed) {
            newWindow.close();
          }
❺  newWindow = window.open("","","height=200,width=420,scrollbars,resizable");
          newWindow.document.write("<HTML><HEAD><TITLE>");
❻  newWindow.document.write(word);
          newWindow.document.write("</TITLE>");
          newWindow.document.writeln("</HEAD><BODY BGCOLOR=#ffffff>");
❼  newWindow.document.writeln("<B>"+word+"</B><br>");
          newWindow.document.writeln(def);
❽  newWindow.document.writeln("<FORM><INPUT TYPE=\"BUTTON\" VALUE=\"Close\"
  onClick=\"self.close()\">");
          newWindow.document.writeln("</FORM>");
          newWindow.document.close();
          newWindow.focus();
        }
      // show me -->
      </script>
      </head>
      <body>
      <a href="#" onClick="newWindowopener('fetal monitoring', 'Fetal monitoring can help
      gauge blah blah blah'); return false;">get info on fetal monitoring</a><br>
      <a href="#" onClick="newWindowopener('eye_drops','Eye treatment of some form is required
      by law blah blah blah'); return false;">get info on eye drops</a><br>
      </body>
      </html>
```

Figure 6-10: Creating help pages on the fly

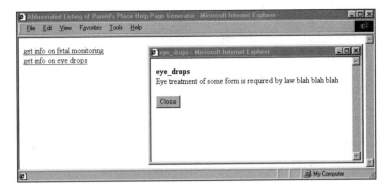

Figure 6-11: A help page created with a JavaScript function

Analysis of the ParentsPlace Code

This example illustrates many interesting features, so let's go through it line by line.

The first two lines introduce two new ideas. ❶ creates a new, generic Object and assigns it to the variable newWindow, just as back in Chapter 2, the line

```
var today = new Date();
```

created a new Date object. You can assign whatever properties and methods you want to a generic object. ❷ adds the closed property to the object and sets the property to true. We'll see where this comes in handy a bit later.

❸ defines the function newWindowopener(). Notice that newWindowopener has two variables in its parentheses: word, the defined word, and def, the definition. Say we call the function with a link like this:

```
<a href="#" onClick="newWindowopener('doe', 'a deer, a female deer'); return false;">doe</a>
```

This sets the variable word to doe and the variable def to a deer, a female deer.

You can read ❹ as "if it's not true that the window newWindow is closed, then close it." The reason to include this line is to make sure two help windows don't open at the same time. Initially, newWindow isn't really a window but a generic object. However, once you open a window, newWindow points to that window.

❺ opens the window. This is just like any other window opening we've seen, except this time the window doesn't have a URL. Generally, you shouldn't open a window without a URL. However, in this case JavaScript will write code to the window, so it's fine.

The next eight lines actually write the HTML to the open window. ❻ puts the variable word into the page's title. Using our previous example, the variable word is doe, so the word doe appears in the title of the Web page.

❼ writes the variable word to the Web page in bold. The code describing the string to print looks like this:

```
("<B>" + word + "</B><br>");
```

and not this:

```
("<B>word</B><br>");
```

The latter won't work, because JavaScript won't recognize word as a variable if it appears inside quotes. The correct version of this line takes the variable word out of the quotes and sandwiches it between the <B> and </B> tags using the plus (+) sign. In the incorrect version, JavaScript doesn't know you mean the variable word, so it just prints <B>word</B> to your Web page instead of <B>doe</B>.

❽ contains a good reminder of how you need to *escape* quote marks when you actually want to print them to a Web page. If you tried to use the following code instead of what actually appears in ❽, JavaScript would have a hard time figuring out which quote marks go with which, and you'd get an error:

```
newWindow.document.writeln("<FORM><INPUT TYPE="BUTTON" VALUE="Close"
 onClick="self.close()">");
```

To avoid confusing JavaScript, you need to put the slash (\) before the quotes JavaScript should print to the Web page, as in ❽.

The rest of the function and the page should be familiar. After JavaScript has written everything it needs to the page, it closes the document, then calls focus() to bring the window forward (see page 82).

Getting Information from Functions

Sometimes you may want to get information from your functions. Consider the prompt() function:

```
var the_answer = prompt("What's your name?","Ishmael");
```

When a user types his or her name into the prompt box and selects OK, the name goes into the variable the_answer. In programming parlance, you'd say that the function prompt() *returns* the words typed into the prompt box. The functions you write can return values as well. Figure 6-12 shows a very simple example of how to make a function return values.

```
<html>
<head>
<title>Date Printer</title>
<script language = "JavaScript">
<!-- hide me
function getNiceDate()
{
    var now = new Date();
    var the_month = now.getMonth()+1; // remember, Jan is month 0
    var the_day = now.getDate();
    var the_year = now.getYear();
    var the_nice_date = the_month + "/" + the_day + "/" + the_year;
❶  return the_nice_date;
}
// hide me -->
</script>
</head>
<body>
Hello! Today is
<script language = "JavaScript">
<!-- hide me
❷ var today = getNiceDate();
document.write(today);
// hide me -->
</script>
</head>
</body>
</html>
```

Figure 6-12: A script with a simple function that returns a value

Analysis of Figure 6-12

Most of the function should be familiar by now. It creates a new Date object, carries out a few method calls, and then creates a nicely formatted date. The magic line is ❶, which tells JavaScript to exit the function and return the value of the_nice_date to whatever variable is waiting for it. In this case, the variable is today in ❷. Whenever JavaScript sees the word return in a function, it exits the function and outputs whatever value comes after return.

❷ calls the function getNiceDate(), which returns a nicely formatted date. The code document.write(today) then puts the date on the Web page (as shown in Figure 6-13).

Figure 6-13: Returning the date

Dealing with Y2K

Figure 6-12 works fine, but it has a little problem. Remember our discussion of the Y2K problem in the getYear() method of the Date object (Chapter 2)? Different browsers deal with years differently. In some versions of Netscape, getYear() returns the year minus 1900. So if it's the year 2010, getYear() returns 110. Other versions return the full four digit year if the year is before 1900 or after 1999. Different versions of Microsoft Internet Explorer give different results for the same date as well.

The way to deal with this problem is to see if the year getYear() returns is less than 1000. If so, your visitor is using a version of either Microsoft Internet Explorer or Netscape which subtracts 1900 from the date if it's after 1899. In this case, you can get the correct four-digit year by adding 1900 to the date. You'll find a concise form for all this convoluted logic in the JavaScript function Y2K() shown in Figure 6-14.

```
function Y2K(the_date)
{
    if (the_date < 1000)
    {
            the_date = the_date + 1900;
    }
    return the_date;
}
```

Figure 6-14: Dealing with the Y2K problem

This function adds 1900 to the year if it is less than 1000. You can drop the Y2K function into the script shown in Figure 6-12 to deal with its Y2K problem. Figure 6-15 demonstrates how the two look together.

```
<html>
<head>
<title>Date Printer</title>
<script language = "JavaScript">
<!-- hide me
function getNiceDate()
{
     var now = new Date();
     var the_month = now.getMonth()+1; // remember, Jan is month 0
     var the_day = now.getDate();
❶   var the_year = now.getYear();
❷   var the_fixed_year = Y2K(the_year);
     var the_nice_date = the_month + "/" + the_day + "/" + the_fixed_year;
     return the_nice_date;
}
❸ function Y2K(the_date)
{
     if (the_date < 1000)
     {
               the_date = the_date + 1900;
     }
     return the_date;
}
// hide me -->
</script>
</head>
<body>
Hello!  Today is
<script language = "JavaScript">
<!-- hide me
var today = getNiceDate();
document.write(today);
// hide me -->
</script>
</head>
</body>
</html>
```

Figure 6-15: The script in Figure 6-12 with the Y2K fix

Analysis of Figure 6-15

❶ in figure 6-15 uses the getYear() method to get the year, and ❷ calls the function Y2K() on the year to fix it up. The variable the_fixed_year is set to whatever Y2K() returns. The JavaScript in Figure 6-15 actually defines the function Y2K() after the getNiceDate() function. It might seem strange that getNiceDate() can call Y2K() even though Y2K() is defined after getNiceDate(). Remember, though, that when you define functions, you're just telling JavaScript their names and what they do, so the order in which you define your functions doesn't matter.

Defining Variables Properly

The getNiceDate() function in Figure 6-15 calls the year variable the_year. However, when you look at how the Y2K() function appears in ❸, you'll see that it calls whatever passes into it the_date. Since we're calling Y2K(the_year), JavaScript looks up the value of the_year and then sends that value to the Y2K() function. The Y2K() function stores that value in the variable the_date. In other words, the functions getNiceDate() and Y2K() have two different names for the same value. It's as if the functions are different countries where people speak different languages. If you try to talk about the_year inside the Y2K() function, it won't know what you're saying, and you'll get an error. Figure 6-16 shows you a graphical representation of how this works.

```
function getNiceDate()
{
  var now = newDate();
  var the_month = now.getMonth()+1;//remember,
    Jan is month 0
  var the_day = now.getDate();
  var the_year = now.getYear();
  var the_fixed_year = Y2K(the_year);
  var the_nice_date = the_month + "/" +
    the_day + "/" + the_fixed_year;
  return the_nice_date;
}
function Y2K(the_date)
{
        if(the_date < 1000)
        {
                the_date = the_date + 1900;
        }
        return the_date;
}
```

Let's say now.getYear() returns 110, meaning that it's 2010 and your visitor is using MSIE. This means that the_year = 110 inside the getNiceDate() function.

Here we're passing the_year into the Y2K() function. First, JavaScript figures out that the_year is a variable equal to 110. Then it passes the value 110 to the Y2K() function.

Here, inside the Y2K() function, the variable the_date takes the value 110, because that's what we passed into the function.

Now the_date gets changed to 2010.

Now the value of the_date is returned to the awaiting variable.

The awaiting variable is the_fixed_year. So now the_fixed_year has the value 2010.

Figure 6-16: How variables work in different functions

The True Nature of var

The reason that the Y2K() function can't access the variable the_year in getNiceDate() is because when you first defined the_year, you put the word var in front of it:

```
var the_year = now.getYear();
```

The word var tells JavaScript to create this variable for this function. Without var you could access the_year inside the Y2K() function. You might think this is a good thing. Why shouldn't you access the_year anywhere in the program—why hide it inside getNiceDate()? Creating variables inside functions that other functions can affect is a major cause of difficult-to-debug problems.

Consider the example in Figure 6-17 to see the headaches you'll avoid if you define your variables with var:

```
<html>
<head>
<title>Bad Encapsulation</title>
<script language="JavaScript">
<!-- hide me

function getNames()
{
    the_name = prompt("what's your name?","");
    dog_name = getDogName();
    alert (the_name + " has a dog named " + dog_name);
}
function getDogName()
{
    the_name = prompt("what's your dog's name?","");
    return the_name;
}

// show me -->
</script>
</head>
<body>
<a href="#" onClick="getNames(); return false;">click here for a survey</a>
</body>
</html>
```

Figure 6-17: The dangers of variables without var

If we run this example and input thau when the prompt asks for a name and fido when the prompt asks for a dog's name, we end up with an alert that says "fido has a dog named fido." Somewhere along the line, the program forgot that the name was thau and replaced it with fido.

This happened because both getNames() and getDogName() use a variable called the_name. Function getNames() saves the user's name in the variable called the_name. Then function getDogName() saves the dog's name in the variable the_name. If I had used var when declaring the variable the_name inside the getDogName() function, JavaScript would have understood that the variable the_name is specific to the function getDogName(), and would have left alone all the_name variables in other functions. Because I didn't use var when I set the variable the_name inside the getDogName() function, I unintentionally replaced the contents of the_name with the dog's name. When getDogName() exits and the alert comes up, we see the dog's name:

```
alert (the_name + " has a dog named " + dog_name);
```

If I had used var inside the getDogName() function, "thau has a dog named fido" would have come up. As your JavaScripts get longer, you're likely to use the same variable in different functions. Without var, it's very difficult to track down what's going wrong in these functions, so save yourself the headache with a little preparation.

Another reason to use var to hide variables inside functions is so that you can write functions that you can cut and paste into other scripts. If you define all your variables with var, you don't have to worry about whether a function you've written will mess up another function when you paste it into a different page. Otherwise you can't tell whether some variable in a program shares a variable name with your function.

Final Words about Functions

There's an art to figuring out when to use a function and knowing the best way to write one. In general, the best time to use a function is for a simple task you need to execute more than once. For example, patching the Y2K bug in JavaScript is a task you'll probably have to do repeatedly, so it's a good idea to create a function to handle it. As we see more complicated examples of JavaScript later in the book, you'll get a sense for what should go into functions. And, of course, as you view the source code on all the great Web pages you see, you'll notice how various JavaScripters use functions.

Almost all complicated JavaScripts use at least one home-made function. In this chapter, you've seen how to write simple functions with no parameters and more complicated functions that take parameters and return values. If you found all of this a bit tricky, don't worry. You'll have many more opportunities to learn how to use functions in JavaScript.

Assignment

Write a page with three images on it, each of them a navigational icon leading to another Web site. Each time the user mouses over a navigational icon, it should do an image swap, and a new window should open with an appropriate URL. For example, the three images could be of an apple, a monkey, and a sun. (see the chapter06 folder on the CD-ROM). When the user mouses over sun, the image could swap to a happy sun, and a window with the Sun Microsystems home page could open up. Create this effect using a function that takes three parameters: the image to swap, the new image to put in its place, and the URL to open in the new window. For example, if the user mouses over the sun icon, the link should look like this:

```
<a href="#" onMouseOver="fancySwap(window.document.sun,'hilight_sun.gif','http://www.sun.com/');"
    onMouseOut="window.document.sun.src='normal_sun.gif';">
<img src="normal_sun.gif" name="sun" border="0">
</a>
```

The first parameter in the function fancySwap() is the location of the image you want to swap. Notice that the image tag inside the link has the name sun. This means JavaScript will refer to this image as window.document.sun. The second parameter is the name of the GIF to swap into the image called sun. The third parameter is the URL that should open in the new window. The function you write will start as follows:

```
function fancySwap(the_image_tag, the_new_image, the_url)
{
    you fill in here...
}
```

The lines of code you write will carry out the image swap (using what you learned in Chapter 4) and open a new window with the_url (using what you learned in Chapter 5).

Good luck—this is a tough one!

7

GIVING AND TAKING
INFORMATION WITH FORMS

So far I've shown you a few ways to get information from your visitors. You can ask questions with the prompt() function, and you can use onClick to tell when they click on a link or onMouseOver to detect when they move over a link. In this chapter, we'll learn a plethora of ways to collect information using HTML forms and JavaScript. You can rely on forms and JavaScript to create very interactive sites that might include surveys and quizzes, calculators, games, and novel navigational tools.

In this chapter you'll learn how to:

- Create HTML forms.

- Use JavaScript to read a form a visitor has filled out.

- Use JavaScript to fill out a form automatically.

- Use forms as navigational tools.

Real-World Examples of Forms

Forms can gather all sorts of information, including demographic input like age and gender, answers to quizzes and polls, and numbers for tricky equations. The mortgage monthly payment calculator shown in Figure 7-1 offers an example of the latter. The form gives you places for the amount, interest rate, and length of a loan. If you enter all this information and push the submit button, JavaScript reads the information off the form, performs a calculation, and displays the results in the monthly payment box.

Figure 7-1: A mortgage calculator

You can also use forms as navigational tools. The front door of the Sun Microsystems Web page has a pull-down menu that functions as a navigational tool. Click on the menu, pull down to highlight the name of the section you'd like to visit, and release the mouse—JavaScript takes you to the page you want. Figure 7-2 shows Sun's home page.

HTML draws the forms in Figures 7-1 and 7-2 on the Web page, and JavaScript reads the information that the visitor fills in. Most forms that use JavaScript follow this pattern. Let's look first at how to write forms to your Web page with HTML.

Form Basics

Figure 7-3 shows a simple form and Figure 7-4 (on page 118) shows the HTML for that form.

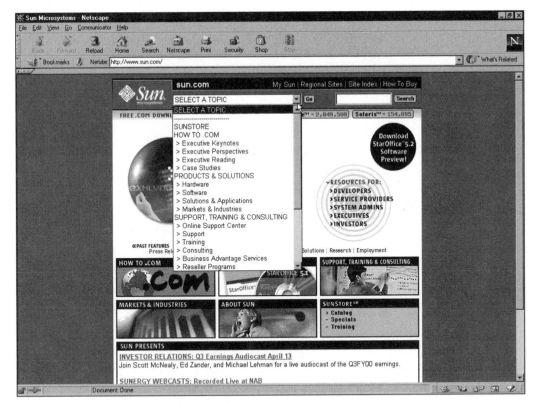

Figure 7-2: Sun's pull-down navigational tool

Figure 7-3: A simple form

Text Fields

As you can see in Figure 7-3, the HTML in Figure 7-4 draws two text boxes on the screen. A visitor to your site can click inside the text boxes and type a name and age.

```
      <html>
      <head>
      <title>A Very Basic HTML Form</title>
      </head>
      <body>
❶    <form>
❷    Name: <input type = "text"> <br>
❸    Age: <input type = "text"> <br>
❹    </form>
      </body>
      </html>
```

Figure 7-4: Code for the basic HTML form in Figure 7-3

Notice that the form is constructed of normal HTML. Like most HTML, the form must go between the <body> and </body> tags. The form begins with a <form> tag and ends with a </form> tag (❶ and ❹). Inside the form tags you'll see the *elements* of the form (❷ and ❸), the parts that hold information. In this chapter, you'll encounter a variety of different form elements, each with special characteristics. The elements in ❷ and ❸ are called *text fields*. These allow the user to type a line of text in a field. Later you'll learn how JavaScript reads the user's typed input.

The part of ❷ that tells the browser to draw a text field is this:

```
<input type = "text">
```

The words before the input tag, as well as the <br> after it, are normal HTML. The input tag itself tells the browser to create an input field of type text. You can embellish the text field a bit—for example, you can make the text box bigger by setting its size:

```
<input type = "text" size = "40">
```

The size of the text field is roughly equal to the number of characters that can fit inside the field.

You can also tell the browser to place some words in the text box. For example, if you want the words type your name in here to appear inside the text box, enter this:

```
<input type = "text" value = "type your name in here">
```

By setting the value of the text box, you determine what goes inside it. Remember the term value—it will come in handy later.

Buttons, Checkboxes, and Radio Buttons

In addition to text fields, you can put buttons, checkboxes, and radio buttons in your forms. Figure 7-5 shows you what each of these elements looks like, and Figure 7-6 shows you the HTML used to draw Figure 7-5.

Figure 7-5: Checkboxes, radio buttons, and buttons

```
    <html>
    <head>
    <title>Checkboxes, Radio Buttons, and Buttons</title>
    </head>
    <body>
    <h1>Tell me about your dog</h1>
    <form>
❶  Name: <input type = "text"> <p>
    Would you like your dog to get our daily newsletter? <br>
❷  <input type = "checkbox"> yes <p>
    How old is your dog? <br>
❸  <input type = "radio" name = "age">between 0 and 1 years<br>
❹  <input type = "radio" name = "age">between 1 and 3 years<br>
❺  <input type = "radio" name = "age">between 3 and 7 years<br>
❻  <input type = "radio" name = "age">older than 7 years<br>
    <p>
❼  <input type = "button" value = "I'm done">
    </form>
    </body>
    </html>
```

Figure 7-6: The HTML for checkboxes, radio buttons, and buttons

The Checkbox

The code in ❷ shows you the HTML for a checkbox. If you want the checkbox checked by default in the above example, put the word checked inside the element tag, like this:

```
<input type = "checkbox" checked>
```

You'll encounter the word checked again, so remember it.

The Radio Button

The next type of input element is the radio button. Radio buttons differ from checkboxes in that you can set up groups of mutually exclusive radio buttons. Since a dog cannot be between 0 and 1 *and* between 1 and 3 years old, I've given the radio buttons in Figure 7-6 the same name (❸ through ❻) so a visitor can only choose one of them. Because all these buttons share the name age, you can only turn on one at a time. For example, if the visitor chooses the first radio button, then the third one, that action deselects the first radio button. If you want the page to open with a radio button already chosen, use the word checked, just as with checkboxes:

```
<input type = "radio" name = "age" checked>
```

The Button

The final type of input element in Figure 7-6 is the button: input type = "button". This input type creates a rectangular button. If you want some words to appear inside the button, set the button's value as in ❼. Right now the button doesn't perform any function, but soon we'll learn how to attach an action to it.

Select Elements

All the form elements we've discussed so far are input elements. The next two elements, pull-down menus and scrolling lists, have a slightly different format.

Figure 7-7: A pull-down menu and a scrolling list

Figure 7-7 shows what these elements look like, and Figure 7-8 shows the HTML used to write that page.

Pull-down menus start with a <select> tag (❶) and end with a </select> tag (❸). An <option> tag (❷) precedes each item in the pull-down menu. You don't have to put each option on its own line, but it makes for cleaner-looking HTML.

Sometimes you want one of the options to appear as the default when the page loads. To do that, put the word selected inside the <option> tag. If you want the word female to appear in the gender pull-down menu when the page loads, you would write this:

```
<option selected>female
```

```
<html>
<head>
<title>A Pull-Down Menu and a List</title>
</head>
<body>
<form>
Your dog's gender:<br>
❶ <select>
❷ <option>Male
<option>Female
❸ </select>
<p>
Your dog's favorite food: <br>
❹ <select size = "3">
<option>beef
<option>chicken
<option>fish
<option>pork
<option>rawhide
<option>lettuce
<option>cactus
</select>
</form>
</body>
</html>
```

Figure 7-8: HTML for a pull-down menu and a scrolling list

The main difference between scrolling lists and pull-down menus is that scrolling lists have `size` set inside the `<select>` tag, as in ❹. Setting the `size` determines how many options appear in the list. In ❹, since we're setting `size` to 3, three options appear in the list. To see more options, a visitor can use the scroll bar on the side of the list.

Choosing More Than One Option

If you want to give your visitors the ability to choose multiple options, put the word `multiple` inside the `<select>` tag, like this:

```
<select size = "3" multiple>
```

This allows a visitor on a PC to choose more than one item by holding down the CTRL key (the apple key for Macintosh users) and clicking on multiple options.

Textarea

If you want to let your visitors input more than one line of text, you'll have to use the textarea form element, which lets your visitors type as much information as they like. Figure 7-9 shows you what a textarea looks like in the browser, and Figure 7-10 shows you the HTML used to draw the textarea.

Figure 7-9: The textarea form element

```
<html>
<head>
<title>A Textarea</title>
</head>
<body>
<form>
<textarea rows = "10" cols = "40">
Default text goes in here
</textarea>
</form>
</body>
</html>
```

Figure 7-10: The HTML for a textarea

Any text that goes between the <textarea> and </textarea> tags appears inside the textarea when the browser renders the page. You can control the size of the textarea by setting its rows and columns. As with the text box, these numbers roughly reflect the number of characters a visitor can enter in the textarea: The rows number controls the textarea's height, and cols controls the width.

Final Form Comments

This covers much of what you need to know about writing HTML forms for the purpose of this book. You'll find other details about forms in any good HTML manual.

Forms and JavaScript

Once you have a form on your Web page, you can use JavaScript to read information from and put information into that form. The mortgage monthly payment calculator, for example, reads the principal, interest rate, and other information the user types into the form, calculates a monthly payment based on this information, and then writes the result into the form.

Naming Form Elements

But before you can read from or write to an element of your form, you need to tell JavaScript which form element you're talking about by naming your form and its elements. The simple form in Figure 7-11 shows you how to name forms (❶) and their elements (❷ and ❸). Notice that you can't name the <option> tag (❹).

```
    <html>
    <head>
    <title>A Form with Names</title>
    </head>
    <body>
    <h1>A Form with Names</h1>
❶  <form name = "my_form">
❷  Age: <input type = "text" name = "the_age_field">
    Gender:
❸  <select name = "the_gender">
❹  <option>male
    <option>female
    </select>
    </form>
    </body>
    </html>
```

Figure 7-11: A form with names

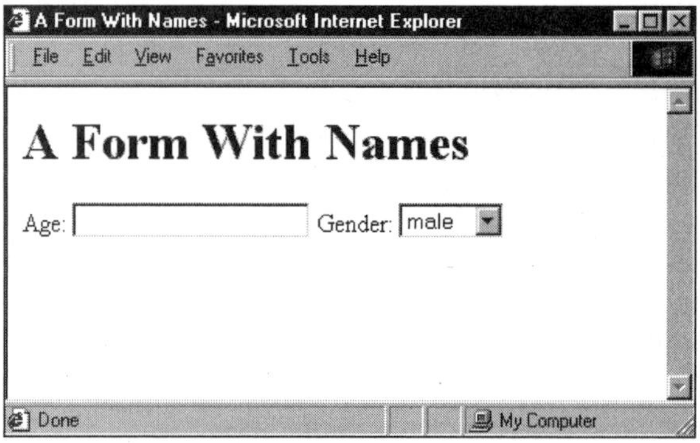

Figure 7-12: The form in Figure 7-11

When naming form elements, you should follow the same principles as in naming an image tag for an image swap: Do not use spaces and make sure no other HTML element has the same name. For example, don't name a text field body, because body is an HTML tag. Some browsers work fine if you do this, but others will give visitors a JavaScript error. You can name buttons, checkboxes, textareas, and radio buttons just as you name text fields and selects.

Naming Radio Buttons

Radio buttons are a special case. Since all radio buttons that belong to a group receive the same name, we can't use the name to figure out which radio button the visitor selected. Putting value = "something" inside a radio button tag lets us differentiate between different radio buttons in the same set (see Figure 7-13).

```
<html>
<head>
<title>Values inside Radio Buttons</title>
</head>
<body>
<form name = "radio_button_form">
How old is your dog? <br>
<input type = "radio" name = "age" value = "puppy">between 0 and 1 years<br>
<input type = "radio" name = "age" value = "young">between 1 and 3 years<br>
<input type = "radio" name = "age" value = "middle_age">between 3 and 7 years<br>
<input type="radio" name="age" value = "older">older than 7 years<br>
</form>
</body>
</html>
```

Figure 7-13: Putting values inside radio buttons

I've named each radio button age to show that it's part of the age group, but each one has its own value.

Naming Options

The same holds true for the <option> tag in select form elements. Although options don't receive names, they do take values. So in order to use JavaScript to determine what a visitor has chosen from a pull-down menu, you need to put values inside the options. Figure 7-14 on page 126 shows a variant on Figure 7-11, with values added to the <option> tags.

In Figure 7-14, the <select> tag still gets a name (❶) and the <option> tags get values (❷ and ❸). When we use JavaScript to determine what option a user selected, it'll be the value of the option we retrieve. If the visitor selects the Female option, we'll retrieve the value female because of the value = "female" inside that option.

```
    <html>
    <head>
    <title>A Form with Values inside the Option Tags</title>
    </head>
    <body>
    <h1>A Form with Names</h1>
    <form name = "my_form">
    Age: <input type = "text" name = "the_age_field">
    Gender:
❶  <select name = "the_gender">
❷  <option value = "male">Male
❸  <option value = "female">Female
    </select>
    </form>
    </body>
    </html>
```

Figure 7-14: Values inside <option> tags

Reading and Setting Form Elements

Once your form and form elements have names, JavaScript can easily find out what your visitors have typed into the form elements. Just tell JavaScript the form and element for which you want information.

Reading Information from Text Fields

If you want to see what value a user has typed into the text field named the_age_field (❷) in Figure 7-11, use this:

```
window.document.my_form.the_age_field.value
```

This line tells JavaScript to look in the window, locate its document, find the form called my_form inside the document, find the form element called the_age_field inside that form, and read its value. Figure 7-15 shows how to build a simple calculator using form elements as inputs.

This example presents two text fields and a link. When a visitor puts numbers in the text field and clicks on the link (Figure 7-16), an alert box appears with the product of those numbers (Figure 7-17). The link next to ❽ calls the function multiplyTheFields() when a user clicks on it.

```
        <html>
        <head>
        <title>A Very Simple Calculator</title>
        <script language = "JavaScript">
        <!-- hide me from old browsers
        function multiplyTheFields()
        {
❶   var number_one = window.document.the_form.field_one.value;
❷   var number_two = window.document.the_form.field_two.value;
❸   var product= number_one * number_two;
❹   alert(number_one + " times " + number_two + " is: " + product);
        }
        // end hiding comment -->
        </script>
        </head>
        <body>
❺   <form name = "the_form">
❻   Number 1: <input type = "text" name = "field_one"> <br>
❼   Number 2: <input type = "text" name = "field_two"> <br>
❽   <a href="#" onClick = "multiplyTheFields(); return false;">multiply them!</a>
        </form>
        </body>
        </html>
```

Figure 7-15: A Very Simple Calculator

Figure 7-16: The multiplying calculator

Figure 7-17: Displaying the results

The function `multiplyTheFields()` does all the work. The code in ❶ looks up the value of the text field `field_one` (❻) inside the form `my_form`, located in the document of the window. It then stores this value in the variable `number_one`. The same thing happens in ❷, except this time JavaScript looks at the text field named `field_two` (❼) and stores it in the variable `number_two`. Once JavaScript reads the values of the two text fields, it multiplies them (❸) and puts the result inside an alert box (❹).

Setting the Value of a Text Field

One difference between Figure 7-15 and the mortgage calculator in Figure 7-1 is that the results of the mortgage calculator go inside a text field instead of in an alert box. To put an item inside a text field using JavaScript, simply set the value of the text field to whatever you want to write inside it.

If Figure 7-15 had a third text field named `the_answer`, we could put the product of the other numbers into it using this line:

```
window.document.the_form.the_answer.value = product;
```

Here we're telling JavaScript to set the value of the text field named `the_answer`, located inside the form called `the_form`, to the value `product`. Figure 7-18 shows you what this looks like in your browser, and Figure 7-19 lists the complete code.

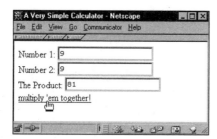

Figure 7-18: Putting the results of the calculation in a text field

The only differences between Figure 7-19 and 7-15 are the addition of a new text field called `the_answer` (❷) and the changed location of the output from an alert box to inside `the_answer` (❶).

Figure 7-19 should give you a basic idea of how the mortgage monthly payment calculator works. I won't go into the guts of the mortgage calculator, but if you'd like to see the mathematics behind your monthly mortgage payment, look on your CD-ROM under sites/mortgage. This might be a little tough to understand until you read the next chapter, though, so tread lightly.

```
<html>
<head>
<title>A Very Simple Calculator</title>
<script language = "JavaScript">
<!-- hide me from old browsers
function multiplyTheFields()
{
    var number_one = window.document.the_form.field_one.value;
    var number_two = window.document.the_form.field_two.value;
    var product = number_one * number_two;
    window.document.the_form.the_answer.value = product;
}
// end hiding comment -->
</script>
</head>
<body>
<form name = "the_form">
Number 1: <input type = "text" name = "field_one"> <br>
Number 2: <input type = "text" name = "field_two"> <br>
The Product: <input type = "text" name = "the_answer"> <br>
<a href="#" onClick = "multiplyTheFields(); return false;">multiply 'em together!</a>
</form>
</body>
</html>
```

❶ (at `window.document.the_form.the_answer.value = product;`)

❷ (at `The Product: <input type = "text" name = "the_answer"> <br>`)

Figure 7-19: The code for Figure 7-18

Reading and Setting Textareas

You can set and read textareas, the form element that lets you enter more than one line of text, just as you can text fields. For example, if you have a textarea named my_text_area inside a form called my_form, you can enter some words like this:

```
window.document.my_form.my_text_area.value = "Here's the story, of a lovely lady...";
```

If your visitor types some input in the textarea, you can read it using this:

```
var the_visitor_input = window.document.my_form.my_text_area.value;
```

Reading and Setting Checkboxes

Checkboxes differ from text fields and textareas. Instead of having a value as text fields and textareas do, they have a Boolean called checked (see Chapter 3 for discussion of Booleans). If a user has clicked on a checkbox so that an *X* or checkmark appears in it, then checked equals true. If the checkbox is not on, then checked equals false (remember—because true and false are Booleans, they don't take quotes). The quiz shown in Figure 7-20 shows how to use the checked property of checkboxes. Figure 7-21 shows the code.

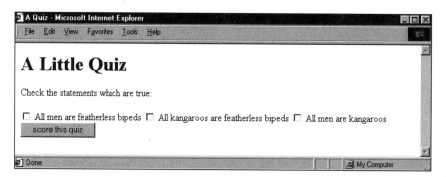

Figure 7-20: A short JavaScript quiz

When someone clicks on the button form element in ❼, it calls the scoreQuiz() function. Line ❶ then creates a variable called correct and sets its value to 0. This variable keeps track of how many answers the visitor answered correctly. The code in ❷ and ❸ gives the visitor one point if he or she clicked on the checkbox next to the first question; line ❷ fetches the value of the checked property in the first checkbox and compares this value to the word true. If the user selects the checkbox, its checked value is true, so ❸ executes, adding a 1 to the variable correct, and ❹ does the same thing for the second question.

The if-then statement in ❺ is slightly different from the other two. It says that if the checked property of the third checkbox is false (that is, the visitor hasn't selected the checkbox), then JavaScript should add 1 to correct.

Finally, ❻ tells visitors how well they did.

To show visitors the correct answers after they click the score button in Figure 7-20, we could use the scoreQuiz() function to determine the value of each checkbox by setting its checked property to true or false. Figure 7-22 on page 132 updates the scoreQuiz() function to give the correct answers.

```
    <html>
    <head>
    <title>A Quiz</title>
    <script language="JavaScript">
    <!-- hide me from old browsers
    function scoreQuiz()
    {
❶   var correct = 0;
❷   if (window.document.the_form.question1.checked == true) {
❸               correct = correct + 1;
        }
❹   if (window.document.the_form.question2.checked == true) {
                correct = correct + 1;
        }
❺   if (window.document.the_form.question3.checked == false) {
                correct = correct + 1;
        }
❻   alert("you got " + correct + " answers right!");
    }
    // end hiding comment -->
    </script>
    </head>
    <body>
    <h1>A Little Quiz</h1>
    Check the statements that are true:
    <form name = "the_form">
    <input type = "checkbox" name = "question1"> All men are featherless bipeds
    <input type = "checkbox" name = "question2"> All kangaroos are featherless bipeds
    <input type = "checkbox" name = "question3"> All men are kangaroos
❼   <input type = "button" value = "score this quiz" onClick = "scoreQuiz();">
    </form>
    </body>
    </html>
```

Figure 7-21: The code for the quiz

In Figure 7-22, I add an else to each if-then clause, which sets the checkbox to the correct answer if the visitor gets the answer wrong. The first if-then clause, starting with ❶, reads in plain English, "If the visitor checks the first checkbox, the answer is correct, so add 1 to the variable correct. Otherwise, check the first checkbox to indicate the correct answer." If the visitor guessed wrong, ❷ selects the first checkbox by setting its checked property to true.

```
    function scoreQuiz()
    {
        var correct = 0;
❶      if (window.document.the_form.question1.checked == true) {
            correct = correct + 1;
        } else {
❷          window.document.the_form.question1.checked = true;
        }
        if (window.document.the_form.question2.checked == true)
        {
            correct = correct + 1;
        } else {
            window.document.the_form.question2.checked = true;
        }
        if (window.document.the_form.question3.checked == false) {
            correct = correct + 1;
        } else {
            window.document.the_form.question3.checked = false;
        }
        alert("you got " + correct + " answers right! The correct answers are now shown");
    }
```

Figure 7-22: The scoreQuiz() function from 7-21, changed to show the correct answers

Reading and Setting Radio Buttons

Reading and setting are slightly more complicated for radio buttons than for text fields and checkboxes. Because all the radio buttons in a group have the same name, you can't just ask about the settings for a radio button with a certain name: JavaScript won't know which button you mean.

To overcome this difficulty, JavaScript puts all of the radio buttons with the same name in a list. Each radio button in the list is given a number. The first radio button in the group is number 0, the second is 1, the third is 2, and so on. (Most programming languages start counting from 0—you just have to get used to this.)

To refer to a radio button, use the notation **radio_button_name[item_number]**. For example, if you have four radio buttons named age, the first one will be age[0], the second will be age[1], the third age[2], and the fourth age[3].

If you want to see whether a visitor has chosen a certain radio button, you have to look at its checked property, just as with checkboxes. Let's say you have four radio buttons named age inside a form called radio_button_form, as in Figure 7-13. If you want to see whether your visitor has selected the first radio button in the age group, write something like this:

```
if (window.document.radio_button_form.age[0].checked == true)
{
    alert("the first radio button was selected!");
}
```

You would use much the same method for a checkbox. The only difference is that you have to refer to the first radio button in the age group as age[0], whereas with a checkbox you can just give its name.

Once you know how to determine whether a radio button is checked, it's easy to understand how to select a radio button with JavaScript. With checkboxes, you use something like this:

```
window.document.form_name.checkbox_name.checked = true;
```

With radio buttons, you have to tell JavaScript which radio button you mean by referring to its list number. To select the first radio button of a set called age, input this:

```
window.document.form_name.age[0].checked = true;
```

Reading and Setting Pull-down Menus and Scrollable Lists

JavaScript can read and set pull-down menus and scrollable lists as it does radio buttons, with two main differences. First, while radio buttons have a checked property, pull-down menus and scrollable lists have a property called selected. Second, the list that keeps track of the options in a pull-down menu or scrollable list differs from that for a radio button. As discussed in the section on reading and setting radio buttons, when a browser sees a group of radio buttons, it creates a list with the same name as the radio buttons. In Figure 7-11, we named the radio buttons gender, so the browser calls the list gender. The first element of this list is called gender[0].

In contrast, the options property, a list of all the options in the pull-down or scrollable list, can tell you what's selected in that menu or list. In the list for the simple pull-down shown in Figure 7-23, male is the first element (item number 0) and female the second (item number 1).

```
<form name = "my_form">
<select name = "the_gender">
<option value = "male">Male
<option value = "female">Female
</select>
</form>
```

Figure 7-23: A simple pull-down menu

Thus the following lines tell you if a visitor has selected the first option in the list (male):

```
if (window.document.my_form.the_gender.options[0].selected == true)
{
    alert("it's a boy!)";
}
```

You can also select an option:

```
window.document.my_form.the_gender.options[1].selected = true;
```

Executing this line of JavaScript would select the female option in the pull-down menu.

The Fast Way to Find Out Which Item Is Chosen in a Pull-down Menu

Sometimes you have a long list of options in a pull-down menu, and you just want to know which one someone selected. Happily, pull-down menus and scrollable lists have a selectedIndex property that contains the number of the selected option. Once you know that number, you can retrieve the option's value.

Let's say you have a pull-down menu like the one in Figure 7-23. To figure out quickly whether a visitor chose male or female in this pull-down menu, you write something like this:

```
❶ var gender_number = window.document.my_form.the_gender.selectedIndex;
❷ var chosen_gender = window.document.my_form.the_gender.options[gender_number].value;
```

❶ determines the selected option in the the_gender pull-down menu by looking at the selectedIndex of the_gender pull-down (in the form my_form within the document of the window). If the user has selected the first pull-down option, gender_number equals 0.

❷ retrieves the value of the selected option by looking at the list of options in the the_gender pull-down menu and finding the value of the option numbered gender_number (the number that the first line found).

Often, the two lines above will be merged into one long line, like this:

```
var chosen_gender =
window.document.my_form.the_gender.options[window.document.my_form.the_gender.selectedIndex].
value;
```

In this line, the part that figures out the chosen option number appears in square brackets. JavaScript first uses selectedIndex to identify the option, then looks up its value.

I'll show you a way to shorten this line when we discuss using pull-down menus as navigation tools. But before that, you need to know a little more about forms in general.

Handling Events Using Form Elements

So far, all the functions in this chapter have been triggered by a visitor clicking on a link or button.

Each type of form element has its own type of list of triggering events. As demonstrated in Figure 7-21, button elements can use onClick to call a function when someone clicks on the button. However, not all form elements take onClick. Table 7-1 shows you some of the events that different form elements handle. You'll find a complete list in Appendix B.

Table 7-1: Some events that different form elements can handle

Form Element	Event	What Triggers the Event
Button	onClick	Self-explanatory
Checkbox	onClick	Self-explanatory
Radio button	onClick	Self-explanatory
Text field	onChange	Change the contents of a text field and then click out of the field (anywhere else on the Web page)
Textarea	onChange	Change what's in a textarea and then click out of it
Select	onChange	Change a selection in the pull-down menu or list
Form	onSubmit	Press ENTER inside a text field or click on a submit button

Note that text fields, textareas, and selects can only trigger events when someone changes them. If a user clicks on a pull-down menu and then chooses an already selected option, that doesn't trigger the onChange event. Similarly, if someone clicks on a text field and then clicks somewhere else without changing anything in the text field, onChange won't register this action.

Notice also that the form element takes an event called onSubmit. A form is *submitted* when somebody presses the ENTER key with the cursor in a text field, or when they push a *submit button*. Figure 7-24 shows you how to build a very simple browser using a form with an onSubmit event.

```
<html>
<head>
<title>A Simple Browser</title>
</head>
<body>
Type in a URL and then either press the submit button or just press the enter key.
❶ <form name="the_form" onSubmit="window.location = window.document.the_form.the_url.value;
   return false;">
<input type = "text" name = "the_url" value = "http://">
❷ <input type = "submit" value="go there!">
</form>
</body>
</html>
```

Figure 7-24: Using onSubmit inside a form

❶ shows you what onSubmit does. In this case, the onSubmit says, "Whenever someone submits this form, look into the form element called the_url and send this person to the URL there." This happens when a visitor presses ENTER in the text field or clicks on the submit button (❷). The return false that appears at the end of ❶ prevents the Web browser from taking control away from JavaScript when the form is submitted. Without it, the JavaScript command never executes.

Make This a Shortcut

You might have noticed that ❶ in Figure 7-24 is a little long. You can shorten it by replacing most of the part identifying the form, window.document.the_form, with the word this, which refers to the thing that contains it. For example, in ❶ of Figure 7-24, the code that looks for the value of the_url is located inside the form tag. That means you can replace all the code identifying the form tag with the word this—in other words, you can write ❶ in Figure 7-24 as follows:

```
<form name="the_form" onSubmit="window.location = this.the_url.value;">
```

I've replaced the elements which identify the form, window.document. the_form, with this, since this is inside the form tag. Though it's sometimes hard to know what this will be, in general it refers to whatever HTML tag contains it.

Here's another example. Imagine we've written a function called check Email() that makes sure an email address entered into a form is valid (we'll be doing this in Chapter 11). The form and text box used to collect the email address could look like this:

```
<form name="the_form">
<input type="text" name="email"
onChange="checkEmail(window.document.the_form.email.value);">
</form>
```

However, the elements `window.document.the_form.email` inside the onChange simply identify the text field that the onChange is part of. Because the text field is sending its own `value` to the `checkEmail()` function, the onChange of the text field can be rewritten like this:

```
onChange="checkEmail(this.value);">
```

Here, the term `this` replaces `window.document.the_form.email` because `this` appears inside the text field.

Using Pull-down Menus as Navigational Tools

Now you're ready to create a navigational pull-down menu, like the one Sun Microsystems uses in Figure 7-2. Figure 7-25 shows you what such a tool typically looks like, and Figure 7-26 on page 138 gives you the script.

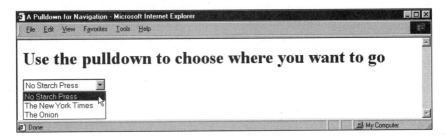

Figure 7-25: A simple navigation tool

You should understand most of the script in Figure 7-26 by now. The onChange in ❶ is the only tricky part (remember that `<select>` tags take the onChange event). When the onChange happens, it calls the function `visitSite()`, which receives this value:

```
this.options[this.selectedIndex].value;
```

```
<html>
<head>
<title>A Pull-Down Menu for Navigation</title>
<script language = "JavaScript">
<!-- hide me from older browsers
function visitSite(the_site)
{
    window.location = the_site;
}
// show me -->
</script>
</head>
<body>
<h1>Use the pull-down menu to choose where you want to go</h1>
<form name = "the_form">
<select name = "the_select" onChange = "visitSite(this.options[this.selectedIndex].value);">
<option value = "http://www.nostarch.com">No Starch Press
<option value = "http://www.nytimes.com">The New York Times
<option value = "http://www.theonion.com">The Onion
</select>
</body>
</html>
```

❶ (marker on `<select` line)

Figure 7-26: Using pull-down menus as navigation tools

The two instances of the word this make this line a bit hard to figure out. Let's expand this into what it stands for. Because the word this appears in the <select> tag, it stands for that <select> tag. The longer version of the line above is

```
window.document.the_form.the_select.options[window.document.the_form.the_select.
selectedIndex].value
```

You can see how this can save a lot of space. In either case, we get the number of the selected option by looking at the selectedIndex of the pull-down menu. Once we know that number, we can obtain the selected value by looking in the options list.

How Sun Microsystems Creates Its Pull-down Navigation Tool

Sun Microsystems' pull-down navigation code is slightly different from that in Figure 7-26. Figure 7-27 shows Sun's code, abbreviated to save space.

```
<html>
<title> Sun Microsystems</title>
<SCRIPT LANGUAGE="JavaScript">
<!--
function gotoFunction() {
        self.location =
document.productGoto.productList.options[document.productGoto.productList.selectedIndex].value;
}
// -->
</SCRIPT>
</HEAD>
<BODY BGCOLOR="#666699" LINK="#666699" VLINK="#666699" ALINK="#FF0000">
<FORM NAME="productGoto" ACTION="/cgi-bin/gotopic.cgi" METHOD="POST">
<SELECT NAME="productList" ONCHANGE="gotoFunction()">
<OPTION VALUE="#">SELECT A TOPIC
<OPTION VALUE="#">————————————————
<OPTION VALUE="/store/">SUNSTORE
<OPTION VALUE="/dot-com/">HOW TO .COM
<OPTION VALUE="/dot-com/keynotes/"> &gt; Executive Keynotes
<OPTION VALUE="/dot-com/perspectives/"> &gt; Executive Perspectives
<OPTION VALUE="/dot-com/reading/"> &gt; Executive Reading
<OPTION VALUE="/dot-com/studies/"> &gt; Case Studies
</SELECT>
</FORM>
</BODY>
</HTML>
```

Figure 7-27: Sun Microsystem's pull-down navigational tool

In line ❷ you see two additions to the <form> tag that I haven't discussed yet—an ACTION and a METHOD. Before JavaScript, you could only use forms with CGI scripts. These two elements send information entered into the form to a server-side CGI script and thus allow a browser that doesn't understand Java-Script to use forms. However, CGI scripting is a completely separate world from JavaScript, so I won't discuss it further here.

Another relatively new aspect of Sun's script is the capitalization of the letters in onChange (❸). As I've mentioned before, according to the World Wide Web Consortium's strictures, you should capitalize all your HTML tags. However, convention strongly favors writing events with incaps notation. Whether you choose regulation or convention is up to you.

Notice also that ❸ doesn't pass the value of the selected option to the function. If you look back at ❶ in Figure 7-26, you'll see that it calls the function inside the <select> tag:

```
onChange = "visitSite(this.options[this.selectedIndex].value);"
```

Inside this tag, we had the option of using the word this to replace the longer version, window.document.the_form.the_select. Because Sun didn't pass the value into the function from inside the select field, it will have to write a bit more code.

❹ in Sun's script is pretty interesting. Each of the options in the pull-down tool has a value, which is the URL to visit if a visitor chooses that pull-down option. However, the first two options just show formatting—Sun doesn't want you to go anywhere if you choose one of these, and has given each a pound sign (#) as its value. In HTML, the pound sign means the top of the page. Since the visitor is already at the top of the page, this doesn't have any effect.

Now let's look at the function that reads the selection and sends the visitor to the appropriate location. This function (❶) first looks for the number of the selected option:

```
document.productGoto.productList.selectedIndex
```

It finds the value of that option, a URL:

```
document.productGoto.productList.options[document.productGoto.productList.selectedIndex].value;
```

Then it uses self.location to send the visitor to that URL. Notice that Sun uses self.location instead of window.location—the two are actually interchangeable, however.

Summary

We covered a lot of ground in this chapter. If you missed any item in the list below, go back and take another look. You should now know:

- How to write HTML forms.

- How to read information entered into a form.

- How to write your own content to a form.

- How to trigger functions from all the form elements.

- How to use the word this as a shortcut.

Most form hassles involve the various form elements. Take a look at Appendix B for a complete review of what kinds of events the different elements trigger and what information your JavaScript can discover from them.

Assignment

Write a clock that tells the time in San Francisco, New York, London, and Tokyo. The clock should have a text field for the time, a button to update the clock, and four radio buttons, each for a different time zone. When you click on one of the radio buttons, the correct time should appear in the text field. When you click on the update button, the clock should update with the time from the zone you've selected with the radio buttons. Figure 7-28 shows an example.

Figure 7-28: Updating the time for different cities

First you'll need some information about looking up time. Remember from Chapter 2 how to get the current hour:

```
var now = new Date();
var the_hour = now.getHours();
```

The Date() object has a few methods that come in handy for dealing with different time zones. In this case, use getUTCHours(), getUTCMinutes(), and getUTCSeconds(). These methods tell you the hour, minutes, and seconds in Coordinated Universal Time (UTC), which has replaced Greenwich mean time as the world standard.

London time is the same as UTC time. New York time is five hours behind London time, California time is eight hours behind London time, and Tokyo is nine hours ahead of London time.

As always, the answer is in Appendix C, but you'll learn a lot more if you give the assignment a good try before looking there. It's not an easy assignment, so don't be surprised if it takes longer than an hour to get it exactly right.

8

KEEPING TRACK OF
INFORMATION WITH
ARRAYS AND LOOPS

The last chapter showed you how JavaScript stores radio buttons and pull-down menu options in lists. In programmer's parlance, lists are called *arrays*. This chapter will teach you how to create your own arrays and use them to keep track of large amounts of information.

In this chapter, you'll learn how to:

- Use JavaScript's built-in arrays to control your HTML.

- Create new arrays of your own information.

- Use loops to search through arrays for information.

Real-World Examples of Arrays

JavaScript's built-in arrays are useful in a wide variety of applications. HotMail, for example, uses JavaScript's built-in arrays to let users move or delete email messages (see Figure 8-1). At the top of a list of HotMail messages you'll see a checkbox. Clicking on this box causes all the other checkboxes to become checked. This trick is easy because the checkboxes are stored in an array, allowing HotMail to use JavaScript to check off each one. Look on your CD-ROM under sites/hotmail to see this in action.

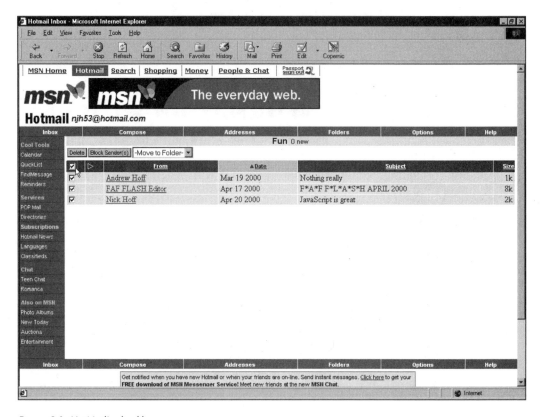

Figure 8-1: HotMail's checkboxes

Creating your own arrays can be useful as well. The Ask Jeeves search engine employs arrays to show users the questions others have asked. In the textarea in Figure 8-2, you'll see one of a dozen questions that rotate through this box. Ask Jeeves stores this list of questions in a JavaScript array and rotates through the array to put different questions into the textarea. The same principle applies to making a timed slide show, which we'll see in the next chapter.

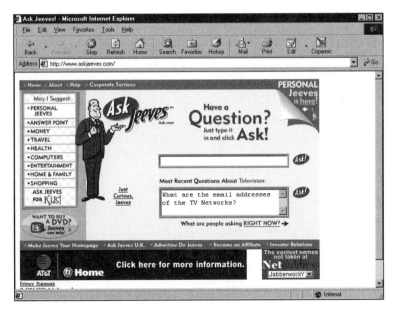

Figure 8-2: Ask Jeeves' rotating questions

JavaScript's Built-in Arrays

When a Web browser reads an HTML page, it automatically creates a number of arrays. In the previous chapter we saw that JavaScript creates an array for each set of radio buttons with the same name. If you create a set of radio buttons named age, you can refer to the first radio button in the set like this:

```
window.document.the_form.age[0]
```

JavaScript also creates an array for the options in each pull-down menu and scrollable list. Here's how you could access the second option in a pull-down menu named gender:

```
window.document.the_form.gender.options[1]
```

These are just two of JavaScript's automatically created arrays. Browsers also automatically create an images array of all the image objects on a Web page. The same holds true for form elements (the array of form elements is called elements). In Figure 8-3 (the Document Object Model), you can see which elements (the boxes with the words array of in them) get automatically created arrays.

Each of these arrays is built based on how the page's creator has written its HTML. In the images array, for example, the first image on a Web page is called images[0], the second is images[1], and so on. If you use the images

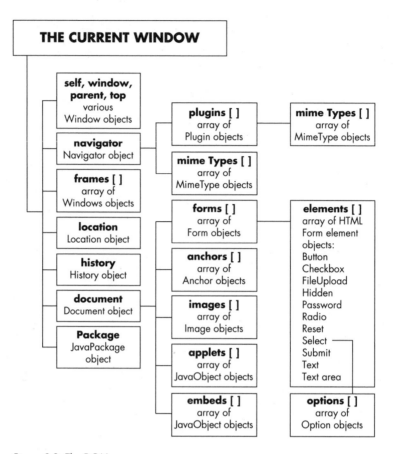

Figure 8-3: The DOM

array, you don't have to name your images to swap them (as in Chapter 4). For example, you can swap the first image on a Web page with an image called happy.gif with this line:

```
window.document.images[0].src = 'happy.gif';
```

Why Built-in Arrays Are Helpful

Why would you want to use built-in arrays instead of just naming HTML elements? Sometimes you have no choice. As we saw in Chapter 7, because all the radio buttons in a set have the same name, you can only access them using the built-in array.

Built-in arrays also come in useful when you have many elements on a page. If you have a Web page with 100 images, naming them all becomes tedious. Instead, you can just refer to each image by its number (for a set of 100 images, the numbers would be 0 to 99).

The best thing about arrays, however, is that a little bit of JavaScript can act on each element in the array—a great time-saving feature if you have a 100-element array. In the HotMail example, clicking on one checkbox checks all the individual message checkboxes. It doesn't matter if you have a lone checkbox or 1,000 of them—the code is the same.

To affect an entire array as the HotMail script does, you need to know how many elements the array contains, and then write some code that goes through each element in the array and does what you want to it. HotMail, for example, figures out how many checkboxes there are, and then checks each one.

Figuring Out How Many Items an Array Contains

In all JavaScript-enabled browsers except for Netscape 2.0, an array's length property contains the number of elements in an array. The script in Figure 8-4 figures out how many images a Web page holds.

```
<script language="JavaScript">

<!-- hide me
❶ var num_images = window.document.images.length;
   alert("there are " + num_images + " images on this page. ");
// show me -->
</script>
```

Figure 8-4: How many images a Web page contains

Drop this JavaScript into the bottom of a Web page with images and you'll see how it works. The critical line is ❶, which tells JavaScript to create a variable called num_images and set it to the number of images in the built-in images array. If the page has ten images, num_images will equal ten.

NOTE   *As mentioned above, Netscape 2.0 arrays don't have the length property. See "Dealing with Netscape 2.0 Arrays" for how to cope with Netscape 2.0 users.*

Going through Arrays

Once you know how many elements are in an array, you need to write some code that goes through each element. If you have a list of four checkboxes and want to check them all, you could write a script like Figure 8-5.

```
<html>
<head>
<title>Checking Four Checkboxes</title>
<script language = "JavaScript">
<!-- hide me
function checkFour()
{
    window.document.the_form.elements[0].checked = true;
    window.document.the_form.elements[1].checked = true;
    window.document.the_form.elements[2].checked = true;
    window.document.the_form.elements[3].checked = true;
}
// show me -->
</script>
</head>
<body>
<form name = "the_form">
<input type = "checkbox"> One <br>
<input type = "checkbox"> Two <br>
<input type = "checkbox"> Three <br>
<input type = "checkbox"> Four <br>
<input type = "button" value = "check 'em" onClick="checkFour();"> <br>
</form>
</body>
</html>
```

Figure 8-5: Checking four checkboxes

The function in this script goes through each of the four checkboxes and sets its checked property to true (see the result in Figure 8-6). But this code is not the best solution, since it only works for four checkboxes. To work with five checkboxes, you'd have to add another line to the function. For the HotMail example, this code would be a disaster, since the number of checkboxes on your HotMail inbox page depends on the number of email messages you've received. The people who programmed HotMail would somehow have to change the JavaScript every time you got a new email message—not a good idea at all.

Even if you have a static number of checkboxes, the code in Figure 8-5 would become problematic with too many checkboxes. With 1,000 checkboxes, for example, the function would end up 1,000 lines long, each line identical to the one before it except for the number between brackets. Not only would this be annoying to write, it would greatly increase the page's download time.

Figure 8-6: The checkboxes checked

You can avoid both these problems with a *loop*. A loop allows you to execute the same lines of JavaScript multiple times with slight variations. For example, a loop could execute the line

```
window.document.the_form.elements[0].checked = true;
```

1,000 times, changing the number in the brackets each time.

while Loops

One kind of loop is called a *while* loop. In plain English, this translates to "While such-and-such is true, do these lines." Figure 8-7 on page 150 shows a while loop that prints the word happy three times.

Loops are a very common programming technique. They may seem strange the first couple of times you see them, but they are so common that after a while you'll understand them on sight.

The typical while loop starts with a variable set to zero, as in Figure 8-7's ❶. The variable index is just like any other variable.

Once you've set this variable, the while loop begins. ❷ reads, "While the variable index is less than three, execute the JavaScript between the curly braces (❸ and ❻)." The format of this line is important. The word while must be lowercase and the boolean test index < 3 must fall between parentheses.

When JavaScript sees ❷, it checks whether the variable index is less than three. If it is, the script runs the lines between the curly braces ❸ and ❻. When we start, index is zero, which is less than three, so the script executes the two lines between ❸ and ❻. ❹ writes the word happy to the Web page, and ❺ adds one to index, changing it from zero to one.

Once we execute ❺ and reach the curly brace ❻, JavaScript jumps back to line ❷ to see if index is still less than three. This is the nature of the while loop. Every time JavaScript reaches ❻, it jumps back to ❷ to see if the test in the parentheses is still true. Because one is less than three, JavaScript executes ❹, which prints happy again; it then executes ❺, adding one to index (which now has a value of two).

```
       <html>
       <head>
       <title>I'm Happy and I Know It</title>
       </head>
       <body>
       I'm <br>
       <script language = "JavaScript">
       <!-- hide me
❶  var index = 0;
❷  while (index < 3)
❸  {
❹    window.document.writeln("happy<br>");
❺    index = index + 1;
❻  }
❼  // show me -->
       </script>
       and I know it!
       </body>
       </html>
```

Figure 8-7: Printing the word happy three times with a while loop

Again, because we're in a while loop, JavaScript jumps from ❻ to ❷ and checks to see if index is still less than three. It is, so ❹ and ❺ execute again. The word happy appears a third time, and the script increments index from two to three.

Once again, JavaScript jumps from ❻ to line ❷ and checks to see if index is less than three. This time, however, index is equal to three, so the test (index < 3) is not true. Thus the while loop stops and JavaScript jumps to ❼, the line after the closing curly brace.

Many people have a hard time with looping, so make sure you understand how it works. You may find it helpful to translate ❷ into plain English: "While index is less than three, write happy and add one to index."

while Loops and Arrays

Now that you know how while loops work, you can apply them to arrays. Look back at the function in Figure 8-5 and notice that each of the four lines is more or less the same:

```
window.document.the_form.elements[some_number].checked = true;
```

The only difference is the number between the square brackets. Now think about the variable index in Figure 8-7. The value of the variable index increases by one each time the script goes through the loop. This feature makes the index variable ideal for accessing each element in an array. Figure 8-8 below uses index to create a more flexible version of Figure 8-5.

```
        <html>
        <head>
        <title>Checking Four Checkboxes</title>
        <script language = "JavaScript">
        <!-- hide me
        function checkFour()
        {
❶         var index = 0;
❷         while (index < 4)
❸         {
❹          window.document.the_form.elements[index].checked = true;
❺          index = index + 1;
❻         }
❼ }
        // show me -->
        </script>
        </head>
        <body>
        <form name = "the_form">
        <input type = "checkbox"> One <br>
        <input type = "checkbox"> Two <br>
        <input type = "checkbox"> Three <br>
        <input type = "checkbox"> Four <br>
        <input type = "button" value = "check 'em" onClick = "checkFour();"> <br>
        </form>
        </body>
        </html>
```

Figure 8-8: Using a loop to check four checkboxes

The critical line is ❹, which says, "Set form element number index to true." The first time through the loop, index is zero, so ❹ checks the first form element (the first checkbox). Then ❺ adds one to index, changing index from zero to one. JavaScript reaches ❻ and jumps back to ❷, executes ❹ and ❺ since index is less than four, and repeats the process until index equals four. When index equals four and JavaScript jumps to line ❷, the while loop ends (since index is no longer less than four) and JavaScript jumps to ❼, the line after the closing curly brace.

Combining while loops and arrays is extremely common, so make sure you comprehend the process. The advantage of this kind of code is that it works whether you have just a few checkboxes or a few thousand. To get the code to work for, say, 4,000 checkboxes, just change the number in ❷ from 4 to 4,000. The loop will then run 4,000 times, starting with 0 and finally ending when index equals 4,000.

Using array.length in Your Loop

The code in Figure 8-8 works well, but it could use one improvement. In general, it's best to have as few numbers in your code as possible: Using specific numbers tends to make code apply only in specific situations. In Figure 8-8, for example, ❷ works only when exactly four checkboxes appear on the page. If you add another checkbox to the Web page, you'll have to remember to change the four in ❷ to five. Rather than rely on your memory, you should rewrite ❷ like this:

```
while (index < window.document.the_form.elements.length)
```

The expression window.document.the_form.elements.length always equals the number of form elements on a page, since adding another checkbox automatically increases the length of the elements array.

An Incremental Shortcut

Lines like ❺ in Figure 8-8 are such frequent occurrences that programmers have come up with the shorthand index++ to replace index = index + 1. That's the variable index followed by two plus signs (++). This saves you the hassle of typing index twice. We'll be seeing many other shortcuts like this later.

Beware of Infinite Loops

You should avoid one common loop mistake like the plague. It's so common that it has a name: the *infinite loop*. Infinite loops happen when your code enters a loop it can never exit. Figure 8-9 shows you the classic error.

```
var index = 0;
while (index < 10)
{
    window.document.write("I am infinite! <br>");
}
```

Figure 8-9: The classic infinite loop—don't try this at home

Running this script will make you sad, so please don't try it. If you do run it, the script will endlessly write "I am infinite!" to the page. To stop the script from running, you'd have to quit the browser, which sometimes isn't easy when you're stuck in an infinite loop.

This loop is infinite because I forgot to add one to index after writing, "I am infinite!" The index variable starts at zero and never changes, so the test while (index < 10) is always true. Since index < 10 is always true, the loop continues until you exit the browser.

The only way to avoid accidentally writing an infinite loop is to exercise caution. Whenever you write a loop, make sure the loop will exit at some point.

for Loops

Another type of loop is the for loop. You format while and for loops differently, but they do the same things. Which loop you use is largely a matter of preference. Though for loops look a little more confusing at first, they are more compact.

Figure 8-10 compares a while loop and a for loop that perform exactly the same task.

```
    while loop
❶ var index = 0;
❷ while (index < 10)
  {
      window.document.writeln("hello<br>");
❸     index++;
  }
    for loop
❹ for (var index = 0; index < 10; index++)
  {
      window.document.writeln("hello<br>");
  }
```

Figure 8-10: Comparing a while loop and a for loop

Both of the loops in Figure 8-10 write the word hello to a Web page ten times. The main difference between them is that ❶, ❷, and ❸ in the while loop collapse into ❹ in the for loop. The format of a for loop is as follows:

```
for (initializer ; test; increment)
{
    // some JavaScript
}
```

All for loops start with the word for, followed by parentheses containing three values, separated by semicolons. The first value is the loop's starting number. In all the previous examples, we've started with something like var index = 0. In ❹ of Figure 8-10, the first value in the parentheses of the for loop is var index = 0 (the same as ❶ in the while loop). The second value in the parentheses of a for loop is the test. In ❹ of Figure 8-10, the test is index < 10 (the same as ❷ in the while loop). The final value in the parentheses of the for loop is the number you're adding to the initializer variable each time the loop repeats (like ❸ in the while loop).

Whether you use while or for loops is a matter of taste. You can write for loops in fewer lines, but while loops are a bit easier to read. Some people prefer for loops because they lower the risk of accidentally getting into an infinite loop. In a while loop, you can easily neglect to put index++ inside the curly braces. In the for loop, it's hard to forget to put this element inside the parentheses because you always have three expressions there.

How HotMail Checks Off All the Message Boxes

Figure 8-11 shows you a stripped-down version of how HotMail uses loops to check off all your messages when you click on the checkbox at the top of your messages list.

I've taken out HotMail's HTML formatting, but the CheckAll() function is exactly the same as HotMail's. To see the HotMail page in all its formatting glory, look in the sites/hotmail directory of your CD-ROM.

Line-by-Line Analysis of Figure 8-11

The first few lines in Figure 8-11 describe the form that contains the messages. ❶ names the form hotmail, and ❷ and the two lines after it name each of the checkboxes that precede an email message. ❸ describes the checkbox that causes the other checkboxes to become checked. This checkbox is named allbox; clicking on it calls the function CheckAll(), which starts on ❹. ❺, the first line in the functions body, sets up a for loop. The loop goes from zero to the number of elements in the form named hotmail. There are four elements in this form, the three message checkboxes and the fourth checkbox that calls CheckAll(). Notice that HotMail uses the variable i for the loop, rather than index, which is what I would use. Naming a variable i is generally a bad idea because you might forget what it stands for; however, it's a fairly common practice to use variables like i and j for loops.

```
      <html>
      <head>
      <title>HotMail's Use of Arrays and Loops</title>
      </head>
      <body>
❶    <form name = "hotmail">
❷    <input type = "checkbox" name = "message1">Message 1<br>
      <input type = "checkbox" name = "message2">Message 2<br>
      <input type = "checkbox" name = "message3">Message 3<br>
❸    <input type = "checkbox" name = "allbox" onClick = "CheckAll();">Select all displayed
      messages<br>
      </form>
      <script language="JavaScript">
      <!--
❹    function CheckAll()
      {
❺      for (var i=0; i<document.hotmail.elements.length;i++)
        {
❻          var e = document.hotmail.elements[i];
❼        if (e.name != 'allbox')
❽              e.checked = document.hotmail.allbox.checked;
        }
      }
      // -->
      </script>
      </body>
      </html>
```

Figure 8-11: HotMail's use of arrays and loops

❻ creates a new variable called e (also a bad name) and assigns it to point to one of the form elements. Which element this is depends on the value of i. The first time through the loop, i will be zero, so e will point to the first element in the hotmail form—the first checkbox. The second time through the loop, i will be one, so e will point to the second checkbox. The loop occurs four times, once for each checkbox. HotMail wants to set the checked value of the first three checkboxes to the value of the last checkbox. If the last checkbox is checked, meaning that a visitor has selected all the other messages, HotMail wants each message checked. If the last checkbox is not checked, the other checkboxes should be unchecked as well. ❽ takes care of this by setting the checked value of the checkbox that e points to—making it the same as the checked value of the last checkbox.

❼ is the last line of interest in this script. This line looks at the name of each form element in the loop. Just as you can get the checked value of a checkbox by looking at the_checkbox.checked, you can get its name by looking at the_checkbox.name.

If the form element is named allbox, **❽** won't execute. In effect, this line is saying, "Don't change the checkbox called allbox." The name property determines the name of a checkbox.

Strictly speaking, **❼** isn't necessary. Leaving **❼** out would mean the script would set the checked value of the last checkbox to—well, the checked value of the last checkbox. Although this wouldn't cause any problems, it's a waste of time, so preventing it with line **❼** is an elegant touch.

Creating Your Own Arrays

Arrays are so handy that you'll often want to create your own. A phone book, for example, is an array of names and phone numbers. You can think of a survey as an array of questions; an array can also store the answers a visitor enters. A slide show is an array of pictures shown in sequence.

Happily, JavaScript gives you the ability to create your own arrays. If you know what you want to store in the array when you create it, use a line like the following:

```
var rainbow_colors = new Array("red", "orange", "yellow", "green", "blue", "indigo", "violet");
```

This line creates a variable called rainbow_colors that stores an array of colors. The words new Array() tell JavaScript to create a new array object, just as new Date() created a new date object back in Chapter 2. To put values in your new array, simply list them in the parentheses.

Everything you've learned about JavaScript's built-in arrays also applies to arrays you create yourself. Figure 8-12 uses the rainbow_colors array to create a psychedelic strobe effect on a Web page.

❶ in Figure 8-12 creates the array and **❷** sets up the loop, saying, "While index is less than the number of items in the array, execute the JavaScript between the curly braces." The first time through the loop, index is zero, so when **❸** looks up rainbow_colors[index], it gets the first item in the array, the value red. **❸** assigns this value to window.document.bgColor, which sets the background color to red. Once the script has set this color, **❹** adds one to index, and the loop begins again. Next time through, index will be one, so **❸** will make the background color orange, **❹** then adds one to index, making it two, and back through the loop we go. If you have a very fast computer, the background may strobe too quickly for you to see it. In this case, add a few more colors to the array in **❶**.

```
<html>
<head>
<title>Strobe</title>
<script language = "JavaScript">
<!-- hide me
function strobeIt()
{
❶ var rainbow_colors =
      new Array("red", "orange", "yellow", "green", "blue", "indigo", "violet");
      var index = 0;
❷    while (index < rainbow_colors.length)
      {
❸      window.document.bgColor = rainbow_colors[index];
❹      index++;
      }
}
// show me -->
</script>
</head>
<body>
<form>
<input type = "button" value = "strobe" onClick="strobeIt();">
</form>
</body>
</html>
```

Figure 8-12: A psychedelic strobe effect

Dealing with Netscape 2.0 Arrays

Netscape 2.0, unlike any other JavaScript-enabled browser, does not have a length property and does not offer a built-in way to create your own arrays.

There are a few ways to deal with these differences. Some JavaScript coders use the techniques covered in Chapter 3 to detect which browser a visitor is using and write appropriate code. Others simply ignore the people using Netscape 2.0. (As of early 2000, Netscape 2.0 accounted for less than one half of one percent of the browsers in use.)

One common technique is to add the function shown in Figure 8-13 to any script that creates its own arrays.

```
function makeArray(len)
{
    for (var index = 0; index < length; index++)
    {
        this[index] = null;
    }
    this.length = len;
}
```

Figure 8-13: A function for Netscape 2.0 users

This function creates a new array specifically for Netscape 2.0 users. Instead of creating a new array like this:

```
var new_array = new Array();
```

you would write this:

```
var new_array = new makeArray(4);
```

if your array contained four elements. This only works when you know exactly how many elements the array will have, but if you need to create your own array and don't want to lock out Netscape 2.0 users, this is your only option.

How Ask Jeeves Uses Arrays It Has Created

The Ask Jeeves search engine has a little textarea that shows examples of previous searches. The script keeps these searches in an array, then uses JavaScript to loop through the array, showing one search at a time. Each search stays in the textarea for 3.5 seconds before the next one appears. The next chapter will discuss how to time events this precisely. For now, pay attention to how Ask Jeeves creates and loops through its array (Figure 8-14).

Line-by-Line Analysis of Figure 8-14

The code in Figure 8-14 contains many little tricks that I haven't yet covered. It starts out simply enough with ❶, which says, "After the page has loaded, call the function scroll()." The first line in the JavaScript tags, ❷, creates an array called text and loads it with a bunch of questions. ❸ creates a variable called count, and sets it equal to the number of questions in the text array.

```
      <html>
      <head>
      <title>Ask Jeeves' Use of Arrays and Loops</title>
      </head>
❶  <body onLoad="scroll();">
      <SCRIPT LANGUAGE="JavaScript">
      <!--
❷  var text = new Array("Where can I learn about the metabolic condition diabetes mellitus?",
      "Where can I learn about general information on smoking?", "Where can I learn about food
      labeling?");
❸  var count = text.length;
      var i = 0;
❹  while (text[count-1] == "")
❺      --count;
      function scroll() {
❻  if (count != null) {
❼      if (document.rotate) {
❽          document.rotate.ask.value = text[i++];
❾          if (i > count - 1)
❿          i= 0;
         }
❶❶      setTimeout("scroll()", 3500);
         }
      }
      // -->
      </SCRIPT>
      <FORM NAME="rotate" ACTION="/main/askjeeves.asp" METHOD="GET">
      <TEXTAREA NAME="ask" ROWS=3 COLS=30 WRAP="VIRTUAL"></TEXTAREA>
      </FORM>
      </BODY>
      </HTML>
```

Figure 8-14: Ask Jeeves' use of arrays and loops

Checking for Blank Questions

The next couple of lines exhibit Ask Jeeves' paranoid programming style.
Paranoid programmers make sure everything is perfect before they execute a
line of code that's going to affect the user experience. ❹ and ❺, for example,
make sure no blank questions (two quotation marks with nothing between
them) appear at the end of the text array. Who knows why that would happen—but just in case, ❹ checks the last element in the array. If it's not blank,
the loop ends. If it is blank, ❺ executes, reducing count by one. The loop

then checks to see if the second to last element is blank. If it's not, the loop ends. If it is, ❺ runs again, reducing count by one once more. Notice that you can subtract one from a variable with variable_name--. You can also use ++variable_name and --variable_name, which is what Ask Jeeves does in ❺.

Checking the Last Element in the Array

You might be wondering how ❹ checks the last element of the array. Remember, count equals the number of items in the array. If the array has three items, count equals three. However, because the first element in the array is zero, the last element in an array will be two—the length of the array minus one. To look at the last element of an array, use the following line:

```
var last_element = the_array[the_array.length - 1];
```

If the array contains three elements, the_array.length equals three, and the_array.length minus one equals two, which is the number JavaScript uses to reference the last element in the array. You may be thinking, "There's no way I'd ever figure that out!" But don't worry—this kind of array mathematics becomes second nature after you've done it a few times.

The scroll() Function

In the scroll() function, we find more programming paranoia. ❻ checks to see if the variable count actually has a setting. If not, its value is the word null. ❼ exhibits more paranoia. Ask Jeeves makes sure the form named rotate has drawn to the page by checking to see if the form named document.rotate exists. If it does not exist, document.rotate is false, and the lines between the brackets of the if-then statement won't execute. I have never encountered any browsers that support JavaScript but not forms. If they're out there, however, ❼ makes sure JavaScript won't try to write to a form that doesn't exist.

❽ looks up a question in the array and writes it into the textarea. This line tells JavaScript to find the form named rotate and the form element named ask and sets its value to whatever appears on the right side of the equal sign. The latter requires some explanation. Instead of just looking up the value of element i in the text array, and then adding one to i as in this line:

```
document.rotate.ask.value = text[i];
i++;
```

❽ looks up the value of element i, then adds one to i right there:

```
document.rotate.ask.value = text[i++];
```

This is legal and saves some space, but it's a little hard to read.

Going back to the notation introduced in ❺, if Ask Jeeves had done this:

```
document.rotate.ask.value = text[++i];
```

putting the plus signs in front of i, the JavaScript would add one to i and *then* look for the value of text[i]. It's the same as this line:

```
i++;
document.rotate.ask.value = text[i];
```

It's rare to see people messing around with the location of the double plus and minus operators. But if you run into this while looking at source code, now you know what's going on.

The next two lines, ❾ and ❿, are important for any program that continuously loops through an array. The Ask Jeeves JavaScript writes a question in the textarea, then moves on to the next question in the array, until it runs out of questions. Once that happens, Ask Jeeves wants the program to return to the first question in the array and start all over. ❾ and ❿ make this happen. ❾ determines whether the last question has appeared. If the variable i is more than count - 1, we've reached the end of the array. Remember, ❷ set count to the length of the array, so count - 1 is the position of the array's last element. If i is greater than count - 1, we've reached the array's end, and ❿ executes. ❿ sets the variable i back to zero, so the next time the script puts text[i] into the textarea, i equals the first question in the array.

❶❶ determines how fast the questions change in the textarea. The next chapter will talk more about ❶❶. For now, you just need to know that it translates as: "In 3.5 seconds, call the function scroll() again." Each time the script calls scroll(), the function puts a new question in the textarea and increments i by one.

Streamlined Jeeves

The code in Figure 8-14 is a bit confusing. Figure 8-15 on page 162 shows you a streamlined version that still works under almost any conditions.

Although the code in Figure 8-15 is more streamlined than Ask Jeeves' code, it's not necessarily better. Paranoia is a good thing in programming. The more checks you put in, the less likely your visitors are to encounter a JavaScript error. Given the choice between the code in Figures 8-14 and 8-15, I'd recommend the former because it's more robust. The code in Figure 8-15 is merely easier to understand.

```
<html>
<head>
<title>Ask Jeeves' Use of Arrays and Loops</title>
</head>
<body onLoad="scroll();">
<SCRIPT LANGUAGE="JavaScript">
<!--
var text = new Array("Where can I learn about the metabolic condition diabetes mellitus?",
"Where can I learn about general information on smoking?", "Where can I learn about food
labeling?");
var i = 0;
function scroll() {
    document.rotate.ask.value = text[i];
    i++;
    if (i == text.length)
    {
        i= 0;
    }
    setTimeout("scroll()", 3500);
}
// -->
</SCRIPT>
<FORM NAME="rotate">
<TEXTAREA NAME="ask" ROWS=3 COLS=30 WRAP="VIRTUAL"></TEXTAREA>
</FORM>
</BODY>
</HTML>
```

Figure 8-15: A more streamlined version of Figure 8-14

Loops Can Nest

As with if-then statements inside other if-then statements, you can also put loops inside other loops. For example, Figure 8-16 shows you a script that writes a solid rectangle of Xs to a Web page 5 Xs high and 10 Xs wide (see the result in Figure 8-17). It's not very useful, but it offers an idea of how nesting loops work.

❶ in Figure 8-16 sets up a loop that will happen five times. Each time through that loop, the second loop (❷ and ❸) runs. That loop writes the letter X to the Web page 10 times. After that loop has run, ❹ writes a <br> to the Web page, creating a line break. After ❹ runs, the loop at ❶ runs again. This happens 5 times. Each time loop ❶ runs, loop ❷ writes a line of 10 Xs, then ❹ writes a <br>. Loops inside loops can seem puzzling at first, but they can come in handy.

```
❶  for (first_loop = 0; first_loop < 5; first_loop++) {
❷      for (second_loop = 0; second_loop < 10; second_loop++) {
❸          window.document.writeln("X");
        }
❹      window.document.writeln("<br>");
    }
```

Figure 8-16: A simple example of nesting loops

Figure 8-17: The rectangle of Xs created
with nested loops in Figure 8-16

Creating Arrays as You Go Along

If you're giving someone a quiz and want to store the answers in an array, you must create an array even though you don't know what it will store. In such cases, you'll need to build your array piece by piece.

Start by creating an empty array, as in this line:

```
var the_answers = new Array();
```

This tells JavaScript to create a new array called the_answers, leaving it empty. Unfortunately, this line won't work in Netscape 2.0 (see "Dealing with Netscape 2.0 Arrays" for how to support Netscape 2.0 users).

Once you've created the array, you can load values into it, like this:

```
the_answers[0] = "yes";
the_answers[1] = "no";
the_answers[2] = "maybe";
```

The first line puts the word yes into the first slot of the array, the next puts no into the second slot, and the third line puts maybe into the third slot. You can store values in an array in any order. Reversing the three lines above wouldn't make any difference. The word *maybe* goes into the third slot of the array because the number 2 appears between the square brackets. Figure 8-18 demonstrates how to use this technique to create a Madlib, that fun seventies party game.

```
<html>
<head>
<title>Madlib</title>
</head>
<body>
<script language = "JavaScript">
<!-- hide me

❶ alert("this is a madlib! please fill in the blanks appropriately");
❷ var answers = new Array();
❸ answers[0] = prompt("an animal","bear");
  answers[1] = prompt("an adjective","happy");
  answers[2] = prompt("a past tense verb","kissed");
  answers[3] = prompt("an object","tree");

❹ var the_string = "";
❺ the_string = the_string + "Once upon a time there was a " + answers[0];
  the_string = the_string + " who was very " + answers[1] + ".";
  the_string = the_string + " In fact, he was so " + answers[1];
  the_string = the_string + " that he " + answers[2] + " a " + answers[3];

❻ window.document.writeln(the_string);

  // show me -->
</script>
</body>
</html>
```

Figure 8-18: A short Madlib

It's not a very long Madlib, but you get the idea. When someone comes to this page, the alert in ❶ greets the visitor. After the alert, the script creates a new, empty array in ❷. The next few lines, starting with ❸, fill the array. Each of these lines uses the prompt() function to ask a question, then loads the answer into the array. The first answer goes into array position zero, the next into array position one, and so on. By the time the script reaches ❹, the visitor has filled the array's first four positions. ❹ initializes a variable that stores the contents of the Madlib. The next few lines, starting with ❺, build this string. Each line adds content to the string. ❺ adds "Once upon a time there was a *user answer*." The next line appends "who was very *user answer*" to the end of the string. ❻ writes the complete string to the Web page.

Associative Arrays

All the arrays we've seen so far have stored values according to their numerical position in the array. An *associative array* uses strings instead of numbers to store values. For example, the lines below create a phone book with an associative array:

```
var phone_book = new Array();
phone_book["dave thau"] = "(415) 555-5555";
phone_book["information"] = "(415) 555-1212";
```

The first line creates a new, empty array, as we've seen before. The next two lines put two associations into the array. The first associates dave thau with (415)555-5555. The second associates the string information with the number to dial for information. To retrieve that number, you would look it up using a line like this:

```
var information_number = phone_book["information"];
```

This tells JavaScript to look in the array phone_book for the value associated with the string information. The string used to retrieve the association must precisely match the string used to store it. Retrieving thau's phone number with the line

```
var thau = phone_book["thau"];
```

won't work if you originally stored the information as

```
phone_book["dave thau"] = "(415) 555-5555";
```

Figure 8-19 shows how to use an associative array for a functional phone book.

```
   <html>
   <head>
   <title>Phone Book</title>
   <script language = "JavaScript">
   <!-- hide me
❶ var phone_book = new Array();
❷ phone_book["happy"] = "(555) 555-1111";
   phone_book["sleepy"] = "(555) 555-2222";
   phone_book["sneezy"] = "(555) 555-3333";
   phone_book["sleezy"] = "(555) 555-4444";
   phone_book["sneary"] = "(555) 555-5555";
   phone_book["bleary"] = "(555) 555-6666";
   phone_book["tweaked"] = "(555) 555-7777";
❸ function displayNumber(the_phone_book, entry)
   {
❹ var the_number = the_phone_book[entry];
❺ window.document.the_form.number_box.value = the_number;
   }
   // show me -->
   </script>
   </head>
   <body>
   <h1>The Dwarves of Multimedia Gulch</h1>
❻ <form name="the_form">
   <b>Name:</b>
❼ <select onChange = "displayNumber(phone_book, this.options[this.selectedIndex].value);">
❽ <option value="happy">Happy
   <option value="sleepy">Sleepy
   <option value="sneezy">Sneezy
   <option value="sleezy">Sleezy
   <option value="sneary">Sneary
   <option value="bleary">Bleary
   <option value="tweaked">Tweaked
   </select>
   <p>
   <b>Number:</b>
❾ <input type="text" name="number_box" value="">
   </form>
   </body>
   </html>
```

Figure 8-19: A phone book using an associative array

Analysis of Figure 8-19

When a browser loads this page, it shows a pull-down menu with some names and a text box that displays a phone number (Figure 8-20). Selecting a name puts that person's phone number in the text box. This neat little application doesn't take too much work to implement.

The script starts by creating a new array called phone_book in ❶ and then filling it with the values in lines ❷ down.

After building the phone_book array, the script defines a function as displayNumber(). This function takes two parameters: an array that holds the phone book we want to use, and a name we want to look up in the phone book. ❹ looks up the name in the phone book and stores it in the_number. ❺ puts the_number in the text box.

❻ starts the form and names it the_form. ❼ is a bit more complicated. This line defines the pull-down menu and describes what should happen when a visitor changes the value there. Changing the pull-down menu selection triggers the onChange event, which calls the displayNumber() function. As described earlier, displayNumber() takes two parameters, the phone book and the name to look up. In this case, we have just one phone book, called phone_book. Later we might expand this script to include several phone books—for example, one for friends, called friends_book; one for business, called business_book; and one for favorite shops, called shop_book. Because we can decide which phone book to use whenever we call the displayNumber() function, switching books is easy. If we wanted to use the business_book phone book, we'd just call the function like this:

```
<select onChange = "displayNumber(business_book, this.options[selectedIndex].value);">
```

The second parameter in the function is the name to look up. If we choose Happy, the person listed first in ❽ of Figure 8-19, the value happy passes to the function.

Play around with this example and make sure you understand how the displayNumber() function works and how the values in line ❼ enter the function.

Figure 8-20: The phone book code in Figure 8-19 in a browser

Summary

This chapter has introduced the last two fundamental ideas behind all programming languages: arrays and loops. Now that you've learned about variables, if-then statements, functions, loops, and arrays, you've learned all of the basic aspects of computer programming—so be happy! From now on, everything we learn is specific to how JavaScript works with the browser. All the tough programming nitty-gritty is behind us.

Before you leave this chapter, make sure you've learned how to:

- Create a new array.

- Access elements in an array.

- Use loops to go through an array's elements.

- Use both `for` and `while` loops.

- Nest loops.

- Use associative arrays.

Assignment

To make sure you understand everything in this chapter, try the following assignment.

Write a script that creates bar charts. This script should first ask a visitor for how many bars he or she would like in the chart. If the visitor wants four bars, the script should then ask for four numbers, ranging from one to ten, and draw a bar for each. Figures 8-21 to 8-23 demonstrate what I mean. To draw the bars, create a square GIF or use square.gif in the assignments/chapter8 directory on your CD-ROM. If someone wants a bar that's ten squares high, use a loop to write `window.document.writeln("<img src='square.gif'>")` ten times to the page.

This is another tough assignment, so give yourself plenty of time to do it.

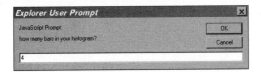

Figure 8-21: Asking visitors how many bars they want

Figure 8-22: Asking for bar values

Figure 8-23: The histogram

9

TIMING EVENTS

Precise timing of events on your Web pages transforms them from static documents to true multimedia applications. If you can time events, you can pace slide shows, create timed games, and control when visitors may perform different actions. In later chapters we'll see how timing events can animate your entire site. In this chapter, you'll learn how to:

- Control when events happen on your Web page.

- Build clocks that update in real time.

- Create slide shows that move at whatever pace you want.

Real-World Examples of Timing Events

We've already seen a few examples of Web pages that use event timing. In the last chapter, we saw how Ask Jeeves presents visitors with a new question every 3.5 seconds. NASA's space shuttle page at http://spaceflight.nasa.gov shows another example of timing on a Web page. As shown in Figure 9-1, NASA has one clock on its page that counts down to the next Space Shuttle launch and another clock that shows how long the space station has been in orbit. These clocks update once a second.

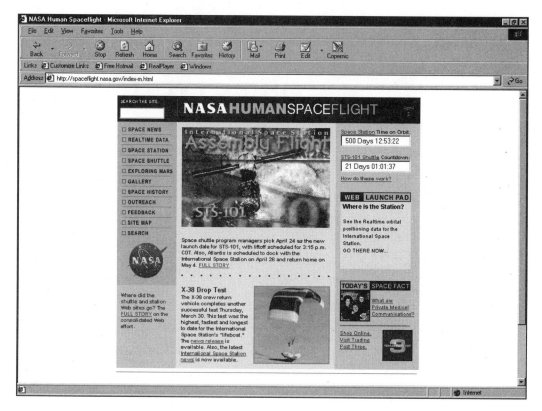

Figure 9-1: NASA's clocks

Timing events is not difficult. In fact, you only need to know two commands: setTimeout() and clearTimeout().

Setting an Alarm with setTimeout()

The built-in JavaScript function setTimeout() tells JavaScript to run a JavaScript command at some time in the future. The function takes two parameters: a JavaScript command and the time (in milliseconds) to wait before running it. For example, the following line causes an alert box to pop up after a visitor has been on a page for three seconds:

```
setTimeout("alert('You have been on this page for 3 seconds!');", 3000);
```

The first parameter contains the JavaScript statement to execute. This statement is between quotes and ends with a semicolon, just like all JavaScript statements. Notice that the string in the alert command is between single quotes rather than double quotes (see Chapter 4).

The second parameter tells JavaScript to execute the first parameter in 3,000 milliseconds, which is three seconds (1,000 milliseconds in a second). Figure 9-2 puts this line in the context of a full Web page.

```
<html>
<head>
<title>A Three-Second Alert</title>
<script language = "JavaScript">
<!-- hide me
setTimeout("alert('You have been on this page for 3 seconds!');", 3000);
// show me -->
</script>
</head>
<body>
<h1>A page so interesting you have to force yourself to stop reading it by having an alert
tell you when you've spent too much time. </h1>
</body>
</html>
```

Figure 9-2: A 3-second alert

Canceling an Alarm with clearTimeout()

Sometimes you'll want to cancel a setTimeout(). Imagine a riddle game in which a player has 10 seconds to guess the riddle's answer. If players don't answer the riddle correctly in 10 seconds, they get sent to a page that gives them the answer. If they do figure out the answer in time, they get congratulated. You could write this game by setting a setTimeout() to send players to the answer page in 10 seconds. If they answer the riddle correctly before the 10 seconds expire, you need to cancel the setTimeout() so they don't end up on the answer page.

To cancel a setTimeout(), you first need to name the time-out by storing it in a variable:

```
var my_timeout = setTimeout("goToAnswerPage();", 10000);
```

This line creates a time-out called my_timeout. Unless clearTimeout() cancels the time-out JavaScript will call the function goToAnswerPage() in 10 seconds. To cancel the time-out when the player answers the riddle correctly, use this line:

```
clearTimeout(my_timeout);
```

This looks up the time-out called my_timeout and cancels it. Figure 9-3 shows a working version of the riddle game.

```
    <html>
    <head>
    <title>A Riddle Game</title>
    <script language = "JavaScript">
    <!-- hide me
❶  var my_timeout = setTimeout("goToAnswerPage();", 10000);
❷  function goToAnswerPage()
    {
        alert("Sorry!");
        window.location = "answer.html";
    }

❸  function checkAnswer(the_answer, the_timeout)
    {
❹    if (the_answer == "a newspaper")
        {
❺          clearTimeout(the_timeout);
❻          alert("Congratulations!  You got it right!");
        }
    }
    // show me -->
    </script>
    </head>
    <body>
    <h1>Riddle Me This</h1>
    What is black, white, and read all over?<br>
❼  <form onSubmit = "checkAnswer(this.the_answer.value, my_timeout); return false;">
    <input type = "text" name = "the_answer">
    <input type = "submit" value = "answer">
    </form>
    </body>
    </html>
```

Figure 9-3: A riddle game

Line-by-Line Analysis of Figure 9-3

❶ initiates setTimeout(). 10 seconds later, unless clearTimeout() cancels the time-out called my_timeout, the function goToAnswerPage(), defined in ❷, is called. This function calls up an alert box and sends the player to answer.html. ❸ defines checkAnswer(), the function called when the player submits an answer (❼). checkAnswer takes two parameters: the answer that the player submits and the time-out to cancel if the answer is correct. The first line of the function, ❹, checks the answer. If it's correct, ❺ cancels the time-out, which stops JavaScript from calling the goToAnswerPage() function, and ❻ congratulates the player. If ❼, which calls the checkAnswer() function when the player submits the form, seems unfamiliar, look at Chapter 7, which discusses the onSubmit event (see the result in Figure 9-4).

NOTE   *If you want to run this script, you'll need to create the answer.html page, which is just a normal Web page with the riddle's answer on it.*

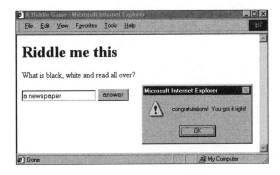

Figure 9-4: What the riddle game looks like

Timing Loops

The real-world time-outs I discussed at the start of the chapter all involve a timed loop of some sort. Ask Jeeves displays each question for 3.5 seconds, and NASA updates its clocks every second. Both of these examples use a time-out in a loop.

Unfortunately, we can't use a while or for loop when timing events. While and for loops happen too quickly, and there's no good way to slow them down. Even if you could slow them, there's no way to time these loops accurately because they run at different speeds on different computers. It might take an old computer two seconds to print "hello" to a Web page 1,000 times, while a newer computer might take just a tenth of a second.

Instead of using a for or while loop, you can accurately time a loop by writing a function that calls itself. The function can control exactly how far in the future it gets called using setTimeout() and clearTimeout(). The simple timing loop in Figure 9-5 should make this clearer.

```
<html>
<head>
<title>A Simple Timing Loop</title>
<script language = "JavaScript">
<!-- hide me
```
❶ `var the_timeout;`
❷ `function upDate()`
```
{
```
❸ `    var the_number = window.document.the_form.the_text.value;`
❹ `    the_number = parseInt(the_number) + 1;`
❺ `    window.document.the_form.the_text.value = the_number;`
❻ `    the_timeout = setTimeout("upDate();", 1000)`
```
}
// show me -->
</script>
</head>
<body>
<form name = "the_form">
```
❼ `<input type = "text" name = "the_text" value = 0><br>`
❽ `<input type = "button" value = "start timer" onClick = "upDate();">`
❾ `<input type = "button" value = "stop timer" onClick = "clearTimeout(the_timeout);">`
```
</form>
</body>
</html>
```

Figure 9-5: A simple timing loop

This simple timing loop (❶ through ❻) forms the basis for the ones we'll see subsequently in this chapter (and in Chapter 13).

The HTML in Figure 9-5 creates a form with three elements: a text box to hold the timer number and two buttons (see Figure 9-6). When a user pushes the Start Timer button, the number in the text box starts to increase by 1 every second. It will keep increasing until the visitor pushes the Stop Timer button.

Figure 9-6: What Figure 9-5 looks like in a browser

Line-by-Line Analysis of Figure 9-5

The key part of this script is the upDate() function starting at ❷. When a user pushes the Start Timer button, its onClick (❽) calls the upDate() function. This function adds 1 to the contents of the text box (❸ through ❺) and then sets a time-out (the_timeout) in ❻ to call itself in one second. After executing ❻, the script just sits around until 1 second passes; then the script remembers the setTimeout() and calls the upDate() function again. The upDate() function adds 1 to the contents of the text box and again sets the_timeout to call upDate() in one second. This cycle of calling the upDate() function, adding 1 to the contents, and setting another time-out to call the function in one second continues until clearTimeout(the_timeout) gets called. When a visitor presses the Stop Timer button in ❾, that activates the statement clearTimeout(the_timeout) and cancels the most recently set time-out, stopping the upDate() function from running again. Figure 9-7 charts this basic loop cycle.

Step	Event
1.	A user presses the Start Timer button, triggering the upDate() function.
2.	upDate() adds 1 to the contents of the text box (making it 1).
3.	The time-out called the_timeout triggers upDate() in one second.
4.	After 1 second passes, upDate() gets triggered.
5.	upDate() adds 1 to the contents of the text box (making it 2).
6.	The time-out called the_timeout triggers upDate() in 1 second.
7.	The user presses the Stop Timer button, which calls clearTimeout(the_timeout).
8.	clearTimeout(the_timeout) cancels the time-out set in step 6.
9.	Because the last time-out was cancelled, upDate() doesn't get called again, so the cycle stops.

Figure 9-7: A chart describing the timing loop cycle

The rest of this chapter covers a few applications of the basic timing loop described above. Don't worry if any of the structure of Figure 9-5 confuses you. You'll get used to it after seeing a few more examples.

Using parseInt() for MSIE 4 and Up

The parseInt() function in ❹ overcomes a peculiarity of Microsoft Internet Explorer versions 3 and higher. These browsers treat all contents of form elements as strings, even when they're numbers. When the text box in Figure 9-5 has the number 2 in it, MSIE reads this as the string '2'. Ordinarily, this wouldn't be too much of a problem. However, remember that the plus (+) operator has two meanings. When you use the plus between two numbers, it adds them: 1 + 2 = 3. But when you use the plus between *strings*, it concatenates them: '1' + '2' = '12'. Because MSIE reads the contents of form elements as strings, in this case it just sticks a 1 at the end of whatever number appears in the timer text box: 0 + 1 = 01, 01 + 1 = 011, 011 + 1 = 0111. This is not what we're looking for.

The parseInt() function overcomes this problem by converting strings and numbers with decimal points into integers. For example, in MSIE 4 and up, the lines

```
var first_number = '2';
var second_number = first_number + 1;
```

result in the variable second_number holding the value "21", while the lines

```
var first_number = '2';
var second_number = parseInt(first_number) + 1;
```

result in the variable second_number holding the value 3 (parseInt(first_number) converts the string '2' to the number 2).

Calling parseInt() with a String That Doesn't Have Numbers

Calling parseInt() with a value that has no numbers in it results in a *NaN*(not a number) value. You can use the isNaN() function to make sure parseInt() returns a number. The following scrap of code asks for a person's age and makes sure he or she has entered a number:

```
var the_age = prompt("how old are you?", "your age here");
if (isNaN(parseInt(the_age)))
{
    alert("that's not a number!");
}
```

Clearing Out a Time-out Before You Set a New One

If you've tried running the code in Figure 9-5, you might have noticed that pressing the Start Timer button multiple times causes the timer to run more quickly. This happens because each time you click on the button, it starts a timer that runs once a second. If you click on the button twice, you have *two* timers that run once a second, which means the value in the text box updates twice a second. To keep this from happening, change the Start Timer button to clear the time-out before setting it. In other words, change ❽ to the following:

```
<input type = "button" value = "start timer" onClick = "clearTimeout(the_timeout); upDate();">
```

Declaring Variables That Hold Time-outs Outside Functions

You may have noticed that ❶ in Figure 9-5 does precisely what I told you not to do—it declares a variable outside a function that uses it. However, variables that hold time-outs are one exception to this rule. Remember that inside a function, the word var means, "This variable only exists inside this function." If we declared the_timeout inside the update() function in Figure 9-5, we wouldn't be able to clear the time-out using the Stop Timer button because the button isn't located inside the function. Declaring the_timeout with var outside all functions allows any JavaScript on the page (including the JavaScript inside the onClick of the Stop Timer button) to access and change the_timeout.

Building a Clock with Timing Loops

Clocks are one obvious application of timing loops. Figure 9-5 provides the code for a simple clock. See if you can understand what's going on before you read the analysis below. Start by looking at the form in the body of the page.

Line-by-Line Analysis of Figure 9-8

The heart of Figure 9-8's script is the writeTime() function. Every second, this function figures out the current time by creating a new date object, puts the time in the text field, and then sets a time-out to run writeTime() a second later (see Figure 9-9).

As usual, the script starts by declaring the variable that will hold the time-outs (❶). Next comes the writeTime() function, which creates a new date object in ❷ (remember, the date object holds the current date and time). ❸ and the two lines following it get the hours, minutes, and seconds from the date object using the getHours(), getMinutes(), and getSeconds() methods. This code hearkens back to Chapter 2, which discussed how NPR updated the date on its Web page.

```
    <html><head><title>A JavaScript Clock</title>
    <script language = "JavaScript">
    <!-- hide me
❶  var the_timeout;
    function writeTime() {
      // get a date object
❷  var today = new Date();
      // ask the object for some information
❸    var hours = today.getHours();
      var minutes = today.getMinutes();
```

Figure 9-8: Code for a JavaScript clock

```
    var seconds = today.getSeconds();
    // make the minutes and seconds look right
❹  minutes = fixTime(minutes);
    seconds = fixTime(seconds);
    // put together the time string and write it out
    var the_time = hours + ":" + minutes + ":" + seconds;
❺  window.document.the_form.the_text.value = the_time;
❻  // run this function again in a second
    the_timeout = setTimeout('writeTime();',1000);
}
❼  function fixTime(the_time) {
    if (the_time < 10)
    {
❽            the_time = "0" + the_time;
    }
    return the_time;
}
// show me -->
</script>
</head>
<body>
The time is now:
<form name="the_form">
<input type="text" name="the_text">
<input type="button" value="start the clock" onClick="writeTime();">
<input type="button" value="stop the clock" onClick="clearTimeout(the_timeout);">
</form>
</body>
</html>
```

Figure 9-8 (continued): Code for a JavaScript clock

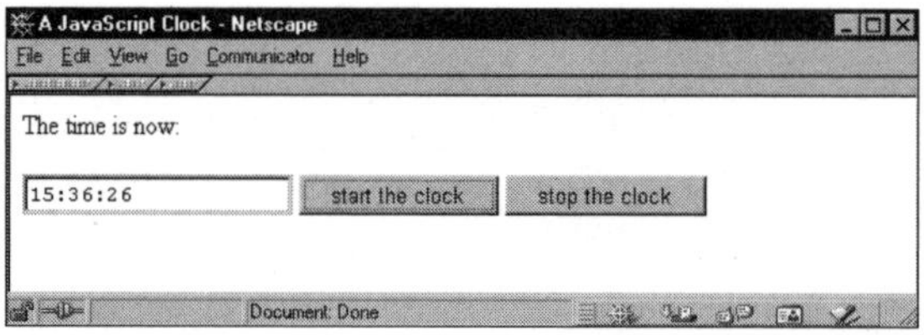

Figure 9-9: A JavaScript clock

❹ in Figure 9-8 is the only really new part of this script. If you look back at Table 2-1 (page 26), you'll see that getMinutes() and getSeconds() each return an integer from 1 to 59. If it's two minutes and three seconds past 9 a.m., the variable hours in ❸ will be 9, minutes will be 2, and seconds will be 3. But putting these numbers together to display the time would create the string 9:2:3 instead of 9:02:03. ❹ takes care of this little problem by sending the minutes and seconds variables to a function I've written called fixTime(). The fixTime() function in ❽ takes a number as its parameter and puts 0 before the number if it is less than 10 (so 2 becomes 02). Make sure you understand how the fixTime() and writeTime() functions work together. It's a good example of how one function can call on another to do its dirty work.

Once fixTime() fixes the minutes and the seconds by inserting 0 where appropriate, ❺ creates the time string and ❻ writes it into the text box. Finally, ❼ sets the time-out that will call writeTime() again in one second. When writeTime() gets called again, it creates a new date object, gets the information out of it, fixes the minutes and seconds if necessary, writes the new time into the text box, and sets the time-out again. The whole process starts when a visitor clicks on the Start The Clock button and ends when the visitor clicks on the Stop The Clock button, which cancels the most recently set time-out.

How NASA's Clock Works

NASA has two clocks on its page. Unlike the clock in Figure 9-8, these clocks work relative to some time in either the past or the future. The first clock keeps track of how long the International Space Station has been in orbit and the second one calculates when the next Space Shuttle will launch. I'm going to focus on the first clock and skip some of the wacky calculations NASA uses to determine the time. To see the full glory of NASA's clocks, look at sites/nasa/index.html on the CD-ROM. Figure 9-10 on page 182 shows the stripped-down NASA code (if you run this code, it gives the time in milliseconds).

Line-by-Line Analysis of Figure 9-10

Function setNewTime() in ❶ in Figure 9-10 is the heart of this script. This function figures out how long the space station has been in orbit by subtracting the original launch time from the current time. The function puts this number in the text field, then calls itself in one second. After one second passes, the function again subtracts the station's launch time from the current time, updates the text field accordingly, and sets another time-out. This continues until the visitor leaves the page.

Converting Dates to Milliseconds

❷ gets the current date and time by creating a new date object, and ❸ converts this date and time into the number of milliseconds since January 1, 1970, with the getTime() method. (For historical reasons, many programming languages consider January 1, 1970, to be the beginning of time.)

```
<HTML>
<HEAD>
<TITLE>NASA Human Spaceflight</TITLE>
</HEAD>
<BODY>
<form name="timeForm">
Space Station</a><br>
<input type="TEXT" name="stationTime" size="18" value="000:00:00:00">
<SCRIPT LANGUAGE="Javascript">
function setNewTimeAgain(){
    setNewTime();
}
❶ function setNewTime(){
❷    now = new Date();
❸    timeNow = now.getTime();
❹    launch = Date.parse("Fri, 20 Nov 1998 00:20:00 CST");
❺    timeLeft = timeNow - launch;
❻    document.timeForm.stationTime.value = timeLeft;
❼    setTimeout("setNewTimeAgain()", 950);
❽    return;
}
❾ setNewTime();
</SCRIPT>
</BODY>
</HTML>
```

Figure 9-10: NASA's clock script

Whenever you want to compare two dates, it's generally best to convert both to milliseconds with the getTime() method. For example, to see if one date falls before or after another, convert both to the number of milliseconds since January 1, 1970 (if the date is prior to January 1, 1970, getTime() returns a negative number; getTime() returns -1000 milliseconds if the time is one second before January 1, 1970). The larger number is the later date. Converting the dates to milliseconds allows you to compare just two numbers. If you didn't want to convert to milliseconds and you had very close dates, you'd have to compare each part of the dates separately. For example, to make sure that January 1, 1970, 1 a.m. does indeed fall earlier than January 1, 1970, 2 a.m., you'd have to check the years, then the months, then the days, then the hours. The difference between these two dates doesn't become apparent until you compare their hours. Converting both dates into milliseconds means you compare just the milliseconds. Messing around with dates is one of the biggest hassles in programming, so if this procedure seems awkward, you're right.

④ uses the parse() method of the date object to calculate the number of milliseconds between January 1, 1970, and the launch of the Space Station. The parse() method takes as a parameter a specially formatted string representing a date and time, then returns the number of milliseconds between that time and January 1, 1970. The formatting is important, so follow **④** precisely. The CST at the end stands for Central Standard Time. Time zones, such as PST for Pacific Standard Time and GMT for Greenwich Mean Time, work as well.

Calculating the Time Since the Launch

Once **③** and **④** have calculated the current time and the launch time in terms of number of milliseconds since January 1, 1970, **⑤** subtracts the launch time from the current time to give the number of milliseconds between them and stores the result in timeLeft.

The original NASA script contains about 40 lines following **⑤** to convert timeLeft into a nicely formatted string. The calculations are long, complicated, and not related to the point of this chapter, so I'm skipping them and putting timeLeft directly into the text box (**⑥**). For those who really care, I'll describe NASA's calculations at the end of this section.

Calling setNewTimeAgain() Again

After **⑥** puts timeLeft into the text box, **⑦** sets a time-out to call the function setNewTimeAgain() in 950 milliseconds. Setting the time-out for slightly less than one second means that the script checks the clock slightly more frequently than once per second. If a computer is running a complicated process, sometimes its internal clock is slightly off for a brief time. Checking the clock more often than once a second means these brief glitches won't affect the accuracy of your script. I'm not sure why **⑦** calls the function setNewTimeAgain() instead of just calling setNewTime(), since setNewTimeAgain() simply calls setNewTime(). It might have to do with NASA's programming style guide. Programmers have style guides just as writers and editors have *The Chicago Manual of Style*. Perhaps some rule in NASA's style guide discourages programmers from writing functions that call themselves directly.

⑧ ends the function with a return. This isn't strictly necessary, but some programming languages require that all functions end with a return. JavaScript does not—however, one school of thought holds that it's a good style to end all functions this way. I don't adhere to this school, but if you're aiming to be the purest, cleanest, most structurally sound programmer possible, you should put return at the end of all your functions.

⑨ calls the setNewTime() function when the page first loads. This starts the timing loop.

Before going on to the next section, take note of the similarities between Figures 9-5, 9-8, and 9-10. All timing loops have more or less the same structure, so make sure you understand that structure thoroughly.

NASA's Calculations

Figure 9-11 shows the code NASA uses to convert the seconds between the current time and the Space Station's launch time into a nicely formatted string (our discussion of timed loops continues on page 187). The code is a bit more complicated than necessary, but it does demonstrate some of the fancier math you can do with JavaScript.

The first few lines of the function are the same as in Figure 9-10. The new code starts right after timeLeft is first calculated. Remember that timeLeft is the number of seconds between the current time and the station's launch. ❶ divides timeLeft by the number of milliseconds in a day, yielding the number of days since launch. Division produces a number with a decimal point, which we don't want, so the parseInt() function creates an integer by taking the number and dropping its decimal point and the numbers that follow the decimal. The variable days stores this integer.

❷ checks to see if days is a number. The function isNaN() returns true if the variable in the parentheses is not a number, and false if the variable is a number. ❷ sets days equal to 0 if days is not a number. The variable days would not be a number if the division or the parseInt() went wrong in ❶. ❷ offers another example of paranoid programming—generally a good thing.

The mod Operator

❸ introduces the *mod* (short for modulo—represented by the percent sign [%]) operator, which calculates the remainder of a division. Here are some examples:

```
5 % 2 = 1  (5 divided by 2 is 2, with 1 left over)
19 % 5 = 4 (19 divided by 5 is 3, with 4 left over)
1 % 3 = 3 (1 divided by 3 is 0, with 3 left over)
```

The mod operator is useful when you need to break down one number into several components (for example, when you have the difference in milliseconds between two times and you want to break that difference into days, hours, minutes, and seconds).

❸ uses mod to figure out what's left over after you subtract the number of milliseconds that represent entire days from timeLeft. Here's a simpler example of how this works:

```
var number_of_hours = 76;
var number_of_days = parseInt(number_of_hours / 24);
var number_of_hours_after_days_removed = number_of_hours % 24;
alert("there are " + number_of_days + " and " + number_hours_after_days_removed + " in " +
number_of_hours + " hours.");
```

```
    function setNewTime(){
        now = new Date();
        launch = Date.parse("Fri, 20 Nov 1998 00:20:00 CST");
        timeNow = now.getTime();
        timeLeft = timeNow - launch;
❶       days = parseInt(timeLeft / 86400000);
❷       if (isNaN(days)){
            days = 0;
        }
❸       timeLeft = parseInt(timeLeft % 86400000);
❹       hours = parseInt(timeLeft / 3600000);
        timeLeft = parseInt(timeLeft % 3600000);
        mins = parseInt(timeLeft / 60000);
        timeLeft = parseInt(timeLeft % 60000);
        secs = parseInt(timeLeft / 1000);
❺       h1 = parseInt(hours / 10);
❻       if ( isNaN(h1))
            h1 = 0;
❼       h2 = parseInt(hours % 10);
        if ( isNaN(h2))
            h2 = 0;
        m1 = parseInt(mins / 10);
        if ( isNaN(m1))
            m1 = 0;
        m2 = parseInt(mins % 10);
        if ( isNaN(m2))
            m2 = 0;
        s1 = parseInt(secs / 10);
        if ( isNaN(s1))
            s1 = 0;
        s2 = parseInt(secs % 10);
        if ( isNaN(s2))
            s2 = 0;
❽       document.timeForm.stationTime.value="  "+days+" Days "+h1+h2+":"+m1+m2+":"+s1+s2;
        setTimeout("setNewTimeAgain()", 950);
        return;
    }
```

Figure 9-11: Converting seconds into a string, the NASA way

If you run the code at the bottom of page 184, the alert will say, "There are 3 days and 4 hours in 76 hours." The mod breaks the number of hours into whole days and remaining hours. In the second line, number_of_days is 3, because 76 / 24 = 3.1667 and parseInt() drops the remainder of .1667. The third line calculates 76 % 24, which is 4, because 76 / 24 is 3, with 4 left over.

Getting Back to the NASA Code

❸ figures out how many milliseconds remain after you subtract all the whole days (in milliseconds) from timeLeft. If the space station launched 444 days ago, this code would subtract the number of milliseconds in 444 days from timeLeft. From this number, we can calculate how many hours, minutes, and seconds after 444 days the station launched.

❹ then takes timeLeft and determines how many hours are in it by dividing it by the number of milliseconds in an hour. Next, mod figures out how many milliseconds remain after subtracting all the hours. The next few lines repeat this process to calculate the number of minutes and seconds left.

By the time we reach ❺, we've calculated the days, hours, minutes, and seconds between the current time and when the station launched. The next bunch of lines format the string written into the text field. Let's say the station launched 444 days, 5 hours, 14 minutes, and 44 seconds ago. ❺ divides the number of hours by 10 and drops the decimal; 5 divided by 10 is 0.5, so h1 equals 0. ❻ does the paranoid check to make sure the division worked, then ❼ uses mod to figure out how many hours remain after you subtract the number of hours calculated in ❺: 5 mod 10 equals five, so h2 equals 5. When ❽ formats the string and writes it to the Web page, the hours appear as 05, since h1 is 0 and h2 is 5. If you had 14 hours, h1 would be 1 and h2 would be 4, so the hours would appear as 14. Personally, I think ❺, ❻, and ❼ seem unnecessarily obscure. I would have written this instead:

```
if (hours < 10)
{
    hours = '0' + hours;
}
```

This achieves the same goal as ❺ through ❼ without the hard-to-follow mod nonsense. As always, though, there's more than one way to code anything, and different programmers have different tastes.

The rest of the function breaks the minutes and seconds into two digits, just as ❺ through ❼ did for hours, and then ❽ writes the time to the text box.

As I said, these calculations seem a bit wacky, but they're worth a look if you ever want to perform a similar task.

A Timed Slide Show

A slide show is another good application of timed loops. Figure 9-12 shows you how to combine arrays and timing loops to create a looping slide show. Again, look the script over before diving into the explanation.

```
       <html>
       <head>
       <title>A Timed Slide Show</title>
       <script language = "JavaScript">
       <!-- hide me
❶     var the_images = new Array();
❷     the_images[0] = new Image();
❸     the_images[0].src = "one.jpg";
       the_images[1] = new Image();
       the_images[1].src = "two.jpg";
       the_images[2] = new Image();
       the_images[2].src = "three.jpg";
❹     var the_timeout;
❺     var index = 0;
       function rotateImage()
       {
❻         window.document.my_image.src = the_images[index].src;
           index++;
❼         if (index >= the_images.length)
             {
                 index = 0;
             }
❽         the_timeout = setTimeout("rotateImage();", 1000);
       }
       // show me -->
       </script>
       </head>
       <body>
❾     <img name = "my_image" src="one.jpg">
       <form>
       <input type = "button" value = "start the show" onClick = "clearTimeout(the_timeout);
       rotateImage();">
       <input type = "button" value = "stop the show" onClick = "clearTimeout(the_timeout);">
       </form>
       </body>
       </html>
```

Figure 9-12: A timed slide show

Line-by-Line Analysis of Figure 9-12

The first few lines set up the array containing the images we'll put in the slide show. ❶ creates the new array, ❷ sets the first item in the array equal to an image object, and ❸ sets the src of that image object to the first picture of the slide show. ❷ and ❸ are just like the lines used to preload images before an image swap (see Chapter 4). The next few lines load the rest of the images.

After the images have loaded, ❹ and ❺ set up two variables for use in the timing loop. ❹ declares the_timeout, which keeps track of each time-out, and ❺ keeps track of which image in the slide show to bring up next time the script calls the rotateImage() function. Keep in mind that declaring the index variable outside the rotateImage() function, as I've done here in ❺, is not the safest programming practice—it's just easier and quicker than the safe solution (see the section "A Safer Version of rotateImage()" below).

Next comes the rotateImage() function, which swaps in a new image and then calls itself in one second. The first line of the function, ❻, does the image swap. It looks up the value of index, finds the src of the element numbered index in the the_images array, and swaps in that image for my_image (the image in ❾).

After swapping the image, the function adds 1 to the index variable. The next time rotateImage() gets called, it looks up the next item in the array and swaps in that item. We have to make sure the number stored in index doesn't exceed the number of images stored in the the_images array. The if-then statement starting at ❼ takes care of this issue by ensuring that if index has incremented past the number of items in the array, it gets set back to 0 (corresponding to the first image in the the_images array). The last line in the function, ❽, should be old hat by now. This line sets a time-out to call the rotateImage() function in one second.

The slide show starts when a visitor presses the button that calls rotateImage() and ends when the user presses the Stop Slide Show button, canceling the most recently set time-out.

A Safer Version of rotateImage()

If you're not interested in perfecting your coding style, you can skip this section; it's a bit advanced. However, if you want to be a supersafe coder, read on.

At a couple of points in this book, I've mentioned that it's best to declare variables inside the functions that use them. As we've seen (see page 179), this won't work for variables that hold time-outs, as in ❹ of Figure 9-12. But in ❺ of Figure 9-12, the variable index, declared outside the function, does not hold a time-out. The only part of the script that uses the index variable is the rotateImage() function—so I really should be declaring index inside the rotateImage() function. Unfortunately, as Figure 9-13 shows, I can't.

Why Declaring a Variable Outside a Function Is Unsafe

Before I describe how to get around this problem, let me first show you once more why declaring index outside rotateImage() is unsafe.

Let's say your script has two functions: rotateImage(), which performs the slide show, and beersOnTheWall(), which counts down from 99. If both rotateImage() and beersOnTheWall() depend on the variable index, and you don't declare index inside the functions, both functions will be looking at the same number—whatever index holds. This is awkward, because you'd probably want index to start at 99 for the beersOnTheWall() function and 0 for the rotateImage() function. You'd also want index to decrease by 1 each time through beersOnTheWall(), but increase by 1 each time through rotateImage(). Having both functions look at the same variable just won't work.

The easy, though dangerous, solution to the problem is to make sure rotateImage() and beersOnTheWall() use different variables. For example, rotateImage() could use the variable index and beersOnTheWall() could use beers. This solution might work in a short script, especially if nobody else is going to change it. However, if the script is lengthy, if more than one person will modify it, or if the script will be changed and expanded frequently, you can't assume the people changing your script will all know they shouldn't name any new variable index. If someone accidentally does create another variable named index, the rotateImage() function probably won't work, because rotateImage() will expect a particular index value, and the newly created index will probably contain another value.

Why You Can't Put var Inside a Timing Loop

Using var and declaring variables inside the functions that use them is the safest, simplest solution to this problem. Unfortunately, this solution doesn't work exactly right in timing loops. To see why, look at the function in Figure 9-13.

```
    function rotateImage()
❶       var index = 0;
        window.document.my_image.src = the_images[index].src;
        index++;
        if (index >= the_images.length)
        {
            index = 0;
        }
        the_timeout = setTimeout("rotateImage();", 1000);
    }
```

Figure 9-13: A faulty rotateImage() function

The addition of ❶ in Figure 9-13 is the only change to Figure 9-12's rotateImage() function. This line declares the variable index inside rotate-Image(), thereby avoiding the problem of having two functions look at the same variable. Unfortunately, each time rotateImage() gets called, index gets set to 0 again. This means only the first image of the_images would ever show up.

The Solution

Figure 9-14 contains the only really safe way to use setTimeout() to call a function that takes a parameter. It's a bit complex, so look closely at it before reading the explanation.

```
<html>
<head>
<title>A Timed Slide Show</title>
<script language = "JavaScript">
<!-- hide me
var the_images = new Array();
the_images[0] = new Image();
the_images[0].src = "one.jpg";
the_images[1] = new Image();
the_images[1].src = "two.jpg";
the_images[2] = new Image();
the_images[2].src = "three.jpg";
var the_timeout;
function rotateImage(index)                             ❶
{
    window.document.my_image.src = the_images[index].src;
    index++;                                            ❷
    if (index >= the_images.length)
    {
        index = 0;
    }
    var the_function_string = "rotateImage(" + index + ");";   ❸
    the_timeout = setTimeout(the_function_string, 1000);       ❹
}
// show me -->
</script>
</head>
<body>
<img name = "my_image" src="one.jpg">
<form>
```

Figure 9-14: Coding timing loops the safe way

```
⑤ <input type = "button" value = "start the show" onClick = "rotateImage(0);">
   <input type = "button" value = "stop the show" onClick = "clearTimeout(the_timeout);">
   </form>
   </body>
   </html>
```

Figure 9-14 (continued): Coding timing loops the safe way

This safer version of rotateImage() never really declares the problematic variable index at all. Instead, rotateImage() gets called with a parameter: the number of the image that should appear. ❶ shows how rotateImage() has changed to accept this parameter. Calling rotateImage(0) in ⑤ calls rotateIndex() and sets index to 0 in ❶. The first line in the body of the function then swaps the image stored in position 0 of the_images with the image on the page. If rotateImage(1) was called instead of rotateImage(0), the second image in the_images would have been swapped into the page, rotateImage(2) swaps in the third image, and so on.

The Hitch

Of course, there is a hitch. After incrementing index in ❷, as we did in Figure 9-14, it would make sense to call rotateImage() again in a setTimeout like this:

```
the_timeout = setTimeout("rotateImage(index);",1000);
```

Unfortunately, this triggers a JavaScript error. When one second passes and the rotateImage(index) command executes, JavaScript tries to remember what the variable index holds, then calls rotateImage() with that value. However, at this point, as far as JavaScript knows, no variable index exists. The variable index exists only inside the function. The setTimeout() in the above line looks up the variable before calling the function, and since nothing called index exists outside the function, JavaScript gives the visitor an error message.

The Solution to the Hitch

The way out of this bizarre situation is in ❸ and ❹ of Figure 9-14. ❸ creates the command that the setTimeout() will call in one second. Instead of using the command

```
"rotateImage(index);"
```

❸ pulls the word index out of the quotes, forcing JavaScript to look up the value of index and put that value into the command. If you have index set to 2, for example, ❸ writes the command that goes into the setTimeout as follows:

```
"rotateImage(2);"
```

❸ may seem confusing, so make sure you understand why it's written that way. Because JavaScript calls rotateImage() with the number 2 instead of the variable index, it doesn't need to look up the value of any variable when the command runs in one second. Instead rotateImage() receives the number 2, and the function proceeds normally.

Once **❸** creates the string that holds the command for the time-out to call, **❹** performs the setTimeout().

What's the moral of this story? It's a bad idea to use setTimeout() to call a function with a variable between its parentheses, as in

```
timeout = setTimeout("rotateImage(index);",1000);
```

because you never know what index will be when you call the function in the future, or even whether index will exist then. If you do use a function inside a setTimeout() and that function takes a parameter, use a line such as **❸** to place the value of the variable into the function.

Why Is image_array Declared Outside the rotateImage() Function?

Since rotateImage() is the only function that makes use of image_array, why not declare it inside the rotateImage() function? Well, I could have, and if I was being extra-safe, I might have. However, re-creating the array every time it calls the function—possibly hundreds or thousands of times—seems wasteful. As written, Figure 9-14 creates the array only once. It's pretty safe to declare image_array outside the function that uses it because the script probably won't ever change this array. Because the values in image_array aren't likely to change, I don't have to worry much about one function changing a value in the array contrary to the needs of another function.

This section has focused entirely on programming style. The code shown in Figure 9-12 will serve you perfectly well in many situations, and you may prefer it for short scripts because it's more comprehensible. The code shown in Figure 9-14 is better for complex scripts, and for those scripts that you or others will change frequently.

Summary

If you have truly mastered this chapter, you now know the following:

- How setTimeout() causes a JavaScript statement to occur in the future.

- How to use clearTimeout() to cancel a time-out.

- How to create a timed loop by writing a function that calls itself.

- How to use parseInt() to convert a string to a number, and why you might have to do this.

If you read the part about coding timing loops the safe way (page 188), you also know how to write a timing loop that calls a function taking parameters.

To make sure you understand timing loops and how to cancel them, try the assignment below.

Assignment

Try enhancing the slide show in Figure 9-12 so that mousing over the image stops the slide show and mousing off the image resumes the slide show. It's a bit trickier than it sounds.

10

FRAMES AND IMAGE MAPS

Frames and image maps are two of the fancier HTML tools available to Web developers. Frames divide a Web page into different sections and are useful for navigation and page layout. Image maps are images that contain multiple HTML links. Clicking on different parts of an image map brings your visitors to different Web pages. JavaScript can enhance both of these HTML features by allowing you to manipulate the contents of frames using image maps and links in other frames.

In this chapter you'll learn how to:

- Create basic frames.

- Use JavaScript to control the contents of frames.

- Use JavaScript to change two frames at once.

- Use frames to share information between Web pages.

- Create basic image maps.

- Use JavaScript to add functionality to your image maps.

A Real-World Example of Frames and Image Maps

My favorite example of integrating image maps, frames, and JavaScript comes from the Salon Web site: It presents a book about eating bugs (see Figure 10-1). (You can view this page at http://www.salon.com/wlust/pass/1999/02/bugs/frame.html or on the CD-ROM in sites/salon/frame.html.) Mousing over the map highlights that area of the world and swaps in two pictures, one of the insects people there eat, and another of them preparing the insect for a meal.

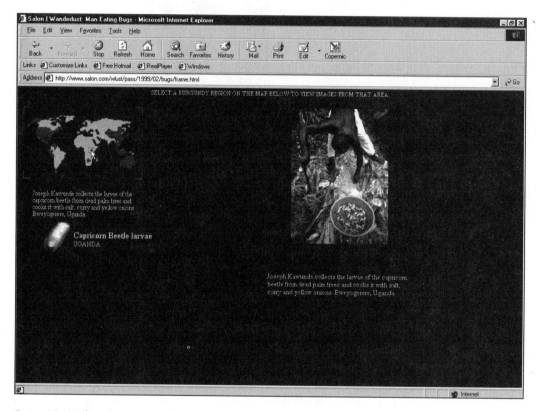

Figure 10-1: Salon's bug-eating pictorial

This page is divided into three frames. One frame holds the map of the world, a second frame holds the picture on the bottom, and a third holds the information along the right side. The world map is an image map; JavaScript causes the frames to change when a visitor mouses over any area of the map.

Frames

If you're already familiar with frames and don't need a review, you can skip to the "Frames and JavaScript" section.

Frame Basics

A Web page with frames is actually a set of HTML pages displayed simultaneously. If a page has two frames, it displays two HTML pages, one for each frame. In addition to the HTML pages that provide the content in the frames, another page describes how to display these HTML pages. Figure 10-2 contains a simple example of a Web page with frames. Figure 10-3 shows you what the code in Figure 10-2 looks like.

```
index.html
<html>
<head>
<title>A Simple Frame Set</title>
</head>
❶ <frameset cols="30%, *">
❷ <frame src = "navigation.html" name = "nav">
<frame src = "contents.html" name = "contents">
❸ </frameset>
</html>


navigation.html
<html><head><title>Nav</title></head>
<body>
<h1> News navigation</h1>
❹ <a href = "http://www.nytimes.com" target = "contents">New York Times</a><br>
<a href = "http://www.wired.com" target = "contents">Wired News</a><br>
<a href = "http://www.news.com" target = "contents">C|Net News</a><br>
</body></html>


news.html
<html><head><title>news</title></head>
<body>
<h1>Choose a link on the left to see some news</h1>
</body></html>
```

Figure 10-2: Code for a simple Web page with frames

There are three separate HTML pages in Figure 10-2. The first page, index.html, describes how the other two pages should appear on the screen. The second page, navigation.html, is on the left side of the screen in Figure 10-3, and the third page, content.html, is on the right side. Clicking on any of the links on the left side loads the corresponding Web page on the right side of the screen.

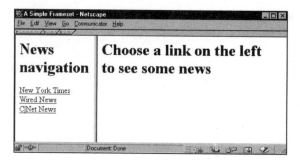

Figure 10-3: A simple Web page with frames

The pages in Figure 10-3 are set next to each other because ❶ in Figure 10-2 tells the browser to set up two frames, arrange them in columns, and make the first column take 30 percent of the page and the second column the rest of the page. Adding more percentages (their sum can't exceed 100) to the cols element (❶) adds more frames to the page. Alternatively, using rows stacks frames on top of each other. You can tweak frame sets in dozens of ways. Any good book about HTML devotes a chapter to them.

The two lines after ❶ tell the browser which HTML pages to load into each frame. ❷ loads navigation.html into the first frame (named nav) and the next line loads news.html into the second frame (named contents). ❸ closes the frame set. Notice that you don't use body tags with frames.

The next two HTML pages are standard Web pages. The first Web page, navigation.html, contains three links, each leading to a news site. Clicking on a link loads the contents into the contents frame because each link contains the element target = "contents" (see ❹). We'll see shortly how to use JavaScript to do the same thing.

Frames and JavaScript

In HTML, the only way an action in one frame can change the contents of another is through standard HTML links. Fortunately, JavaScript allows you to expand your repertoire of frame tricks immensely. The JavaScript in Figure 10-4, for example, makes the contents of the right frame change when a visitor mouses over one of the links on the left. The pages index.html and news.html are the same as in Figure 10-2; only navigation.html has changed.

Line-by-Line Analysis of Figure 10-4

The key to this script is the function changeContents(). When a visitor mouses over the *New York Times* link, ❹ calls changeContents() and sends it the string http://www.nytimes.com.

```
navigation.html
<html><head><title>Nav</title>
<script language = "JavaScript">
<!-- hide me
❶ function changeContents(the_url)
  {
❷    var content_frame = parent.contents;
❸    content_frame.location = the_url;
  }
  // show me -->
  </script>
  </head>
  <body>
  <h1> News navigation</h1>
❹ <a href = "http://www.nytimes.com" onMouseOver="changeContents('http://www.nytimes.com');
  ">New York Times</a><br>
  <a href = "http://www.wired.com" onMouseOver="changeContents('http://www.wired.com');
  ">Wired News</a><br>
  <a href = "http://www.news.com" onMouseOver="changeContents('http://www.news.com');
  ">C|Net News</a><br>
  </body></html>
```

Figure 10-4: Using JavaScript to change a frame with a mouse-over

The changeContents() function starts at ❶, where the_url gets set to whatever string passes into the function. ❷ tells JavaScript to look for the thing named contents inside its parent (the frame set containing a frame is the frame's parent—see Figure 10-5), and sets the variable content_frame to point to the contents frame.

Referring to frames is just like referring to windows. Just as you can change the URL shown in a window like this:

```
window_name.location = "http://www.nytimes.com";
```

you can change the URL shown in a frame like this:

```
the_frame.location = "http://www.nytimes.com";
```

This is precisely what ❸ in Figure 10-4 does. After ❷ assigns content_frame to point to the frame we want to change, ❸ changes that frame's location by setting content_frame.location to the_url.

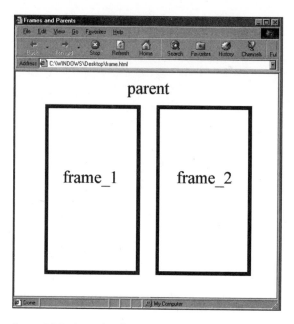

Figure 10-5: A graphical representation of frames and their parents

Frames and Image Swaps

In the Chapter 5 assignment, I described how clicking on a JavaScript-enhanced link in one window can change an image in another window. Because JavaScript treats frames and windows similarly, the same trick enables a link in one frame to change an image in another.

Here's a refresher: Figure 10-6 contains the code necessary to swap an image in one window by clicking on a link in a second window. Figure 10-7 shows how the same trick works with frames.

There are two HTML pages in Figure 10-6. The first page, first_page.html, starts by launching a new window in ❶ and calling it image_window. This window will open to image_page.html, which only has one item in it—an image of a happy face named the_image (❸). When someone clicks on the link in ❷, JavaScript looks for the window called image_window and looks in its document for the_image. Once it finds the_image, it changes its src to sad.gif. The link in ❸ changes the image back to happy.gif.

Figure 10-7 shows you how to do the same thing with frames instead of windows.

```
first_page.html
<html>
<head>
<title>Control Panel</title>
<script language = "JavaScript">
<!-- hide me
```
❶ ```
var image_window = window.open("image_page.html","image_window","width=100,height=100");
// show me -->
</script>
</head>
<body>
```
❷ ```
<a href = "#" onClick = "image_window.document.the_image.src = 'sad.gif'; return
false;">sad</a>
<br>
<a href = "#" onClick = "image_window.document.the_image.src = 'happy.gif'; return
false;">happy</a>
</body>
</html>
```
```
image_page.html
<html><head><title>The Image Page</title></head>
<body>
```
❸ ```
<img src="happy.gif" name="the_image">
</body>
</html>
```

Figure 10-6: Swapping an image in one window with a link in another

```
frameset.html
<html>
<head>
<title>Image Swapping in Frames</title>
</head>
<frameset rows = "30%, *">
<frame src = "navigation.html" name="navigate">
<frame src = "image_page.html" name="image_frame">
</frameset>
</html>
```

Figure 10-7: Swapping an image in one frame with a link in another
```

```
navigation.html
<html>
<head>
<title>Control Panel</title>
</head>
<body>

❶ <a href = "#" onClick = "parent.image_frame.document.the_image.src = 'sad.gif'; return
  false;">sad</a>
  <br>
  <a href = "#" onClick = "parent.image_frame.document.the_image.src = 'happy.gif'; return
  false;">happy</a>
  </body>
  </html>

image_page.html
<html><head><title>The Image Page</title></head>
<body>
❷ <img src="happy.gif" name="the_image">
  </body>
  </html>
```

Figure 10-7 (continued): Swapping an image in one frame with a link in another

The page frameset.html in Figure 10-7 sets up the page shown in Figure 10-8: navigation.html in the top frame (which takes up 30 percent of the window) and image_page.html in the bottom frame with happy.gif (called the_image in ❷). ❶ is the link in the top frame that changes happy.gif in the bottom frame to sad.gif. The critical part of ❶ is

```
parent.image_frame.document.the_image.src = 'sad.gif';
```

which is similar to ❷ in Figure 10-6:

```
image_window.document.the_image.src = 'sad.gif';
```

The only difference is that in Figure 10-6 we refer directly to the window image_window, while in Figure 10-7 we tell the JavaScript in the navigation.html to go up to its parent, then down to the frame image_frame.

Figure 10-8: Interframe image swapping

Changing the Contents of Two Frames at Once

In some situations, you may want to change the contents of two or more frames at once. In Salon's bug-eating piece, for example, mousing over part of the world in the map frame changes the contents of all three frames.

Figure 10-9 contains the JavaScript for a simple example of changing more than one frame: a Spanish-language tutorial. As you can see in Figure 10-10, clicking on a Spanish word in one frame shows you an image of what that word means in a second frame, and translates the word into English inside a form element in a third frame.

```
frameset.html
<html>
<head>
<title>Changing Two Frames at Once</title>
</head>
❶ <frameset cols = "30%, 30%, *">
<frame src = "navigation.html" name = "navigate">
<frame src = "form_page.html" name = "form_frame">
<frame src = "image_page.html" name = "image_frame">
</frameset>
</html>


navigation.html
<html>
<head>
<title>Navigation Frame</title>
<script language = "JavaScript">
<!-- hide me
```

Figure 10-9: Changing two frames at once

```
     function changeFrames(new_image, new_words)
     {
❷ parent.image_frame.document.the_image.src = new_image;
❸ parent.form_frame.document.the_form.the_name.value = new_words;
     }
     // show me -->
     </script>
     </head>
     <body>
❹ <a href = "#" onClick = "changeFrames('apple.gif','apple'); return false;">manzana</a>
     <br>
     <a href = "#" onClick = "changeFrames('orange.gif','orange'); return false;">naranja</a>
     </body>
     </html>
```

form_page.html
```
<html><head><title>The Form Page</title></head>
<body>
<form name = "the_form">
<input type = "text" name = "the_name">
</form>
</body>
</html>
```

image_page.html
```
<html><head><title>The Image Page</title></head>
<body>
❺ <img src="blank.gif" name="the_image">
</body>
</html>
```

Figure 10-9 (continued): Changing two frames at once

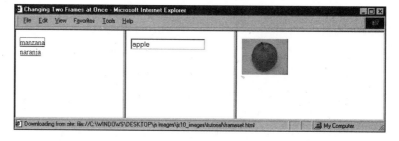

Figure 10-10: A simple Spanish tutorial—after clicking on the word manzana

Line-by-Line Analysis of Figure 10-9

The tutorial involves four different HTML pages. The first, frameset.html, describes the layout of the frames (❶).

In the first frame, navigation.html contains the JavaScript function and the links that change the contents of the other two frames. Function change-Frames() takes the parameters new_image, the name of the image to swap in the third frame, and new_words, the words to put into the form element in the second frame. ❷ performs the image swap by telling JavaScript to find the parent of the navigation frame (frameset.html), then the frame image_frame inside the frame set, and inside that frame the image named the_image (❺). Once JavaScript has found the_image, changeFrames() changes the_image.src to whatever new_image was set to when the script called the function. ❸ changes the contents of the text box in form_frame in a similar fashion.

Clicking on the manzana link in the navigation frame (❹) calls the changeFrames() function, with apple.gif as the image to swap in and *apple* as the word to go into the form. Although changeFrames() only changes two frames, you could easily expand it to change as many frames as the frame set holds.

Frames Inside Frames

Sometimes you need to mix side-by-side frames with stacked frames. For example, the page shown in Figure 10-11 has one wide frame on top and two narrower frames next to each other, below the wider top frame. You would achieve this effect by creating one frame set with two frames, one on top of the other, and loading the bottom frame with a second frame set that has two frames next to each other. Figure 10-12 shows the code for Figure 10-11.

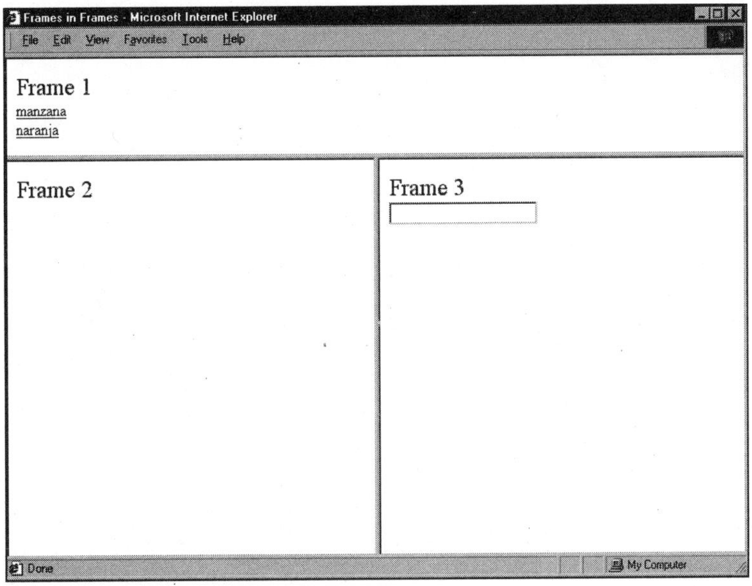

Figure 10-11: Frames inside frames

The pages navigation.html, image_page.html, and form_page.html in Figure 10-12 are the same as in Figure 10-9. The first frame set (call it the outer frame set) sets up two frames, one on top of the other (❶). The top frame (❷) holds navigation.html, which contains the navigation links and the JavaScript controlling how the links affect the other frames. The bottom frame (❸) loads bottom_frame.html, which holds the second frame set (call it the inner frame set). This frame set (❹) creates two frames: The left frame contains image_page.html and the right, form_page.html. Each of these pages could also have a frame set, since you can nest frame sets infinitely. Be careful, though—having more than one level of frame sets quickly boggles the minds of even the best Web page producers.

```
index.html
<html>
<head><title>Frames in Frames</title></head>
❶   <frameset rows="20%,*">
❷       <frame src = "navigation.html" name = "navigate">
❸       <frame src = "bottom_frame.html" name = "bottom">
</frameset>
</html>


bottom_frame.html
<html>
<head><title>Bottom Frames</title></head>
❹ <frameset cols="50%,*">
          <frame src = "image_page.html" name ="image_frame">
          <frame src = "form_page.html" name = "form_frame">
   </frameset>
</html>
```

Figure 10-12: The frame set for Figure 10-11

JavaScript and Frames Inside Frames

As long as you have only one frame set, JavaScript in one frame can influence any other frame by referring to it as parent.frame_name. Matters get a bit more complicated if you have nested frame sets. Consider frame 3 in Figure 10-11. The parent of this frame is the inner frame set (bottom_frame.html) containing frames 2 and 3. The appropriate JavaScript in frame 3 could influence frame 2 using parent.image_frame. For example, to change the URL shown in frame 2, frame 3 could run the following script:

```
parent.image_frame.location = "http://www.webmonkey.com/";
```

How can JavaScript in frame 3 change the contents of frame 1? The inner frame set (which contains frames 2 and 3) doesn't "know" anything about frame 1 because it's located in another frame set. The outer frame set (index.html), however, *does* "know" about frame 1 and the inner frame set because it set them up. In order for a frame in the inner frame set to affect a frame in the outer frame set, the inner frame must ask the outer frame set to find the frame to change. In this case, you could achieve this by calling the parent of frame 3's parent:

```
parent.parent.top_frame.location = "http://www.webmonkey.com/";
```

Running this script in frame 3 changes the URL in frame 1. The line in frame 3 tells JavaScript to go up to frame 3's parent, the inner frame set; find that frame set's parent, the frame set in frameset.html; and then find the frame top_frame inside that frame set.

Alternatively, frame 3 can refer directly to the outermost frame set by using the word top in your script:

```
top.navigate.location = "http://www.webmonkey.com";
```

This tells JavaScript to find the topmost frame set and look for the frame named navigate inside that frame set. The top object contains everything in the Web browser window, so if there are frame sets on the page, top refers to the outermost frame set. If there are no frames in the browser, top means the same thing as window.

Whether you use top or a chain of parents to deal with nested frame sets depends on the circumstances. If you have a link in a frame buried four frame sets deep that you want to affect a frame on the top level, using top probably makes sense. If you want the link in the buried frame set to affect a frame in its own frame set, parent is the way to go.

Frame Busting

Some sites use frames to keep you in their site even after you try to leave it. For example, when you do a search on Ask Jeeves and click on a result, the result appears on a page that has Ask Jeeves in the upper frame (see Figure 10-13). The result site is generally not an Ask Jeeves site. It might even be a Web page *you've* written.

Ask Jeeves allows its users to get rid of the top frame by clicking on a button, but you might not want your Web page showing up in an Ask Jeeves frame at all. To prevent this from happening, insert the script shown in Figure 10-14 in the header of your page.

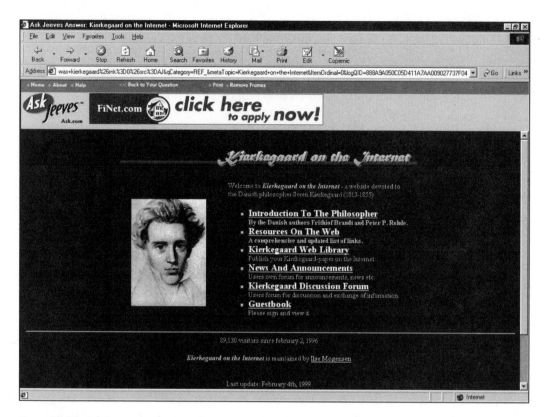

Figure 10-13: Ask Jeeves uses frames to keep you in its site

```
<script language="JavaScript">
<!-- hide me
❶ if (self != top)
   {
❷   top.location = self.location;
   }
   // show me -->
</script>
```

Figure 10-14: Frame-busting code

❶ checks to see if the HTML page containing this JavaScript is the top frame of the frame hierarchy (remember, self means "this page"). ❶ translates to "If this page is not on top, perform the statements between the curly braces." If the HTML page is not on top, it's inside an alien frame set. To escape the frame set, the page puts itself on top by setting the top.location of the window to self.location (❷—self.location stores the URL of a Web page).

Using Frames to Store Information

Web pages have lousy memories. Unless you do something fancy, the moment a visitor leaves your Web page, the page forgets any information it has collected. If, for example, you have a long quiz and you want to tell a visitor his or her score at the end, you'll find it tough to break the quiz into several pages—the second page can't keep track of what answers the visitor gave on the first page.

There are a few ways around this problem. If you want to store the information for a long time on your visitor's computer, cookies are the way to go (see Chapter 12). But if you only want to save the information briefly, there's a neat trick using frames to store information between pages.

The trick involves setting up an invisible frame containing a JavaScript function with an array that saves the information from each page as your visitors move from page to page inside your site. When you need to retrieve the information, simply access an array in the invisible frame. Figure 10-15 lists four Web pages to show how you would do this for a quiz. Figure 10-16 shows you what the code in Figure 10-15 generates.

```
frameset.html
<html>
<head>
<title>A Quiz</title>
</head>
❶ <frameset rows="100%,*" frameborder="0">
❷ <frame src="quiz_page_1.html" noresize>
❸ <frame src="secret_code.html" name="tracker" noresize>
</frameset>
</html>


secret_code.html
<html>
<head>
<title>A Quiz</title>
<script language = "JavaScript">
<!-- hide me
❹ var answers = new Array();
❺ function score(answers)
  {
     var correct = 0;
     var correct_answers = new Array("true","true","false","true");
     for (var loop=0; loop < correct_answers.length; loop++)
      {
```

Figure 10-15: Preserving information between pages with frames

```
        if (answers[loop] == correct_answers[loop])
        {
            correct++;
        }
    }
    percent_correct = (correct/4) * 100;
    alert("you got " + percent_correct + " percent right!");
}
// show me -->
</script>
</head>
<body>
Nothing to see here!
</body>
</html>
```

quiz_page_1.html

```
<html>
<head>
<title>Quiz Page 1</title>
</head>
<body>
Answer the following true/false questions:
<p>
<form>
A chicken is a bird:<br>
<input type="radio" name="bird" onClick="parent.tracker.answers[0]='true';">True<br>
<input type="radio" name="bird" onClick="parent.tracker.answers[0]='false';">False<br>
<p>
A skink is a lizard:<br>
<input type="radio" name="skink" onClick="parent.tracker.answers[1]='true';">True<br>
<input type="radio" name="skink" onClick="parent.tracker.answers[1]='false';">False<br>
<p>
</form>
<p>
```
❻ `<a href="quiz_page_2.html">Next Page</a>`
```
</body>
</html>
```

quiz_page_2.html

```
<html>
<head>
```

Figure 10-15 (continued): Preserving information between pages with frames

```
<title>Quiz Page 2</title>
</head>
<body>
Answer the following true/false questions:
<p>
<form>
A whale is a fish:<br>
<input type="radio" name="whale" onClick="parent.tracker.answers[2]='true';">True<br>
<input type="radio" name="whale" onClick="parent.tracker.answers[2]='false';">False<br>
<p>
A human is a primate:<br>
<input type="radio" name="human" onClick="parent.tracker.answers[3]='true';">True<br>
<input type="radio" name="human" onClick="parent.tracker.answers[3]='false';">False<br>
<p>
❼ <input type="button" value="score the quiz"
onClick="parent.tracker.score(parent.tracker.answers);">
</form>
</body>
</html>
```

Figure 10-15 (continued): Preserving information between pages with frames

As you can see in Figure 10-16, the quiz doesn't look like it's in frames. In fact, it has two frames, but one is invisible. The visible frame holds two true-false questions and a link to go to the next page (see Figure 10-17). Although clicking on the link apparently brings the visitor to a completely new Web page, it's actually the same page with new contents in the visible frame.

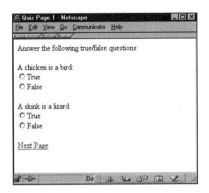

Figure 10-16: Page 1 of the quiz generated by Figure 10-15

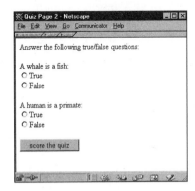

Figure 10-17: Page 2 of the quiz generated by Figure 10-15

Line-by-Line Analysis of Figure 10-15

The invisible frame stores the visitor's answers as he or she moves from page to page. If you didn't put the quiz in frames, the browser would forget the visitor's answers each time it loaded a new Web page. Here's how the invisible frame stores information.

The first page in Figure 10-15, frameset.html, sets up the frames as we've seen before, but with a few changes. ❶ describes two frames; the first one takes up 100 percent of the window, making it seem as if the page had no second frame. We've set frameborder, which controls the thickness of the line between the two frames, to 0 to eliminate any trace of the invisible frame.

❷ and ❸ contain another new element: noresize. This element tells the browser to prevent visitors from resizing the frames. Without this element, a visitor might accidentally click on the bottom of the window and pull the hidden frame up. Putting noresize inside the frame tags prevents this from happening. Also note that the invisible frame, called tracker, holds the HTML page secret_code.html—this is where we'll be storing the information. Because the frame is hidden, visitors can't see the contents of secret_code.html.

The next page, secret_code.html, holds the visitor's answers in the answers array (❹) and scores the quiz at the end.

The scoring function starts at ❺. This function creates an array called correct_answers, which holds the correct answers and loops through the array, comparing each correct answer with the answer the visitor gave. If the answers match, the script increments the variable correct. Once the script has checked all the answers, the function calculates what percentage the visitor got right and announces the score in an alert.

The two quiz pages show how the script stores the visitors' answers in the invisible frame and how it calls the score() function.

The page quiz_page_1.html contains a form with two quiz questions and a link. Each quiz question is true or false; the visitor answers by clicking on the appropriate radio button. Clicking the True radio button on the first question runs the following code:

```
parent.tracker.answers[0]='true';
```

This line goes to the frame tracker in the page's parent (that is, the frame set) and stores the string 'true' in the first slot (answers[0]) of the array. Clicking on the False radio button on the second question runs the following code, then stores the string 'false' in the second slot of the answers array:

```
parent.tracker.answers[1]='false';
```

Clicking on the link at ❻ loads the new page, quiz_page_2.html, into the visible frame. The invisible frame, however, sticks around, storing the values from the last page. It keeps the visitor's answers to the two questions on quiz_page_2.html in the third and fourth slots in the answers array. Clicking on the "score the quiz" button at ❼ calls the following code:

```
parent.tracker.score(parent.tracker.answers);
```

This line invokes the score() function found inside the tracker frame. The function takes an array containing the visitor's answers as a parameter. Because the tracker frame stores the answers array, the script can pass the array to the score function by referring to parent.tracker.answers.

This example uses practically every major element of programming this book has covered to date, so take a long look at it and make sure you understand everything that's going on. I've introduced two major new concepts:

- One frame refers to a variable stored in another frame with parent.other_frame.variable (as in parent.tracker.answers).

- One frame calls a function declared in another frame with parent.other_frame.function() (as in parent.tracker.score()).

Image Maps

JavaScript allows you to expand the capabilities of image maps by letting you call JavaScript statements when users click, mouse over, or mouse out of different parts of an image map.

Image Map Basics

To construct an image map, you need an image and a map that describes which parts of the image should go to which URLs. Figure 10-18 shows you part of the code for the image map Salon uses in its bug-eating piece. Figure 10-19 shows you what this HTML looks like in a browser. Clicking on any of the dark areas in the image brings you to a Web page about that area.

❶ in Figure 10-18 tells the browser to display left.gif and associate it with the map called left. The element isMap tells the browser this is an image map, and the element useMap tells the browser which map to use.

```
      <html>
      <head>
      <title>Image Map Example</title>
      </head>
      <body>
❶    <img src="left.gif" isMap useMap="#left">
❷    <MAP name="left">
❸    <AREA coords="9,23,41,42"
❹        href="http://www.salon.com/wlust/pass/1999/02/bugs/us.html"
❺        shape="RECT">
      <AREA coords="26,42,75,64"
          href="http://www.salon.com/wlust/pass/1999/02/bugs/us.html"
          shape="RECT">
      <AREA coords="28,65,55,78"
          href="http://www.salon.com/wlust/pass/1999/02/bugs/mexico.html"
          shape="RECT">
      <AREA coords="58,70,78,86"
          href="http://www.salon.com/wlust/pass/1999/02/bugs/venezuela.html"
          shape="RECT">
      <AREA coords="51,88,63,103"
          href="http://www.salon.com/wlust/pass/1999/02/bugs/peru.html"
          shape="RECT">
❻    </MAP>
      </body>
      </html>
```

Figure 10-18: Part of Salon's bug-eating image map

The rest of the page defines the map. ❷ starts the map and gives it a name, ❷ through ❻ define the different regions of the map (called *areas*), and ❻ ends the map. Three elements define each area: shape, coordinates, and URL link. In Salon's image, each area is rectangular (❺). ❹ associates the first area with a URL that discusses bug eating in the United States, and ❸ defines which part of the image this area covers. The four numbers are the *x* (horizontal) and *y* (vertical) coordinate of the upper left corner, and the *x* and *y* coordinate of the lower right corner, in pixels. So the first area in 10-19 goes from the (9, 23) point of the image to the (41, 42) point of the image, where the numbers represent the number of pixels from the upper left corner (see Figure 10-20).

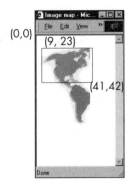

Figure 10-19: What the HTML
in Figure 10-18 looks like

Figure 10-20: Graphical representation of the
area described by ❸ through ❺ in Figure 10-18

Image Maps and JavaScript

Adding JavaScript to an image map is just like adding JavaScript to an HTML
link. The area tag can handle onClick, onMouseOver, and (in the 4.0 browsers)
onMouseOut events. For example, if you want an alert box to pop up when a
visitor moves the mouse over Alaska, you could rewrite the first area in Figure
10-18 as follows:

```
<AREA coords="9,23,41,42"
    href="http://www.salon.com/wlust/pass/1999/02/bugs/us.html"
    onMouseOver = "alert('it's cooooold in Alaska!');"
    shape="RECT">
```

Adding onClick and onMouseOut is equally simple.

Frames and Image Maps: How Salon's Bug-Eating Script Works

Because Salon's bug-eating piece involves so many pages (see Figure 10-1 for
what the page looks like in a browser), the code in Figure 10-21 describes only
the frame set and navigation pages. One large difference between Figure 10-21
and Salon's actual code is that Salon has divided its image map into three separate images to minimize download times. Figure 10-21 assumes the site has just
one image. To see how the code for handling three separate images differs,
look at the scripts in sites/salon on the accompanying CD.

```
     index.html
     <html>
     <HEAD>
     <TITLE>Salon | Wanderlust: Man Eating Bugs</TITLE>
     </HEAD>
❶  <FRAMESET frameborder=no border=0 COLS="280,*">
❷  <FRAMESET frameborder=no border=0 ROWS="165,*">
        <FRAME SRC="nav.html" NORESIZE SCROLLING="no" border="0" NAME="map">
        <FRAME SRC="teaser.html" NORESIZE SCROLLING="no" border="0" NAME="teaser">
      </FRAMESET>
      <FRAME SRC="eatbug.html" NORESIZE SCROLLING="no" border="0" NAME="thePicture">
     </FRAMESET>

     nav.html
     <html>
     <head>
     <title>Image Map Example</title>
     <script language="javascript">
     <!-- hide me
❸  var hold="notta";
❹  function changeMe(theMap,theOne,theBug) {
❺  window.document.left.src=theMap;
❻  if (hold == theOne)
       {
❼        return;
       } else   {
❽        parent.thePicture.location = theOne;
❾        parent.teaser.location=theBug;
❿        hold=theOne;
       }
     }
     //end hiding --></script></head>
     <body>
⓫  <img src="left.gif" name="left" isMap useMap="#left">
     <MAP name="left">
⓬  <AREA coords="9,23,41,42" shape="RECT" href="us.html"
⓭  target="thePicture"
⓮  onmouseOver="changeMe('us.gif','us.html','usteaser.html');"
⓯  onMouseOut="window.document.left.src='left.gif';">
     <AREA coords="26,42,75,64" shape="RECT" href="us.html"
     target="thePicture"
     onmouseOver="changeMe('us.gif','us.html','usteaser.html');"
```

Figure 10-21: Salon's bug-eating script

```
onMouseOut="window.document.left.src='left.gif';">
<AREA coords="28,65,55,78" shape="RECT" href="mexico.html"
target="thePicture"
onmouseOver="changeMe('mexico.gif','mexico.html','mteaser.html');"
onMouseOut="window.document.left.src='left.gif';">
</MAP>
</body>
</html>
```

Figure 10-21 (continued): Salon's bug-eating script

The top page of the site, index.html, uses two frame sets to describe three frames. The frame in the upper left, called map, contains the image map; the one below the map, called teaser, contains a little picture and some text; and the third frame on the right, called thePicture, contains a bigger image of the appropriate bug. The content of all three frames changes when a visitor mouses over part of the map.

Salon's Nested Frames

Salon nested its frames using a different method than the one I described in the section "Frames Inside Frames." Instead of having a frame call in a second file containing a frame set, as in ❸ in Figure 10-12, Salon puts a second frame set right inside the first one (❷ in Figure 10-21). This works fine in HTML, but it confuses JavaScript a little, as we'll see.

Salon's Image Map

Most of the action happens in the frame containing the map, defined starting with ⓫ in nav.html in Figure 10-21. This line puts the image of the world map on the page and tells the browser to use the image map left. ⓬ sets the coordinates for the first region of the left image map and the URL link. ⓭ targets the frame thePicture (on the right side of the screen) and ⓬ tells the browser to load us.html into thePicture when a visitor clicks on the region. ⓮ and ⓯ tell the browser what to do when a visitor moves his or her mouse over or out of this region. Mousing over a region calls the changeMe() function, which changes the contents of the frames appropriately.

The changeMe() Function

Function changeMe(), which starts at ❹, changes the contents of the frames. It takes three parameters: theMap, the name of a new map to swap with the standard one; theOne, the name of the page that holds the big image to swap into thePicture frame; and theBug, the name of the page with the teaser information to swap into the teaser frame. Each region of the map calls changeMe() with a different map, pictureFrame page, and teaser page. For example, the mouseOver in ⑭ calls changeMe() like this:

```
changeMe('us.gif','us.html','usteaser.html');
```

which tells changeMe() to swap the us.gif map into one frame, us.html into another frame, and usteaser.html into a third frame.

⑤ swaps the map of the world with another map with the appropriate region colored green—us.gif for example. ⑥ then checks to see if the visitor has actually chosen a new area. If the visitor mouses over Alaska, then moves over to the continental United States, the picture in thePicture frame shouldn't change. The variable hold, declared at ③, keeps track of the currently selected region. The if-then-else statement in ⑥ checks to see if the page to load into thePicture frame is already loaded there. If it is, the function just returns (⑦) and no more swaps happen. Whenever JavaScript sees the word *return* inside a function, it leaves that function. Putting a return inside an if-then statement, as in ⑦, is a handy way to quit in the middle of a function.

If the visitor has moused over a new area, the else part of the clause runs. ⑧ puts the page theOne into the frame named thePicture, and ⑨ puts the page theBug into the frame named teaser.

Summary

Frames and image maps add a lot of power to Web page design. Enhanced with JavaScript's ability to change the contents of Web pages, they add functionality that would otherwise be impossible. The examples shown here just scratch the surface of what you can do with JavaScript, frames, and image maps. Keep practicing and playing with them, and you're bound to come up with amazing designs.

If you've read this whole chapter, you should know how to:

- Create frames.

- Trigger image swaps in one frame with an event in another one.

- Change the contents of a form in one frame following an event in another one.

- Change the URL shown in a frame using both JavaScript and HTML.

- Change more than one frame at the same time.

- Deal with nested frames.

- Use frames to save information after a visitor leaves a Web page.

- Create an image map.

- Add JavaScript to image maps.

- Say *apple* in Spanish!

If you have all of that down, you should feel very powerful. Here's an assignment to test your knowledge.

Assignment

Create your own browser page using forms and frames. The page should have at least two frames: a frame with a text box that allows a visitor to type in a URL, and a frame that shows the URL after submission of the form. Figure 10-22 shows an example of what I mean, but you can build a browser page to suit your taste. In addition to providing a location box, the browser page in Figure 10-22 uses Salon's image map to display various URLs in the display frame.

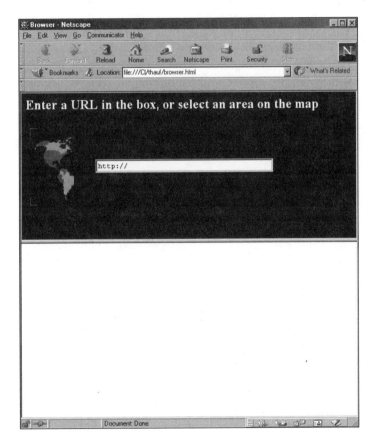

Figure 10-22: A homemade browser

11

VALIDATING FORMS, MASSAGING STRINGS, AND WORKING WITH CGI

Even with the advent of JavaScript, CGI scripting is an important way to add interactivity to a Web page. Used in conjunction with JavaScript, CGI scripts can run more quickly and give your visitors a better experience of your Web site. One of the most common ways to use JavaScript with CGI is as a *form validator*. Making sure visitors have filled out a form correctly before sending it to a CGI script speeds up the process immensely by cutting down on the number of times they have to submit forms to your Web server.

In this chapter you'll learn how to:

- Make sure visitors fill out HTML forms correctly.

- Make sure they have formatted strings (for example, email addresses) correctly.

- Make JavaScript work with CGI scripts.

A Real-World Example of Form Validation

Before saving the information you've entered in a form, many sites use JavaScript to make sure you've filled out the form correctly. When you open an account at Pets.com, for example, you must provide your name, a correctly formatted email address, and a password. Before the Pets.com site saves your information, it checks your email address and password for correct formatting and tells you if it sees any mistakes (see Figure 11-1).

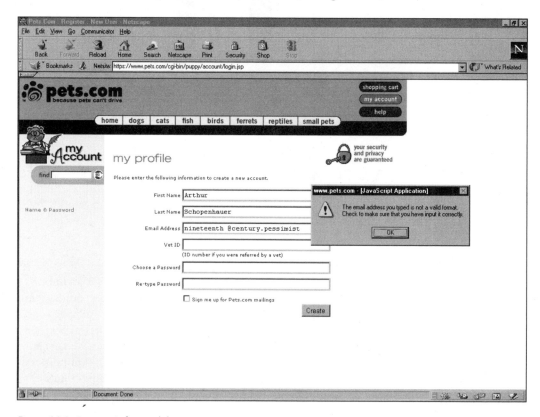

Figure 11-1: Pets.com's form validator in action

Making Sure a Visitor Has Filled Out a Form Element

Making sure a visitor has supplied all the mandatory information in an HTML form is the most basic type of form validation. If you want to require your visitors to provide a name and age, you need a JavaScript function to make sure they've entered this information before the form goes to the CGI script.

Chapter 7 covers *almost* everything you need to know to do this. If you're feeling hazy about how JavaScript and forms work together, review that chapter before reading on. If you feel confident, try to understand the code in Figure 11-2, which checks whether a user has filled out the mandatory form elements.

```
      <html>
      <head>
      <title>Checking Mandatory Fields</title>
      <script language = "JavaScript">
      <!--
      function checkMandatory()
      {
❶     var error_string = "";
         // check the text field
❷     if (window.document.the_form.the_text.value == "")
         {
              error_string += "You must give your name.\n";
         }
         // check the scrollable list
❸     if (window.document.the_form.state.selectedIndex < 0)
         {
              error_string += "You must select a state.\n";
         }
         // check the radio buttons
❹     var rad_select = "no";
❺     for (var loop = 0; loop < window.document.the_form.gender.length; loop++)
         {
❻         if (window.document.the_form.gender[loop].checked == true)
            {
                 rad_select = "yes";
            }
         }
❼     if (rad_select == "no")
         {
              error_string += "You must select a gender.\n";
         }
❽     if (error_string == "")
         {
❾        return true;
         } else {
              error_string = "We found the following omissions in your form: \n" + error_string;
❿        alert(error_string);
                 return false;
         }
      }
      // end hide -->
      </script>
```

Figure 11-2: Making sure your visitor has filled in mandatory fields

```
    </head>
    <form name = "the_form" action="#" method="post"
⑪  onSubmit="var the_result = checkMandatory(); return the_result;">
    Name:<input type="text" name="the_text">
    <br>
    State you live in:<br>
    <select name="state" size="3">
    <option value="alabama">Alabama
    <option value="arizona">Arizona
    <option value="california">California
    <option value="colorado">Colorado
    <option value="connecticut">Connecticut
    <option value="delaware">Delaware
    <option value="illinois">Illinois
    </select>
    <p>
    Gender:<br>
    <input type="radio" name="gender">Female<br>
    <input type="radio" name="gender">Male<br>
    <p>
    <input type="submit" value="Submit me!">
    </form>
    </body>
    </html>
```

Figure 11-2 (continued): Making sure your visitor has filled in mandatory fields

Line-by-Line Analysis of Figure 11-2

⑪ calls checkMandatory() after your visitor clicks the Submit Me button. If there are any empty form elements, an alert box pops up explaining what needs filling out. (Figure 11-3 shows you what happens if the visitor hasn't filled out any of the form elements when he or she clicks the button.)

In brief, the checkMandatory() function works by returning the value true if the visitor has filled out all the fields, false if something's missing. If the function returns false, the script sets the variable the_result to false in ⑪. If you hearken back to Chapter 7, you'll remember that browsers won't submit a form if a JavaScript returns false inside the onSubmit function.

The checkMandatory() function checks each of the form elements and, if the user fails to fill out an element, adds a phrase describing the error to the error_string variable, declared at ❶. Once the function has made all the checks, the error_string will contain a blurb for each form element not filled in, or it will be blank if the user has entered all the elements.

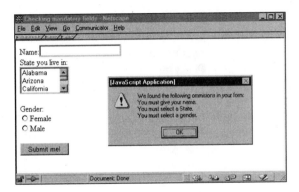

Figure 11-3: When your visitor hasn't filled in any of the elements

Checking Text Fields and Scrollable Lists

The first check is at ❷, where the function determines if there's anything in the name field. If not, it adds some text to the error_string variable. Notice the use of the plus and equal signs (+=) in the body of the if-then statement at ❷. When dealing with strings, += tells the function to add the following item to the end of the variable. The body of ❷ adds the string "You must give your name.\n" to the variable error_string (the \n at the end creates a line break in the alert box). ❸ checks the scrollable list to see if the user has selected anything. If the visitor has selected a state, selectedIndex equals the position of the selected element: 0 with the first option selected, 1 with the second option selected, and so on. If the visitor has not selected a state, selectedIndex equals -1. If the selectedIndex of this form element is less than 0, the script adds the appropriate message to error_string.

Checking Radio Buttons

The trickiest type of form element to check is the radio button. To check whether a user has selected a particular radio button, you have to loop through all the buttons in a series and check them one at a time. In Figure 11-2, ❹ declares the variable rad_select to keep track of whether the guest has chosen a radio button. Initially, the function sets rad_select to "no". If we encounter a selected radio button when we loop through them, we'll set rad_select to "yes" to show that we've found a selected radio button.

The loop begins at ❺ and is the standard loop for checking a list of radio buttons. The loop might look strange at first, but if you study it long enough to understand what's going on, it soon becomes second nature.

The variable loop starts at 0 and goes until it has checked the last radio button named gender. Each time through the loop, ❻ checks to see if the radio button has been selected and, if it has, changes rad_select from "no" to "yes". After the loop has looked at all the radio buttons, ❼ checks whether rad_select is still "no". If it is, the visitor hasn't selected any of the radio buttons, so the script adds the appropriate error message to error_string.

Checking error_string

Now that all the checks are done, ❽ determines whether any error messages have been added to error_string. If not, error_string still equals the null string (""), which is what ❶ set it to. If error_string is null, no error messages have been added, which means the form is complete and can be sent to the CGI script.

To send the form to the CGI script specified in the action of the form tag, the onSubmit in ⓫ must return true. If nothing has been added to error_string, ❾ returns true, which sets the variable the_result in ⓫ to true. Thus the onSubmit returns true and the form is submitted.

> **NOTE** *In the script in Figure 11-2, the action does not specify any CGI script. Instead, there's a hash mark (#). If it named another script, the script would probably store the information in a database somewhere and thank the user for filling out the survey. In this case, since there is no CGI script, the page just reloads, clearing the values entered into the form. The hash mark is there to satisfy Netscape 2, which behaves strangely if it sees nothing in the quotes of an action.*

If the error_string contains something, meaning that the form is incomplete, the script adds "We found the following omissions in your form: \n" to the front of error_string and puts the string in an alert box (❿). After the visitor clicks OK in that box, checkMandatory() returns false, setting the_result to false in ⓫. As a result, the onSubmit then returns false, the form does not go to the CGI, and the page doesn't reload.

Much of the code in Figure 11-2 applies to all form validation scripts. The main differences between form validation scripts are the types of things they check. If, for example, you wanted a script to check a form element for a valid email address, you'd add some code to do that check in the checkMandatory() function. Before you can do so, however, you have to know a bit about analyzing strings.

String Handling

You'll often want to verify that a string has a certain format: that an email address looks valid, or a date is formatted the way you want, or perhaps that a credit card number passes a basic validity test. To verify string formats, you need these five useful string methods: indexOf(), lastIndexOf(), charAt(), substring(), and split(). I'll cover each method separately and also show how to use them to verify an email address or date (since the credit card script is long, I don't discuss it here, but you'll find a good example on the **CD-ROM** under libraries/form validators/netscape's suite/index.html).

indexOf() and lastIndexOf()

The indexOf() method finds the location of a specified set of characters (called a *substring*) inside a string and tells you at what position the substring starts (the first character of a string is in position 0, the second in position 1, and so on). If the string doesn't contain the specified substring, indexOf() returns -1.

A compliment to indexOf(), lastIndexOf() gives you the position of the last occurrence of a character or substring. Table 11-1 shows the value of various calls to indexOf() and lastIndexOf() when the variable the_word holds the string superduper (var the_word = "superduper").

Table 11-1: Some example calls to indexOf()

Call to indexOf()	Result	Reason
the_word.indexOf("s")	0	The letter s is in position 0 of the_word.
the_word.indexOf("u")	1	The letter u is in position 1 of the_word.
the_word.indexOf("dupe")	5	The substring dupe starts at position 5 in superduper.
the_word.indexOf("z")	-1	There's no z in superduper.
the_word.lastIndexOf("u")	6	The last u is in position 6 of the_word.

Figure 11-4, which checks an email address for valid formatting, illustrates a more realistic use of indexOf() and lastIndexOf().

```
<html><head><title>Validating an Email Address</title>
<script language = "JavaScript">
<!-- hide me
function checkEmail(the_email)
{
❶   var the_at = the_email.indexOf("@");
❷   var the_dot = the_email.lastIndexOf(".");
❸   var a_space = the_email.indexOf(" ");
❹   if ((the_at != -1) &&  // if there's an '@'
❺       (the_at != 0) &&  // and it's not at position 0
❻       (the_dot != -1) && // and there's a '.'
❼       (the_dot > the_at + 1) && // and something between the '@' and '.'
❽       (the_dot < the_email.length - 1) && // and something after the '.'
❾       (a_space  == -1)) // and there are no spaces
    {
                alert("looks good to me!");
                return true;
    } else {
```

Figure 11-4: Validating an email address

```
                    alert("sorry, your email address is invalid!");
                    return false;
            }
        }
        // show me -->
        </script>
        </head>
        <body>
        <form method="POST" action="#"
❿         onSubmit = "var result = checkEmail(this.emailbox.value); return result;">
        Email Address: <input type="text" name = "emailbox"><br>
        <input type="submit" value="submit me!">
        </form>
        </body>
        </html>
```

Figure 11-4 (continued): Validating an email address

Line-by-Line Analysis of Figure 11-4

When the form is submitted, the onSubmit at ❿ calls the checkEmail() function and sends it the contents of the emailbox form element. If the visitor filled out the form correctly, checkEmail() returns true, the form will be submitted, and the page reloads. If the form has been completed incorrectly the function returns false, the form won't be submitted, and the page won't reload.

The checkEmail() function works by checking for the six basic formatting rules all email addresses must follow:

1. There must be an @ sign.

2. The @ sign can't be the first character.

3. There must be a period in the address.

4. There must be at least one character between the @ and the last period.

5. There must be at least one character between the last period and the email's end.

6. There can be no blank spaces in the address.

To test all six rules, we need a few pieces of information. ❶ through ❸ determine the location of the first @ sign, the location of the last period, and the location of the first space (if any) in the string. ❹ through ❾ check to see if the address violates any of the above rules. Since these lines are and'ed (&&)

together (see Chapter 3 if you've forgotten about &&), they must all be true to trigger the then part of the if-then-else clause (which tells the visitor he or she filled out the form correctly). If one or more of the tests turns up false, that triggers the else part of the if-then-else clause, telling the visitor he or she entered the email address incorrectly.

Table 11-2 shows you each rule and the line that tests it.

Table 11-2: Checking email addresses

Line	Rule	Comment
❹	1	If there's an @, the_at doesn't equal –1.
❺	2	If the @ sign is not the first character, the_at is greater than 0.
❻	3	If there's a period, the_dot doesn't equal –1.
❼	4	If there's something between @ and the last period, the_dot is greater than the_at +1.
❽	5	If a period is the last character, the_dot equals the_email.length –1.
❾	6	If there are no spaces, a_space equals –1.

charAt()

The charAt() method finds the position of a specific character inside a string. To find the character in the first position of the string stored in the_word, you'd type something like this:

```
var the_character = the_word.charAt(1);
```

Table 11-3 shows some more examples of charAt() at work. Let's say the_word holds superduper again.

Table 11-3: Some example calls to charAt()

Call to indexOf()	Result	Reason
the_word.charAt(0)	"s"	The letter s is in position 0 of the_word.
the_word.charAt(1)	"u"	The letter u is in position 1 of the_word.
the_word.charAt(the_word.length-1)	"r"	The last character is the_word.length-1.
the_word.charAt(100)	""	There's no position 100 in superduper.

Finding the last character in a string is a bit tricky. After you find out how many characters are in a string using string_name.length, you have to remember to subtract 1 from the length, since the first character of a string is at position 0. Thus the last character will be in position the_word.length-1.

Checking Strings Character by Character

The charAt() method is useful for analyzing strings on a character-by-character basis. Figure 11-5 lists a function that makes sure there are no characters that are illegal in email addresses in a string (!#$%^&*()/:;,+). You can add this function to the email checker to make sure the address doesn't contain any illegal characters.

```
function hasIllegalCharacters(test_string, illegal_string)
{
❶    var is_illegal = false;
❷    var the_char = "";
❸    for (var loop=0; loop < illegal_string.length; loop++)
    {
❹        the_char = illegal_string.charAt(loop);
❺        if (test_string.indexOf(the_char) != -1)
        {
❻            is_illegal = true;
        }
    }
❼    return is_illegal;
}
```

Figure 11-5: Using charAt() with a loop

The hasIllegalCharacters() function takes two parameters, a string to check for illegal characters and a string that lists which characters are illegal. To add this to the email checking script in Figure 11-4, drop in the hasIllegalCharacters() function and call it as follows:

```
var bad_news = "!#$%^&*()/:;,+";
var the_email = "happy@javascript.is.my.friend.com";
var is_bad = hasIllegalCharacters(the_email, bad_news);
```

After hasIllegalCharacters has done its work, is_bad will be true if one or more of the bad characters appear in the string or false if the string is fine. To use hasIllegalCharacters() in Figure 11-4, you also need to add an (is_bad == true) clause to the if-then statement starting on line ❹ of Figure 11-4.

NOTE *If you use the above code, make sure to pass* hasIllegalCharacters() *the email address you want checked— happy@javascript.is.my.friend.com is just an example.*

Line-by-Line Analysis of hasIllegalCharacters()

The two parameters in hasIllegalChararcters() are test_string, the string we're making sure does or doesn't have illegal characters, and illegal_string, the string that lists the illegal characters. The function goes through each character in illegal_string and determines whether test_string contains that character. The loop at ❸ does most of the work, going from the first character of illegal_string (0) to the last (one less than illegal_string.length). Each time through the loop, ❹ sets the_char to a different character in illegal_string. ❺ checks to see if the character stored in the_char is in the test_string string. If it's not, indexOf() returns -1. If the bad character appears in the string, indexOf() returns something other than -1 and line ❻ changes is_illegal (❶) from false to true. At the end of the loop, is_illegal will be true if the script has found a bad character and false if it hasn't. The last line of the function (❼) returns this value to the function of part of the script called hasIllegalCharacters().

substring()

The substring() method is just like charAt() except that it can grab entire substrings from a word, not just individual characters. The format is as follows:

```
var the_substring = the_string.substring(from, until);
```

Here from is the position of the first character of the substring, and until is, strangely enough, one greater than the last position of the substring. In other words, the substring grabs characters from the first parameter of the call up to, but not including, the second parameter of the call. Here it is in use:

```
  var the_string = "superduper";
❶ var where = the_string.substring(1,3);
❷ var who = the_string.substring(0,5);
```

❶ sets where to up because the letter u is in position 1 of the string and the letter e is in postion 3 of the string. Remember, substring() grabs characters up to, but not including, the character in the position listed in the second parameter of the function.

❷ sets who to super because the letter s is in postion 0 and the letter d is in position 5.

You can use substring() with indexOf() to break strings apart. Figure 11-6 shows how to use substring() and indexOf() to take an email address and separate the person's user name from the domain of the address.

```
<html><head><title>User Name Yanker</title>
<script language = "JavaScript">
<!-- hide me
function getUserName(the_string)
{
❶    var the_at = the_string.indexOf('@');
❷    if (the_at == -1)
     {
         alert("you must type in a valid email address");
     } else {
❸          var user_name = the_string.substring(0, the_at);
            alert("The user name is " + user_name);
     }
}
// show me -->
</script>
</head>
<body>
<form onSubmit = "getUserName(this.the_email.value); return false;">
Email: <input type = "text" name = "the_email"><br>
</form>
</body>
</html>
```

Figure 11-6: indexOf() and substring() working together

The script calls the getUserName() function when the visitor submits the form. ❶ uses indexOf() to find the position of the @ sign and ❷ warns the visitor if the @ sign is missing. If there is an @ sign, ❸ uses substring() to get everything from the beginning of the string to the @ sign. Remember that the second parameter of substring() is one past the last position you want to grab.

Combining indexOf() and substring() in this way is quite common. Sometimes you have to use them together multiple times to get what you want. For example, if you want to grab the domain name out of a URL, you have to use indexOf() and substring() a couple of times. Figure 11-7 shows you the scrap of code that does this.

```
   var the_url = "http://www.webmonkey.com/javascript/";
❶ var two_slashes = the_url.indexOf('//');
❷ var all_but_lead = the_url.substring(two_slashes+2, the_url.length);
❸ var next_slash = all_but_lead.indexOf('/');
❹ var the_domain = all_but_lead.substring(0,next_slash);
```

Figure 11-7: Grabbing the domain from a URL

Figure 11-7 first locates the two slashes at the beginning of the string. The variable two_slashes holds the value 5 because the two slashes start at position 5. ❷ grabs everything two characters from the beginning of the two slashes until the end of the string. When it's done, all_but_lead will hold www.webmonkey.com/javascript. ❸ looks at that string and finds the next slash, then ❹ grabs everything from the start of all_but_lead to the next slash, resulting in www.webmonkey.com.

If it makes you feel any better, string handling is a pain in most languages. It's just something you have to get used to. An even more complicated use of substring() that performs simple checks on credit card numbers appears on the accompanying CD-ROM under libraries/form validators/netscape's suite/ccnums.html.

NOTE *Figure 11-7 only works for URLs with a slash (/) as their last character. You'll find a more general version of the above code on the CD-ROM under libraries/form validation/isValidUrl().*

split()

The split() method makes extracting the domain name from a URL a little easier. Unfortunately, it only works in Netscape 3.0 and up and in Microsoft Internet Explorer 4.0 and up. split() uses a character or group of characters to divide a string into a bunch of substrings, then loads the substrings into an array, as in the following example:

```
var my_friends = "eenie,meenie,miney,mo";
var friend_array = my_friends.split(",");
```

This splits the my_friends string along its commas, creating an array called friend_array in which element 0 is eenie, element 1 is meenie, element 2 is miney, and element 3 is mo. split() simplifies the URL example in Figure 11-7 to this:

```
var the_url = "http://www.webmonkey.com/javascript/";
var the_array = the_url.split("/");
var the_domain = the_array[2];
```

split() creates an array in which element 0 is http:, element 1 is null (nothing at all), element 2 is www.webmonkey.com, and element 3 is javascript. Though split() can't always simplify string handling, it does come in handy when you have a character that breaks up a string, like the slash (/) in the URL example or the comma (,) in the example before that. Figure 11-8 shows you a function that uses split() to make sure a date is formatted as mm/dd/yy (for example, 12/05/68 for December 5, 1968).

```
function checkDate(the_date)
{
❶    var date_array = the_date.split("/");
❷    if ((date_array.length == 3) &&
❸        (date_array[0] > 0) && (date_array[0] < 13) &&
         (date_array[1] > 0) && (date_array[1] < 32) &&
         (date_array[2] >= 0) && (date_array[1] < 100))
    {
         return true;
    } else {
         alert("please type in the date in a mm/dd/yy format.");
         return false;
    }
}
```

Figure 11-8: Checking a date's format

This simple function splits a string into pieces along the slash character in ❶. The first check, at ❷, makes sure there are three pieces of information in the array (for month, day, and year). ❸ makes sure the first number, which should represent the month, is between 0 and 13 (noninclusive). The next two lines perform analogous checks for the day and year. If the tests in all three of these lines are true, the date is formatted correctly.

NOTE *This code doesn't make sure the date is valid. The date 2/31/99 would pass the test, even though there are only 28 days in February. On the CD-ROM under libraries/form_validation, you'll find a complete set of date validation functions you can use to make sure an entered date is real.*

Bringing It Together: Pets.com's Form Validators

As usual, there are many ways to write any bit of JavaScript. Figure 11-9 shows you the code Pets.com uses to validate its forms (also see Figure 11-1). Don't let the code's length intimidate you—after all, you know 90 percent of it already.

This is only part of Pets.com's form validating script, and it's still pretty long. You should understand most of it, so I'll just cover the broad strokes and then point out a few details I haven't covered yet.

```
<HTML>
<HEAD>
    <TITLE>Pets.Com : Register : New User</TITLE>
    <SCRIPT LANGUAGE="Javascript">
<!--
❶  var fields = new Array();
   fields[0] = "EMAIL_ADDRESS";
   fields[1] = "PASSWORD";
   fields[2] = "VERIFY";
   fields[3] = "FIRST_NAME";
   fields[4] = "LAST_NAME";
errArray = new Array();
errArray['FIRST_NAME'] = "Please enter a first name.";
errArray['LAST_NAME'] = "Please enter a last name.";
errArray['EMAIL_ADDRESS'] = "Please enter a valid email address.";
errArray['emptyError'] = "Please enter information in required fields.";
errArray['emailError'] = "Your email address is invalid";
errArray['passwordError'] =
"Your password and verify password must be the same.";
❷ function checkForm(form,array)
  {
      for (var x=0; x<parseInt(form.elements.length); x++)
      {
          for (var i=0;i<array.length;i++) {
              if (form.elements[x].name == array[i]) {
                  if (form.elements[x].value == "") {
                      return alertError(form.elements[x],'emptyError');
                  }
❸              else if
                  ((form.elements[x].name.toUpperCase().indexOf("EMAIL") > -1) &&
❹                  !isEmail(form.elements[x].value))
                  {
❺                  return alertError(form.elements[x],'emptyError');
                  }
                  else
                    if ((form.elements[x].name.toUpperCase().indexOf("VERIFY") > -1) &&
  !doesMatch(form.elements[x].value, form.elements["PASSWORD"].value))
                    {
❻            return alertError(form.elements[x],'passwordError');
                    }
              }
          }
      }
```

Figure 11-9: Pets.com's form validator

```
        }
        return true;
    }
❼ function doesMatch (p,v)
    {
    return (p == v)
    }
    function alertError(error,field){
❽ var errStr = (field == "emptyError" && errArray[error.name]) ?
            errArray[error.name] : errArray[field];
    alert(errStr);
❾  error.focus();
    return false;
    }

    function isEmail(email)
    {
        // valid format "a@b.cd"
        invalidChars = " /;,:";
        if (email == "")
        {
                return false;
        }
        for (var i=0; i< invalidChars.length; i++)
        {
                badChar = invalidChars.charAt(i)
                if (email.indexOf(badChar,0) > -1)
                {
                        return false;
                }
        }
        atPos = email.indexOf("@",1)
        // there must be one "@" symbol
        if (atPos == -1)
        {
                return false;
        }

        if (email.indexOf("@", atPos+1) != -1)
```

Figure 11-9 (continued): Pets.com's form validator

```
        {
        // and only one "@" symbol
                return false;


        }


        periodPos = email.indexOf(".",atPos)
        if(periodPos == -1)
        {
        // and at least one "." after the "@"
                return false;
        }


        if ( atPos +2 > periodPos)
        // and at least one character between "@" and "."
        {
                return false;
        }


        if ( periodPos +3 > email.length)
        {
                return false;
        }
        return true;
}
// -->
</SCRIPT>
</HEAD>
<BODY>
```

⑩ `<FORM ACTION="" METHOD=post name="register" onSubmit="return checkForm(this, fields)">`

```
Please enter the following information to create a new account.<p>
First Name: <input type=text name="FIRST_NAME" value="" maxlength=30 size=36><p>
Last Name: <input type=text name="LAST_NAME" value="" maxlength=30 size=36><p>
Email Address: <input type=text name="EMAIL_ADDRESS" value="" maxlength=255 size=36><p>
Password: <input type=password name="PASSWORD" maxlength="255" value="" size="36"><p>
Retype Password: <input input type=password name="VERIFY" maxlength="255" value=""
size="36"><p>
<input type=submit name="checkout" value="Create">
</BODY>
</HTML>
```

Figure 11-9 (continued): Pets.com's form validator

Analysis of Figure 11-9

The checkForm() function (❷) does most of the work in this script. This function takes two parameters: form, a form to check, and array, a list of fields in the form to check. Having the form as a parameter would be a good idea if you intended to cut and paste these functions to different pages. If Pets.com puts the functions on five pages, each with a differently named form, it won't have to change the functions to accommodate the different form names. The script can just call the function with the name of the form.

At the top, ❶ defines the list of fields to check. Notice that when ❿ calls the function, the term this tells the function which form to work on. Remember from Chapter 8 that the term this refers to whatever this appears in. In ❿, this shows up inside the form tag and therefore refers to the form. Inside the function, the form parameter equals the form we're checking.

The function works by looping through each element in the form and then through the list of elements the function is supposed to validate. When the function finds an element that's on the list of elements to validate, it first determines whether the visitor has filled in the element. If the element is an email address, the function makes sure the address is formatted correctly using Pets.com's isEmail() function. If the element is a password, the function makes sure both passwords (most forms ask for a password twice to make sure there are no typos) match exactly using the doesMatch() function (❼). If any of these checks fail, a function called alertError() tells visitors what they did wrong.

toUpperCase()

Most of the code in each of these functions should make sense to you, but you'll see a few totally new lines. The if-then clause starting at ❸ has a couple of unfamiliar elements. The first test in the clause contains a method, toUpperCase(), which turns a string into all uppercase characters:

```
(form.elements[x].name.toUpperCase().indexOf("EMAIL") > -1)
```

This line determines if the *xth* array element is an email element by capitalizing all the letters of that element's name and checking to see whether the capitalized name contains the letters EMAIL.

Here's how it works: The third element of the form is named EMAIL_ADDRESS. When *x* is 2, form.elements[2].name is EMAIL_ADDRESS. The toUpperCase() method makes sure all the letters are uppercase. If the form was instead named Email_Address, the statement form.elements[2].name. toUpperCase() would result in EMAIL_ADDRESS. Once the function has capitalized the form name, it uses the indexOf() method to see if the name contains the letters EMAIL. Capitalizing the name of the form is another example of paranoid programming (in a good way): Pets.com doesn't want to have to remember to capitalize its form element names correctly when it creates new forms.

The Exclamation Point

❹ has something new, too:

```
!isEmail(form.elements[x].value)
```

The exclamation point at the beginning of isEmail means *not*. This part of the if-then clause reads, "If isEmail(form.elements[x].value) is not true." isEmail(form.elements[x].value) will be false (that is, not true) if the email address in the form is invalid. Taken together, the two clauses in **❹** read, "If this is an email element and it's not filled in correctly, then call alertError()."

The alertError() Function

Pets.com's alertError() function is very strange and hard to understand. The function has two parameters (**❺**), the incorrectly filled-in element (form.elements[x]) and a string (emptyError). The first line of the alertError() function, **❽**, contains a totally new concept:

```
var errStr = (field == "emptyError" && errArray[error.name]) ?
        errArray[error.name] : errArray[field];
```

This is a fancy if-then-else statement, called a *trinary operator* because it has three parts. The clause before the question mark in the trinary operator is like the Boolean test in the parentheses of an if-then statement, the clause between the question mark and the colon is like the contents of the then clause, and the clause after the colon is like the else clause. The trinary operator above translates into the following statement:

```
var errStr;
if (field == "emptyError" && errArray[error.name])
{
    errStr = errArray[error.name];
} else {
    errStr = errArray[field];
}
```

Translated into English, the above reads, "If the string passed to the function is emptyError and the form element passed into the function has a name that appears in the errArray array (defined right after the fields array at the top of the script), set the variable errStr to whatever is associated with the name of the form element in errArray." Consider **❺** in Figure 11-9. Because the string is emptyError and the form element has a name (EMAIL_ADDRESS), errStr gets set to the string associated with EMAIL_ADDRESS: "Please enter a valid email address."

If either the string passed to the function is not emptyError or the element passed into the function doesn't have a name, errStr gets set to whatever is associated with the string. In the case of the password check at ❻, the string passed to alertError() is not emptyError but passwordError, so the test at ❽ is false, meaning that errStr gets set to whatever is associated with passwordError in errArray: "Your password and verify password must be the same."

I have no idea why Pets.com made the alertError() code so complicated. Perhaps several people worked on the script and the form, and each person worked a little differently. Regardless, this offers a great example of how hard it is to understand other people's code and why you should try to code in the most straightforward, standard way possible. Figure 11-10 contains a simpler version of alertError().

```
function alertError(problem_field)
{
    var the_field_name = problem_field.name;
    if (errArray[the_field_name])
    {
        alert(errArray[the_field_name]);
        problem_field.focus();
    } else {
        alert("Sorry, there's something wrong with " + the_field_name);
        problem_field.focus();
    }
return false;
}
```

Figure 11-10: A simpler version of Pets.com's alertError() function

The focus() Method

Pets.com's alertError() function introduces another new method in ❾: the focus() method. The focus() method of a form element causes the cursor in the Web browser to move to that form element. So if a visitor has not filled in the EMAIL_ADDRESS element correctly, he or she will see an alert, and the cursor will move to the EMAIL_ADDRESS form element. It's a neat trick.

Beyond those few lines, you should find everything in this script clear. It's not as straightforward as it could be, but it does the job.

Summary

This chapter has covered the rest of what you need to know about forms, shown you how to use JavaScript to check a form before sending it to a CGI script, and demonstrated some of the string handling methods that come in handy when checking forms for valid completion.

If you understood everything in this chapter, you should know how to:

- Make sure visitors have filled out all fields in a form.

- Check an email address for valid formatting.

- Submit a correctly filled-out form to a CGI script.

- Use a bunch of string handling methods to manipulate strings.

The string handling methods described here just scratch the surface. Check Appendix B to see what other tricks you can perform with strings; it provides a full list of string handling instructions.

Assignment

The assignment in the last chapter was to make your own browser using frames. For this assignment, you will add code to your browser that makes sure the URLs entered in the browser's location bar are correct Web addresses, meaning that the URL starts with http:// or https://, has no spaces, and has at least two words with a period between them. The URLs below are *not* valid:

- The URL www.nytimes.com is missing the http:// beginning.

- The URL http://nytimes needs the .com ending.

- The URL http://www..nytimes.com has two periods with nothing between them.

Enjoy!

12

COOKIES

It's often helpful to remember a little bit of information about a visitor after he or she has left your site: a log-in name, the last time the visitor visited, or, if you have a shopping site, purchases the visitor made. To remember this information, you'll have to save it somewhere.

Chapter 10 showed you how to use frames to create a shopping cart. Unfortunately, this method does not retain the information the visitor entered after closing the browser. Cookies provide a solution to this problem: They let you save information on your visitor's computer for a specified length of time.

Cookies aren't hard to use, but the code for saving and retrieving them can pose quite a challenge. You can use other people's code (I'll point out some good cookie libraries), but it's still a good idea to know how cookies work so you can alter the code from libraries to suit your own needs.

In this chapter you'll learn:

- What cookies are.

- What you can and can't do with them.

- How to set a cookie.

- How to read a cookie you've set.

- How to remember names and dates with cookies.

- How to build a basic shopping cart with cookies.

- Where to get good prewritten cookie code.

A Real-World Example of Cookies

Cookies are used in all sorts of applications. A common use is to determine whether a visitor has seen a page before. For example, the first time you visit http://book_of_javascript.tripod.com/survey.html, you'll receive a survey to fill out. After you've seen the survey once, you'll never see it again, because the page stores a cookie on your computer to record that first visit. Every time you visit the page, the page checks to see if you have the cookie; if you do, it won't give you the survey.

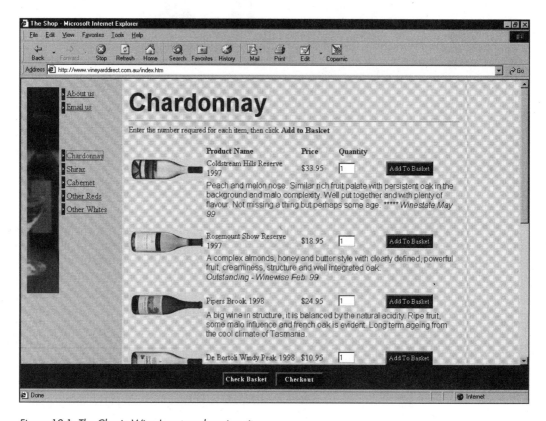

Figure 12-1: The Classic Wine Investors shopping site

A more complex cookie example is the Classic Wine Investors Australia shopping site at http://www.vineyarddirect.com.au/index.html (Figure 12-1). This wine seller's shopping cart, called JShop, comes from http://www.jshop. co.uk/ and depends almost entirely on JavaScript and cookies. Figure 12-2 shows you a page listing a sample purchase.

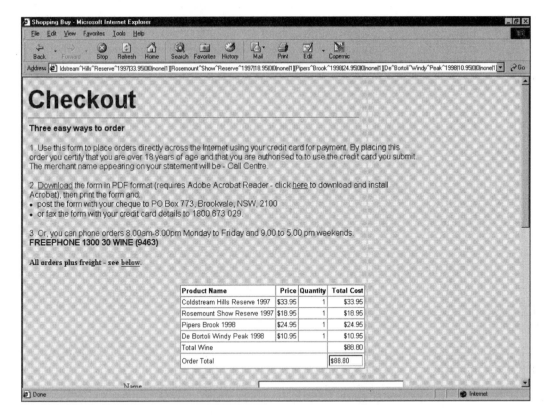

Figure 12-2: A wine purchase

What Are Cookies?

Cookies are little bits of information a site leaves on the hard drive of visitors. Because the information ends up on the hard drive, it remains after they leave the current page and even after they turn the computer off. You'll find this feature extremely useful when you want to remember information about a user each time he or she visits your site.

Cookies were introduced in Netscape 2.0 and Microsoft Internet Explorer 3.0. Unfortunately, MSIE 3.0 offers a less-than-perfect implementation: While you can use cookies to save and read information on other people's computers, you can't save cookies to *your own* computer. This means you can't test your cookie code in MSIE 3.0. If you're still using MSIE 3.0, it's probably time to either upgrade to a more recent version or switch to Netscape.

You can see the cookies saved on your computer by looking for the cookies.txt file for Netscape or the Cookies directory for MSIE. In either case, you'll see a long list of site names, each with a string of text. The text might seem incomprehensible to you since most sites encrypt cookies in some way to pack more information into them. But take a look to see who's left these little treats on your system—you'll find it very educational.

What Cookies Can and Can't Do

Because cookies involve writing to and reading from your visitors' hard drives, cookie-friendly browsers deal with lots of security issues. As a result, using cookies has many limitations. The most important ones for the purposes of this chapter are these:

1. Not everyone has a cookie-friendly browser.

2. Not everyone who has a cookie-friendly browser chooses to accept cookies (but most people do).

3. Each domain may only have 20 cookies (so use them sparingly).

4. Cookies can't exceed 4 kilobytes. That's just over 4,000 characters—actually quite a lot.

5. A Web site can only set and read its own cookies (for example, Yahoo can't read AOL's cookies).

Keep these limitations in mind when you consider using cookies on your site.

Working with Cookies

This section covers all the basic cookie operations: setting, reading, resetting, and setting expiration dates.

Setting Cookies

Setting a basic cookie is simple. Just create a string in the form *cookie_name=value* and then set the document.cookie property to that string. The only trick is that cookie values can't include spaces, commas, or semicolons. Happily, the escape() and unescape() functions will code and decode cookies, so you don't have to worry about this restriction.

Figure 12-3 lists a simple example that stores a visitor's name in a cookie named username.

The first line of the function in Figure 12-3 (❶) asks for a visitor's name and saves it in the_name. ❷ creates the string to store in the cookie. The escape() function replaces characters that cookies can't handle with legal characters. For example, if I entered dave thau at the prompt, this line would create the string username=dave%20thau. The percent sign and 20 (%20) replace the space between dave and thau.

❸ sets the cookie. To make sure you've set a cookie, type the following into your browser's location bar:

```
javascript:alert(document.cookie)
```

```
    function setCookie()
    {
❶      var the_name = prompt("What's your name?","");
❷      var the_cookie = "username=" + escape(the_name);
❸      document.cookie = the_cookie;
       alert("Thanks!");
    }
```

Figure 12-3: A cookie-setting function

Reading Cookies

It's pretty easy to read a cookie you've saved to someone's hard disk. Figure 12-4 shows you code that can read the cookie set in Figure 12-3.

```
    function readCookie()
    {
❶      var the_cookie = document.cookie;
❷      var broken_cookie = the_cookie.split("=");
❸      var the_name = broken_cookie[1];
❹      var the_name = unescape(the_name);
       alert("Your name is: " + the_name);
    }
```

Figure 12-4: Reading a cookie

The first line (❶) in Figure 12-4 is the important one. Whenever your browser opens a Web page, the browser reads whatever cookies that site has stored on your machine and loads them into the document.cookie property.

The tricky part about reading cookies is getting just the information you want from them. In Figure 12-4, everything after the first line of the function pulls the user's name out of the cookie. Once ❶ gets the cookie, ❷ breaks the cookie into a two-element array using the split() method we learned in Chapter 11. The first element in the array consists of everything in the cookie preceding the equal sign (=). In this case, it's username, so that is the first element in the array. The second element in the array is everything following the equal sign, which is dave%20. ❸ grabs this string from the array and stores it in the_name, and ❹ decodes the_name with the unescape() function by swapping %20 for a space.

If you get a JavaScript error while trying these examples, quit your browser after trying each example to erase the cookies you've set. Because cookies can store more than one value, the examples in this chapter would require additional—and complicated—code to separate the different cookie values. The "Setting Multiple Cookies" section covers a more robust way of reading JavaScript cookies.

Resetting Cookies

To *reset* (change the value of) a cookie, simply set its name to another value. For example, to keep track of the last time a visitor came to your site, set a cookie named date each time that person visits your site. Figure 12-5 lists a complete Web page that keeps track of the last time a given visitor entered the Web page.

Loading this page calls the JavaScript functions readCookie() (❷) and setCookie() (❸). The readCookie() function checks to see if the site has set a cookie (❶). If the string between the parentheses of the if-then clause is false or the null string (""), the lines in the body of the if-then statement won't execute. If the string finds a cookie, document.cookie will return whatever that cookie is, so the lines in the body of the if-then statement will execute, extracting the date from the cookie and writing it to the Web page using document.write().

After readCookie() does its thing, setCookie() sets a new cookie. This function gets the current date and sets a cookie named date to that date. Each time setCookie() is called, it replaces the last cookie named date with a new one. This is just like setting a variable.

Setting More Than One Piece of Information

Adding more than one piece of information to a cookie is no problem. For example, to store a person's name, age, and phone number, you could set a cookie like this:

```
var the_cookie = "username:thau/age:just a tyke/phone:411";
document.cookie= "my_cookie=" + escape(the_cookie);
```

A slash separates property names (username, age, and phone) and a colon distinguishes the property names and values (username:thau, phone:411). The slash and colon are arbitrary; you can use any symbols—so long as you're consistent.

It's a bit harder to pull multiple pieces of information out of a cookie. Try using associative arrays (Chapter 8) to store the information. For example, if you saved

```
my_cookie=username:thau/age:just a tyke/phone:411
```

to someone's hard drive, you could read the information into an associative array using the readTheCookie() function in Figure 12-6.

```
    <html><head><title>Date Cookie</title>
    <script language="JavaScript">
    <!-- hide me
    function setCookie()
    {
        var the_date = new Date();
        var the_cookie = "date=" + escape(the_date);
        document.cookie = the_cookie;
    }

    function readCookie()
    {
❶   if (document.cookie)
    {
        var the_cookie = document.cookie;
        var the_cookie_array = the_cookie.split("date=");
        var the_date = unescape(the_cookie_array[1]);
        document.write("The last time you visited here was: " + the_date);
        document.write("<br>");
    }
    }
    // end hide me -->
    </script>
    </head>
    <body>
    <h1>Welcome!</h1>
    <script language="JavaScript">
    <!-- hide me
❷ readCookie();
❸ setCookie();
    // end hide -->
    </script>
    </body>
    </html>
```

Figure 12-5: Tracking a visitor's last visit to a Web page

```
       <html>
       <head>
       <title>Complex Cookie</title>
       <script language="JavaScript">
       <!-- hide me
       function readTheCookie(the_info)
       {
           // load the cookie into a variable and unescape it
           var the_cookie = document.cookie;
           var the_cookie = unescape(the_cookie);

           // separate the values from the cookie name
           var broken_cookie = the_cookie.split("=");
❶         var the_values = broken_cookie[1];

           // break each name:value pair into an array
❷         var separated_values = the_values.split("/");

           // loop through the list of name:values and load
           // up the associate array
           var property_value = "";
❸         for (loop = 0; loop < separated_values.length; loop++)
           {
               property_value = separated_values[loop];
               var broken_info = property_value.split(":");
               var the_property = broken_info[0];
               var the_value = broken_info[1];
❹             the_info[the_property] = the_value;
           }
       }
       function setCookie()
       {
           var the_cookie = "my_cookie=name:thau/age:just a tyke/phone:411";
           document.cookie = escape(the_cookie);
       }
❺     setCookie();
❻     var cookie_information = new Array();
❼     readTheCookie(cookie_information);

       // end hide -->
       </script>
       </head>
```

Figure 12-6: Loading a complex cookie into an associative array

```
<body>
<h1>This Is What I Know about You</h1>
<script language="JavaScript">
<!-- hide me
❽ document.write("Name: " + cookie_information["name"] + "<br>");
document.write("Age: " + cookie_information["age"] + "<br>");
document.write("Phone: " + cookie_information["phone"] + "<br>");
// end hide -->
</script>
</body>
</html>
```

Figure 12-6 (continued): Loading a complex cookie into an associative array

When this page loads, ❺ sets a cookie, ❻ creates a new array, and ❼ sends the new, empty array to the readTheCookie() function. The function first gets the cookie and splits off the cookie's name (my_cookie). After ❶, the_values will equal name:thau/age:just a tyke/phone:411 because that's how we set the cookie in the setCookie() function.

Next, ❷ splits the_values into its component parts, loading name:thau into separated_values[0], age:just a tyke into separated_values[1], and phone:411 into separated_values[2].

After the function breaks up the_values, ❸ loops through each of the three elements (home, age, phone) in separated_values. Each time through the loop, the function breaks the element into two pieces along the colon. It then loads the first part of the element into the_property and the second part into the_value. The first time through the loop, the_property is name and the_value is thau. Once the element is split like this, the associative array the_info gets loaded up in ❹. After the loop has occurred three times, you get these results: the_info["name"] = thau, the_info["age"] = "just a tyke", and the_info["phone"] = 411.

With the associative array loaded up properly, the three lines starting at ❽ retrieve the information and display it on a Web page.

Setting the Duration of a Cookie

Until now, we've been creating cookies that disappear when a user exits the browser. Sometimes this is for the best. Since each domain can have only 20 cookies on a user's machine, you don't want to waste space by saving unnecessary cookies between browser sessions. However, if you *do* want your cookies to remain on a user's hard drive after he or she quits the browser, you have to set an expiration date in a special format called GMT.[1] For example,

1 In MSIE 5.0, and probably in future browsers, GMT (Greenwich Mean Time) has been replaced by UTC (Universal Time Code). They're just different names for the same thing, but don't be surprised if you see UTC instead of GMT.

```
Sun, 12-Jan-1992 00:00:00 GMT
```

is the supposed birth date in Greenwich Mean Time of HAL9000, the intelligent computer from *2001: A Space Odyssey*. (HAL? HAL? Are you out there?)

The GMT format can be sort of a pain, especially since you must figure out if the day was a Monday, Friday, or whatever. Luckily, JavaScript's toGMTString() date method converts a date in a simpler format to a date in GMT format. Here's an easy way to set a date far into the future:

```
var the_date = new Date("December 31, 2023");
var the_cookie_date = the_date.toGMTString();
```

To set your cookie to expire, you have to add the expiration date to the cookie. Add expires=date to the string and separate the cookie components with a semicolon:

```
cookie_name=whatever;expires=date
```

Figure 12-7 shows you how to build a cookie that will last until the end of the Mayan calendar:

```
function setCookie()
{
    // get the information
    //
    var the_name = prompt("What's your name?","");
    var the_date = new Date("December 31, 2023");
    var the_cookie_date = the_date.toGMTString();

    // build and save the cookie
    //
    var the_cookie = "my_cookie=" + escape(the_name);
    the_cookie = the_cookie + ";expires=" + the_cookie_date;
    document.cookie = the_cookie;
}
```

Figure 12-7: Setting a cookie that will expire far in the future

Before the_cookie in Figure 12-7 is escaped (using the escape() function), it will resemble the following line:

```
my_cookie=thau;expires=Fri, 31-Dec-2023 00:00:00 GMT
```

Once set, this cookie lives on your visitor's hard drive until the expiration date.

You can also use the expiration date to delete cookies by setting the date to a time in the past. This can come in handy if you're using cookies to log people in and out of your site. When a visitor logs in, give him or her a cookie that shows they've done so. When he or she wants to log out, delete the cookie.

Who Can Read the Cookie?

I've already mentioned that only the Web site that set a cookie can read it—McDonald's can't read Burger King's cookies, and vice versa. The full story is a little more complicated than that, however.

Letting One Page Read a Cookie Set on Another

By default, only the Web page that set the cookie can read it. If one of your pages sets a cookie, to let other pages on your site read the cookie you must set the path of the cookie. The cookie's path sets the top-level directory from which a cookie can be read. Setting the path of a cookie to the root-level directory of your site makes it possible for all your Web pages to read the cookie.

To do this, add path=/; to your cookie. If you just want the cookie readable in a directory called food, add path=/food;.

Dealing with Multiple Domains

Some Web sites have lots of little domains. For example, the Yahoo Web portal has a main site (www.yahoo.com), a finances site (finance.yahoo.com), a personalized site (my.yahoo.com), and many others. By default, if a Web page on finances.yahoo.com sets a cookie, pages on my.yahoo.com can't read that cookie. But if you add domain=domain_name to a cookie, all domains ending in domain_name can read the cookie. To allow all the machines in the yahoo.com domain to read a cookie, Yahoo has to add domain=yahoo.com to the cookie.

The Whole Cookie

Adding an expiration date, domain, and path to a cookie makes it pretty big. Figure 12-8 lists a function that sets all these variables so you can see the whole picture in one example.

Figure 12-8 results in a cookie that looks like this (before escaping it):

```
my_cookie=thau;path=/;domain=nostarch.com;expires=Sun, 31 Dec 2023 00:00:00 GMT;
```

Of course, because I'm setting the domain to nostarch.com, only a No Starch Press computer can read this cookie.

```
function setCookie()
{
    var the_name = prompt("What's your name?","");
    var the_date = new Date("December 31, 2023");
    var the_cookie = escape(the_name) + ";" ;
    var the_cookie = the_cookie + "path=/;";
    var the_cookie = the_cookie + "domain=nostarch.com;";
    var the_cookie = the_cookie + "expires=" + the_date.toGMTString() + ";";
    document.cookie = "my_cookie=" + the_cookie;
}
```

Figure 12-8: Setting all the cookie properties

Setting Multiple Cookies

Sometimes one cookie just isn't enough. For instance, if your Web site has two different JavaScript applications—one that uses cookies to store information about your visitors and one that uses cookies to keep track of their purchases—you'll probably want to store these two types of information in different cookies.

To save multiple cookies, just give each cookie a different name. Setting document.cookie to a cookie with a new name won't delete the cookies that are already there. Here's some code that sets two cookies:

```
var visitor_cookie = "this_person=" +
    escape("name:thau/occupation:slacker/phone:411");
document.cookie = visitor_cookie;
var purchase_cookie= "purchases=" + escape("tshirt:1/furbie:15/burrito:400");
document.cookie = purchase_cookie;
```

This code sets document.cookie twice, but because the cookies have different names, you can store both in document.cookie. After running the four lines above, document.cookie looks like this (except for the escaped characters):

```
this_person=name:thau/occupation:slacker/phone:411;purchases=tshirt:1/furbie:15/burrito:400
```

In the above example, storing two cookies in document.cookie works well because the JavaScript that looks at purchase information doesn't have to deal with the information in the other cookie. Unfortunately, it's a bit difficult to pull the contents of one cookie out of document.cookie because it contains multiple cookies. Here's where prewritten JavaScript libraries come in handy.

Cookie Libraries

You'll find many free cookie libraries on the Web. Just use any search engine and search for *javascript cookie* to get a list. The functions in the libraries generally come ready to run, so you can just cut and paste them into your Web pages. Webmonkey has exceptionally well-commented libraries, so we'll use its code here. You can find more of Webmonkey's free JavaScript code at http://hotwired.lycos.com/webmonkey/programming/javascript/code_library/.

Webmonkey's Code for Accessing Multiple Cookies

Figure 12-9 shows you Webmonkey's code for accessing one cookie when document.cookie is storing multiple cookies.

```
function WM_readCookie(name) {
    if(document.cookie == '') { // there's no cookie, so go no further
    return false;
    } else { // there is a cookie
    var firstChar, lastChar;
    var theBigCookie = document.cookie;
    firstChar = theBigCookie.indexOf(name);        // find the start of 'name'
    var NN2Hack = firstChar + name.length;
    { // if you found the cookie
    if((firstChar != -1) && (theBigCookie.charAt(NN2Hack) == '=')) {
        firstChar += name.length + 1; // skip 'name' and '='
        // Find the end of the value string (the next ';').
        lastChar = theBigCookie.indexOf(';', firstChar);
        if(lastChar == -1) lastChar = theBigCookie.length;
        return unescape(theBigCookie.substring(firstChar, lastChar));
    } else { // If there was no cookie of that name, return false.
        return false;
    }
    }
    }
} // WM_readCookie
```

Figure 12-9: Reading one cookie from document.cookie

To use these functions, cut and paste them into the page and call the functions appropriately. To retrieve a cookie named thisuser, call the function WM_readCookie("thisuser").

Webmonkey's well-commented functions speak for themselves. If you use these, read them over first and make sure you understand how they work.

Shopping Cart Basics

This section discusses code that represents the start of a shopping cart script. You definitely do not want to use this code to run your own shopping cart—it's much too simplistic. For example, you can't remove an item from the basket once you've selected it. You'll find a more complete (free or very inexpensive) JavaScript shopping cart program on the Web. Just search for *javascript shopping cart* on any search engine and you'll find a list of applications.

A complete shopping cart application is quite long, but the code below should give you a feel for what's involved in building your own JavaScript shopping basket or understanding someone else's. Figure 12-10 shows you the code for a main page of a simple shopping cart (see Figure 12-11) with simple links to pages that contain items to buy.

```
<html><head><title>Welcome to My Store</title>
</head>
<body>
<h1>Welcome to My Store!</h1>
Here you can buy:<br>
<a href="parts.html">Computer parts!</a> and <br>
<a href="clothes.html">Clothes!</a><br>
<p>
When you're done choosing items, you can
<form>
❶ <input type="button" value="check out" onClick="window.location='checkout.html';">
</form>
</body>
</html>
```

Figure 12-10: The shopping cart main page

Figure 12-11: What the shopping cart main page looks like

The only new and interesting feature in Figure 12-10 is ❶, which redirects visitors to the page checkout.html (discussed in Figure 12-15) when they click the checkout button. Figure 12-12 shows you the code for one of the pages where you can buy a product.

```
   <html><head><title>Clothes</title>
❶  <script language="JavaScript" src="shopping.js"></script>
   </head>
   <body>
   <h1>Buy these clothes!</h1>
   <form name="clothes">
   Tshirt:
   <input type="text" name="tshirt" size="3" value="1">
❷  <input type="button" value="add" onClick="addToCart(window.document.clothes.tshirt.value,
   'tshirt',14);">
   ($14 each)
   <p>
   Jeans:
   <input type="text" name="jeans" size="3" value="1">
   <input type="button" value="add"
   onClick="addToCart(window.document.clothes.jeans.value,'jeans',30);">
   ($30 each)
   <p>
   <a href="main.html">Go back to main page</a>
   or <br>
   <form>
   <input type="button" value="check out" onClick="window.location='checkout.html';">
   </form>
   </body>
   </html>
```

Figure 12-12: Code for a page where you can purchase goods

Most of this page describes the form that lists what visitors can buy. Each item has a button next to it that lets you buy the item (see Figure 12-13). Pushing that button (as in ❷) calls the function addToCart(), which takes three parameters: the quantity of the item to buy, what the item is, and how much it costs. Interestingly, the addToCart() function isn't stored on this Web page but in a file called shopping.js (Figure 12-14), a normal text file that contains all the functions the shopping cart needs to work. The browser reads the shopping.js file into the page and interprets it at ❶. This technique is very handy when you have a set of functions that apply to many pages. In our example, all the shopping pages on the site will need the addToCart() function, so rather than cut and paste this function onto every page, we can use ❶ to call the functions from shopping.js. You'll also find this feature extremely useful when you want to change the function. Instead of having to track down every place you've cut and pasted it in, you just need to change it once in the shopping.js file. Once you've changed it there, any page that uses the shopping.js file will load the changed version.

Figure 12-13: A shopping page

```
    function addToCart(amount, item, price)
    {
❶      var purch_string = escape(item + ":" + amount + ":" + price);
❷      var the_cookie = WM_readCookie("purchases");
❸      if (the_cookie)
        {
❹        purch_string = the_cookie + "/" + purch_string;
        }
❺    WM_setCookie("purchases",purch_string,0,"/");
    }
```

Figure 12-14: shopping.js

The addToCart() function in shopping.js creates a string to save into a cookie (❶) in the form item:amount:price. The function then uses the Webmonkey WM_readCookie() function to see if the visitor has already received a cookie named purchases (❷ and ❸). If there is already a cookie, ❹ puts a forward slash (/) at its end and adds the string created in ❶. Each time a visitor buys an item, the cookie gets a slash followed by the item name. If you bought one T-shirt and one pair of jeans, the cookie would look like this:

```
purchases=tshirt:1:14/jeans:1:30
```

If you then bought another T-shirt, the cookie would look like this:

```
purchases=tshirt:1:14/jeans:1:30/tshirt:1:14
```

A more complete version of addToCart() would realize that you had already bought a T-shirt and, instead of tacking another tshirt:1:14 to the end of the cookie, would add one to the T-shirt amount:

```
purchases=tshirt:2:14/jeans:1:30
```

However, since that small change involves a fair amount of code, I'm leaving it out. Check out demos/jshop on your CD-ROM to see the code for a complete shopping cart.

After the new cookie string has been constructed, ❺ uses the Webmonkey library function WM_setCookie() to save the visitor's cookie information.

The final page to consider is the checkout page listing in Figure 12-15.

```
     <html><head><title>Checkout</title>
❶   <script language="JavaScript" src="shopping.js"></script>
     </head>
     <body>
     <h1>Here's your Basket So Far</h1>
     <script language="JavaScript">
❷   checkOut();
     </script>
     </body>
     </html>
```

Figure 12-15: Code for the checkout page

The checkout page loads in the shopping.js file in ❶ just like the product page in Figure 12-12. Although there is a little HTML on this page, most of what you see when you visit this page is generated by the checkOut() function, which is stored in the shopping.js file. Figure 12-17 lists the checkOut() function, which writes the contents of the shopping cookie to the page, and the readTheCookie() function, which reads the cookie and formats it in a way that makes the checkOut() function's job easier.

Figure 12-16: What the checkout page looks like

```
❶ function readTheCookie(the_info)
   {
       var split_stuff;

       // load the cookie into a variable and unescape it

❷      var the_cookie = WM_readCookie("purchases");
       if (the_cookie)
       {
❸          if (the_cookie.indexOf('/') != -1)
           {
               split_stuff = the_cookie.split("/");
❹              for (var loop=0; loop < split_stuff.length; loop++)
               {
❺                  the_info[loop] = split_stuff[loop];
               }
           } else {
❻                  the_info[0] = the_cookie;
           }
       }
   }

   function checkOut()
   {
       var total=0;
       var the_stuff = new Array();
❼      readTheCookie(the_stuff);
```

Figure 12-17: Code for the functions used by the checkout page

```
        document.writeln("<table border=2>");
    document.writeln("<th>Item</th><th>Amount</th><th>Price</th><th>Subtotal</th>");
❽      for (var loop=0; loop<the_stuff.length; loop++)
    {
❾        var this_item = the_stuff[loop].split(":");
❿        document.writeln("<tr>");
⓫           for (var inloop = 0; inloop < this_item.length; inloop++)
        {
            document.writeln("<td>");
            document.writeln(this_item[inloop]);
            document.writeln("</td>");
        }
⓬  sub_total = this_item[1] * this_item[2];
⓭           total += sub_total;
        document.writeln("<td>" + sub_total + "</td>");
          document.writeln("</tr>");
    }
    document.writeln("<tr>");
    document.writeln("<td><b>total</b></td>");
⓮    document.writeln("<td></td><td></td><td><b>" + total + "</b></td>");
    document.writeln("</tr>");
    document.writeln("</table>");
    }
```

Figure 12-17 (continued): Code for the functions used by the checkout page

The readTheCookie() Function

The checkOut() function creates a new, empty array and passes the array to
the readTheCookie() function (❼). The readTheCookie() function breaks up
the cookie into each item bought and loads the items in the array. ❷ reads
the cookie using the WM_readCookie() function. If there is a purchases cookie
(which the visitor would have set by clicking on an item—see Figure 12-13),
❸ determines if the visitor bought more than one item. If he or she
purchased only one item, that item gets loaded into the array in position 0
(❻). If he or she purchased two or more items, a forward slash appears
between them and the cookie gets split up into the split_stuff array. Then
the loop at ❺ copies everything in the split_stuff array into the_info, the
array sent into the function at ❶. At the end of readTheCookie(), the_info
contains all the items purchased.

The checkOut() Function

Once readTheCookie() loads the information from the cookie into the_info, checkOut() writes the purchased items to the Web page. ❽ loops through the_info, each element of which contains a purchased item. If the first item bought is one pair of jeans, the first element in the array appears as jeans:1:14. ❾ then splits this element along the colon, loading the three resulting elements into the this_item array.

The rest of the code writes the table. ❿ begins a new row and ⓫ sandwiches each element in this_item between <td> and </td> tags.

⓬ calculates how much this_item costs by multiplying the price of the item (this_item[1]) by the quantity bought (this_item[2]). If the first element in the_info is jeans:1:14, then this_item[0] is jeans, this_item[1] is 1, and this_item[2] is 14 because of the split in ❾. ⓬ then multiplies 1 by 14 to get the subtotal, and ⓭ adds this subtotal to the total, written to the page in ⓮.

Even though the above shopping cart requires a lot of JavaScript, each of its functions is short and fairly easy to understand. Complicated applications like shopping carts are usually just groups of smaller functions that work together.

Once you understand the basics of JavaScript, the hard part of writing an application is figuring out what functions you need and how they interrelate. This is the art of programming, and comes only with a lot of practice. If you understand the shopping cart code above but don't think you could write it yourself, practice writing smaller scripts—you'll soon get the hang of it.

Summary

Cookies are an advanced JavaScript feature and can add a lot of functionality to your site. In addition to setting up a shopping cart, you can use cookies to keep track of when and how often a visitor comes to your site and to save customization preferences visitors might set. If you've thoroughly grasped this chapter, you now know:

- What cookies are.

- How to set a basic cookie.

- How to make a cookie last after the user has turned off their computer.

- How to control which pages can read your cookie.

- How to store more than one piece of information in a cookie.

- How to set and read more than one cookie.

- How to create a separate JavaScript file that other HTML files can include.

- Where to find JavaScript cookie libraries.

- The basics of how a shopping cart script works.

Assignment

Write a page that works like the survey page described at the beginning of the chapter. The first time a visitor sees the page, he or she should get an alert box that says, "Welcome, new-timer!" At the next visit, that alert box shouldn't appear.

13

DYNAMIC HTML

Dynamic HTML (DHTML) combines JavaScript, HTML, and Cascading Style Sheets (CSS) to give Web page designers an incredible amount of freedom to animate and add interactivity to their pages. If you have a 4.0 or higher browser and you've seen sites that have hierarchical menus (a menu where clicking on an option reveals a submenu of further selections) or images that dance all over the screen, you've seen DHTML in action.

DHTML is an immense subject. This chapter will introduce DHTML and show you how what you've learned so far fits into the DHTML puzzle.[1]

This chapter covers:

- CSS basics.

- How JavaScript, HTML, and CSS work together to make objects fly around your screen.

- Hierarchical menu basics.

- How to write DHTML that works across browsers.

---

1 If you want to learn all the details about DHTML, I suggest you buy *Dynamic HTML: The Definitive Resource* by Danny Goodman (O'Reilly & Associates, 1998).

Real-World Examples of DHTML

DHTML can enhance your Web pages in a variety of ways. There are entire sites devoted to DHTML examples and tutorials. A few good ones are:

http://www.dhtmlzone.com/index.html

http://hotwired.lycos.com/webmonkey/authoring/dynamic_html

http://www.webreference.com/dhtml

Typing dynamic html into any search engine will show you dozens more choices.

One common application for DHTML is for creating a *hierarchical menu*. On its Web site, http://www.microsoft.com, Microsoft uses DHTML to create a hierarchical menu (Figure 13-1). Choosing the About Microsoft option on the menu pulls down several other options. Microsoft's code for this menu is quite complicated, but by the end of this chapter, you should have a good sense of how it works.

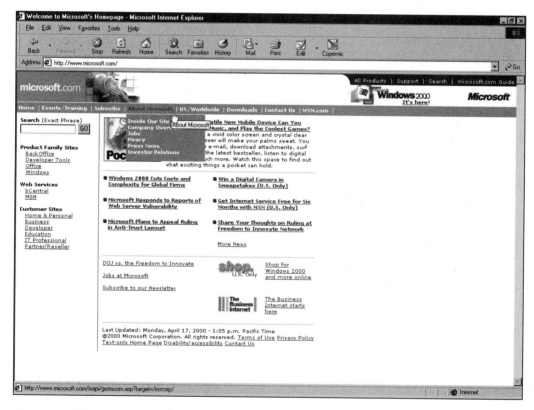

Figure 13-1: A DHTML hierarchical menu

CSS Basics

As mentioned in the opening of the chapter, DHTML is a combination of HTML, JavaScript, and CSS. CSS enables you to position HTML precisely on your pages—no longer will you have to use bizarre tables and invisible GIFs to position elements. With a CSS you can easily place a GIF precisely in the center of your page or a block of text in the lower right corner. Unfortunately, CSS didn't make it into Netscape and Microsoft Internet Explorer until version 4.0, so older browsers won't understand CSS positioning instructions. Perhaps even worse, these browsers implement CSS differently, making it somewhat difficult to use. However, CSS basics work similarly in both browsers.

The div Tag

Before you can position any HTML, you have to use the `<div>` and `</div>` tags to tell your browser which HTML you want to position. Figure 13-2 shows a simple use of `div` tags.

```
<html><head><title>Divide and Conquer</title></head>
<body>
<h1>Divide and Conquer</h1>
This text is not inside a div.
<p>
❶ <div id = "myFirstDiv">
But this text is.<br>
And so is this text.<br>
❷ </div>
<p>
But this text is not.
</body>
</html>
```

Figure 13-2: Basic div usage

The page in Figure 13-3 looks just like any other HTML page. However, ❶ and ❷ create a div that gives the lines between ❶ and ❷ the id `myFirstDiv`. You can use any set of letters or numbers for a div's id, but it can't contain spaces or underscores, and the first character has to be a letter. Now we can use the div's id to position the block with CSS or move it around dynamically with JavaScript.

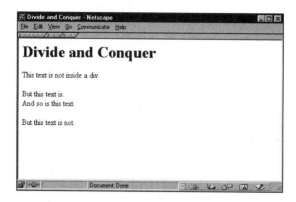

Figure 13-3: An HTML page with divs

Positioning a div Tag with CSS

You can position the contents of a div tag anywhere on a Web page using the HTML style element. Replacing ❶ in Figure 13-2 with the following line moves the block of text called myFirstDiv into the lower middle of the page:

```
<div id = "myFirstDiv" style="position:absolute; top:150; left:100;">
```

Figure 13-4 shows what this looks like.

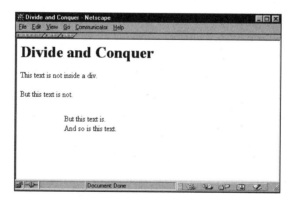

Figure 13-4: Moving a div into the lower middle of the page

As you can see, the style goes inside the div tag and has three components separated by semicolons. The position component gives the div a reference point (with position:absolute, the reference point is the browser window's upper left corner). The top component determines how many pixels down from the reference point the div appears, and the left component determines how many pixels to the right of the reference point the div appears.

Instead of positioning the div relative to the upper left corner of the browser window, you can position it relative to where it would normally appear in the HTML. If you did not include any positioning information in the div, it would follow the line "This text is not inside a div." However, if you use the style shown on page 268 but replace position:absolute with position:relative, the div appears 150 pixels below and 100 pixels to the right of that point. Figure 13-5 shows you what this would look like.

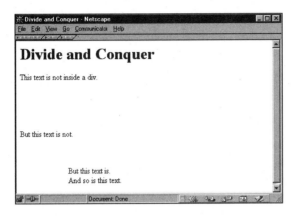

Figure 13-5: Using position:relative instead of position:absolute

Whether you use position:absolute or position:relative depends on what you're aiming for. If you want one block of HTML to appear directly to the right of another block, you might find it easier to use position:relative. But if you want to make sure an image appears in the center of the screen, you'll find position:absolute more useful.

Hiding a div

You can display or hide the contents of a div by setting its visibility to either visible or hidden. The style below puts the div in the lower center of the page and hides it.

```
<div id = "myFirstDiv" style="position:absolute; top:150; left:100; visibility:hidden">
```

You can change the visibility of a div with JavaScript. Sometimes it makes sense to create a bunch of invisible divs on a page and use JavaScript to make them appear when you need them. For example, you could make an entire section of HTML blink on and off by alternately hiding and showing it. Later in the chapter, when we talk about hierarchical menus, I'll show you how to hide divs.

Layering divs

Another nice feature of divs is that you can layer them on top of each other. For example, you could put an image of a mouse in one div and an image of a maze in another div, then put the mouse in the maze by layering the mouse div on top of the maze div. Once you've done that, you can move the position of the mouse div to make it look like the mouse is exploring the maze.

To layer one div on top of another, set the div's z-index. A div with a higher z-index value appears on top of a div with a lower z-index. Figure 13-6 shows the code for a page with one GIF (a small white square) on top of another GIF (a bigger black square). In Figure 13-7, the small white GIF has a higher z-index, and in Figure 13-8, the black square has a higher z-index.

```
<html><head><title>Layering Divs</title></head>
<body>
<div id="whiteSquare" style="position:absolute; top:100; left:100; z-index:2">
<img src="white.gif">
</div>
<div id="blackSquare" style="position:absolute; top:0; left:0; z-index:1">
<img src="black.gif">
</div>
</body>
</html>
```

Figure 13-6: Layering divs with z-index

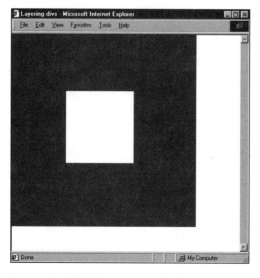

Figure 13-7: The white square with a higher z-index than the black square

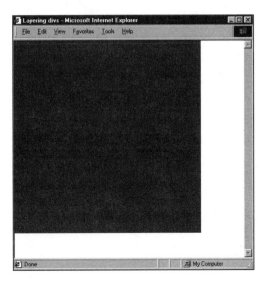

Figure 13-8: The black square with a higher z-index than the white square

Normal HTML is at z-index 0. If you set the z-index of a div to a negative number, it appears behind the normal HTML, like a background image.

JavaScript and DHTML

DHTML becomes dynamic when you start using JavaScript to manipulate divs. Here's where Netscape and Microsoft Internet Explorer start to diverge. If you have a div named myFirstDiv (as in Figure 13-2) and you want to use JavaScript to hide the div, you'd use this JavaScript in Netscape:

```
window.document.myFirstDiv.visibility = "hidden";
```

You'd use this JavaScript in MSIE:

```
window.document.all.myFirstDiv.style.visibility = "hidden";
```

Figure 13-9 on page 272 combines the two lines above in a function that hides the div when the user clicks the link. This function works in both Netscape and MSIE.

The body in Figure 13-9 is exactly the same as in Figure 13-2 except for the addition of the link at ❾. Clicking on this link calls the function hideDiv().

```
    <html><head><title>Cross-Browser Div Hiding</title>
    <script language = "JavaScript">
    <!--
    function hideDiv()
    {
❶    var the_div;
❷    if (window.document.all)
     {
❸        the_div = window.document.all.myFirstDiv.style;
❹    } else if (document.layers) {
❺        the_div = window.document.myFirstDiv;
     } else {
❻        alert("sorry, this only works in 4.0 browsers");
❼        return;
     }

❽    the_div.visibility = "hidden";
    }
    // -->
    </script>
    </head>
    <body>
    <h1>Hide the Div</h1>
    This text is not inside a div.
    <p>
    <div id = "myFirstDiv" style="position:absolute; top:150; left:100; visibility:visible">
    But this text is.<br>
    And so is this text.<br>
    </div>
    <p>
    But this text is not.
    <br>
❾ <a href="#" onClick="hideDiv(); return false;">hide the div</a>
    </body>
    </html>
```

Figure 13-9: Cross-browser div hiding

Line-by-Line Analysis of Figure 13-9

The variable the_div in ❶ points to the div we want to change (the_div varies depending on which browser the visitor is using). ❷ checks to see if the visitor is using a version of MSIE that can handle DHTML (that is, MSIE version 4 and higher). If so, the expression window.document.all is true, so ❸ executes. ❸ uses the MSIE code to point the_div to the style of myFirstDiv.

If ❷ returns false—that is, the user's browser is not a DHTML-capable version of MSIE—❹ checks to see if the browser is a DHTML-capable version of Netscape. If it is, document.layers is true and ❺ executes. ❺ uses the Netscape code to point the_div to myFirstDiv. If the browser isn't a DHTML-capable version of either MSIE or Netscape, ❻ lets visitors know they should upgrade their browser, then ❼ exits the function. If the browser hasn't exited the function in ❼ (which only happens if the visitor is using a browser that can't handle DHTML), ❽ changes the visibility of the_div to hidden.

I used window.document.all in Figure 13-9 to check for MSIE and window.document.layers for Netscape. I could also have used navigator.appName and navigator.appVersion to determine what type of browser the visitor was using (see the section titled "Browser Detection" in Chapter 3). However, window.document.all and window.document.layers have the benefit of possibly including other browsers that can run DHTML. If I wanted to create an entirely new browser called ThauScape that could run DHTML, I could write the browser so window.document.layers was true. Then any script that checked for window.document.layers would think ThauScape ran DHTML, even though the person writing the script had never heard of ThauScape.

Making divs Move

Changing the div's top or left property moves the div around the screen. For example, to move a div 5 pixels to the right, add 5 to the left property. Of course, the way to do this differs a little between browsers.

In Netscape

To move a div 5 pixels to the right in Netscape, use this line:

```
window.document.myDiv.left = window.document.myDiv.left + 5;
```

Or try a shorter version:

```
document.myDiv.left += 5;
```

The shorter version works because, as mentioned in Chapter 2, you can just drop the window part, and if you remember from Chapter 12, += 5 means "add 5 to this variable."

To move a div 5 pixels to the left, subtract 5 from the `left` property:

```
document.myDiv.left -= 5;
```

This line subtracts 5 from the `left` property of `myDiv` using the `-=` operator.

In MSIE

MSIE considers the value stored in `window.document.all.myDiv.style.left` a string. This means when we add 5 to it, we have to use the `parseInt()` function to change the value from a string to an integer. To move a `div` 5 pixels to the right in MSIE, use this line:

```
document.all.myDiv.style.left = parseInt(document.all.myDiv.style.left) + 5;
```

Cross-Browser

To write cross-browser JavaScript that moves a `div` around, just use the code in Figure 13-9 to detect the visitor's browser and use `parseInt()` when reading the value of the `left`, `right`, or `z-index` property of a `div`. Figure 13-10 lists cross-browser code for moving the `div` in Figure 13-2 100 pixels to the right.

Figure 13-10 is almost exactly the same as Figure 13-9. Clicking on the link in ❸ of Figure 13-10 calls the `moveDiv()` function (❶). Except for ❷, this function is identical to `hideDiv()` in Figure 13-9. All of the code up to ❷ sets `the_div` according to the visitor's browser. After setting `the_div` to point to the `div` we want to change, ❷ adds `100` to the `left` property. The `parseInt()` function makes sure MSIE does the arithmetic correctly.

Using setTimeout() and clearTimeout() to Animate a Page

The code in Figure 13-10 makes a `div` *jump* across the screen. If you want the `div` to drift more slowly across the screen or to move along a specific path, you can use timing loops (Chapter 9) to animate your `div`.

To make a `div` move smoothly across the screen, write a function that moves the `div` a little bit, then uses `setTimeout()` to call itself in a few milliseconds. Figure 13-11 on page 276 contains code that causes an image of the number 1 to roam randomly around the screen.

Line-by-Line Analysis of Figure 13-11

In Figure 13-11, the image of the 1 starts wandering when a visitor clicks on the link at ❻, calling the `moveNumber()` function. The `moveNumber()` function sets `the_div` based on the visitor's browser and then determines how far the `div` moves.

```
    <html><head><title>Cross-Browser Div Moving</title>
    <script language = "JavaScript">
    <!--
❶  function moveDiv()
    {
        var the_div;
        if (window.document.all)
        {
            the_div = window.document.all.myFirstDiv.style;
        } else if (document.layers) {
            the_div = window.document.myFirstDiv;
        } else {
            alert("sorry, this only works in 4.0 browsers");
            return;
        }
❷      the_div.left = parseInt(the_div.left) + 100;
    }
    // -->
    </script>
    </head>
    <body>
    <h1>Moving the Div</h1>
    This text is not inside a div.
    <p>
    <div id = "myFirstDiv" style="position:absolute; top:150; left:100;">

    But this text is.<br>
    And so is this text.<br>
    </div>
    <p>
    But this text is not.
    <br>
❸  <a href="#" onClick="moveDiv(); return false;">move the div</a>
    </body>
    </html>
```

Figure 13-10: Cross-browser code for moving a div

```
<html><head><title>The Wandering One</title>
<script language = "JavaScript">
<!--
var the_timeout;
function moveNumber()
{
    var the_div, move_amount;
    if (window.document.all)
    {
        the_div = window.document.all.numberOne.style;
    } else if (document.layers) {
        the_div = window.document.numberOne;
    } else {
        alert("sorry, this only works in 4.0 browsers");
        return;
    }
❶  move_amount = Math.floor(Math.random() * 10);
❷  if (Math.floor(Math.random()*10) < 5)    {
        the_div.left = parseInt(the_div.left) + move_amount;
    } else {
        the_div.left = parseInt(the_div.left) - move_amount;
    }
❸  random_number = Math.floor(Math.random() * 10);
❹  if (Math.floor(Math.random()*10) < 5)
    {
        the_div.top = parseInt(the_div.top) + move_amount;
    } else {
        the_div.top = parseInt(the_div.top) - move_amount;
    }
❺  the_timeout = setTimeout("moveNumber();", 100);
}
// -->
</script>
</head>
<body>
<h1>The Wandering One</h1>
<div id = "numberOne" style="position:absolute; top:150; left:100; z-index:-1">
<img src="one.jpg">
</div>
<br>
❻ <a href="#" onClick="the_timeout=setTimeout('moveNumber();',100); return false;">start
  wandering</a> <br>
❼ <a href="#" onClick="clearTimeout(the_timeout); return false;">stop wandering</a>
</body>
</html>
```

Figure 13-11: The Wandering One

Generating Random Numbers

❶ chooses a random number between 0 and 9 by generating a random number from 0 to $.\overline{9}$ (that is, .9 repeating, a decimal point with infinite nines after it) with the `Math.random()` method and multiplying it by 10. This yields a number between 0 and $9.\overline{9}$. `Math.floor()` then drops the digits to the right of the decimal point. If `Math.random()` generates 0.543, multiplying by 10 gives you 5.43, and `Math.floor()` turns that into 5. The `parseInt()` function, which acts pretty much the same as `Math.floor()`, gives an error in Netscape if it's parsing a number less than 1, so `Math.floor()` is better for this purpose. This combination of `Math.random()` and `Math.floor()` is the traditional way to generate a random whole number between 0 and 9.

Determining the Direction of an Image's Motion

The if-then statement starting at ❷ generates another number between 0 and 9. If the number is below 5 (which happens exactly half the time), the amount generated at ❶ gets added to the `left` property, moving the number 1 on the screen a little to the right. If the number is 5 or above, the amount gets subtracted from the `left` property, moving the 1 to the left. ❸ and ❹ act similarly, moving the 1 up or down.

After the 1 has moved a little horizontally and a little vertically, ❺ calls `setTimeout()` to call the function again in a tenth of a second (remember, there are 1,000 milliseconds in a second so 100 milliseconds is one tenth of a second). When 100 milliseconds pass, the `moveNumber()` function gets called again, moving the number a little more and again setting `setTimeout()`. The 1 keeps wandering until the visitor clicks the link at ❼, clearing the last timeout set and ending the cycle.

Using eval() to Work with More Than One div

Figure 13-11 shows you how to animate one image, but if you wanted to animate more than one div you'd have a problem: The `moveNumber()` function works only for the div named `numberOne`. Previously, we added a parameter to a function when we wanted the function to perform a different task depending on the situation. If we could write `moveNumber()` so that it took a div as a parameter, we could animate any div and call the function once for each div we wanted to animate.

Unfortunately, it's not that easy—we can't just pass a div into a function, because we don't know how to refer to it. Let's say we've written a page that has two divs, `divOne` and `divTwo`, and a function called `moveDiv()` that takes a div as a parameter and moves it a random distance to the right. It would be nice if we could use an `onClick` to pass the div we want to move into `moveDiv()`, like this:

```
<a href="#" onClick="moveDiv(divOne); return false;">move div one</a>
```

The problem is that divOne will be one thing in Netscape and something different in MSIE (see Figure 13-9).

Pointing to a div with eval()

Happily, the eval() JavaScript function allows us to turn the name of a div into the div itself. It's important to differentiate between a variable that holds the name of an HTML element and a variable that actually points to the element itself. For example, in the line

```
var the_div_name = "window.document.divOne";
```

the variable the_div_name holds a string. To JavaScript, that string is just a series of characters that don't have any meaning. However, in the line

```
var the_div = window.document.divOne;
```

the variable the_div actually describes a div called divOne. In programming parlance, we say the_div points to the HTML element window.document.divOne. The difference between this line and the former one is the quotes. When JavaScript sees quotes around a set of characters, it doesn't try to interpret what you mean by them. When it finds no quotes, JavaScript assumes it should pay attention to that item because it is, for example, a variable or an HTML element such as a div.

What eval() Does

The eval() function takes a string and forces JavaScript to evaluate it. For example, if we run the following two lines, we'll end up with the_solution as 8:

```
var the_add_string = "3 + 5";
var the_solution = eval(the_add_string);
```

Notice that the_add_string is a string. If we printed the_add_string using a document.write() or alert() statement, it would print out "3 + 5." The eval() function takes the string 3 + 5 and evaluates it as if it were a JavaScript statement.

You can also use eval() to get a pointer to a div by using the div's name:

```
var the_div_name = "window.document.divOne";
var the_div = eval(the_div_name);
```

Here, the_div_name is just a string. It doesn't point to the actual div, so it doesn't have any of the div's properties. The following line would yield an error:

```
the_div_name.visibility = "hidden";
```

JavaScript would tell us that the_div_name doesn't have a property called visibility (it's a string, not a div). The eval() function evaluates the_div_name, returning a pointer to the div itself. After running the second line above, we can change the visibility of the div as follows:

```
the_div.visibility = "hidden";
```

How to Use eval()

Figure 13-12 lists a function that takes the name of a div and moves it a random distance to the right. The great thing about the function is that it takes the name of any div.

```
function moveDiv(the_div_name)
{
    var the_div, div_string;
    if (document.all)
    {
❶      div_string = "window.document.all. " + the_div_name + ".style";
        the_div = eval(div_string);
❷    } else if (document.layers) {
❸      div_string = "window.document. " + the_div_name;
❹      the_div = eval(div_string);
    } else {
        alert("sorry, this only works in 4.0 browsers");
        return;
    }
❺    the_div.left = parseInt(the_div.left) + Math.floor(Math.random()*10);
}
```

Figure 13-12: Using eval() when passing the name of a JavaScript object to a function

If we had one div called divOne and another called divTwo, we could use moveDiv() like this:

```
<a href="#" onClick="moveDiv('divOne'); return false;">move div one</a>  <br>
<a href="#" onClick="moveDiv('divTwo'); return false;">move div two</a>
```

When we call moveDiv()in the first case, the parameter the_div_name gets set to the string divOne. The function then determines which browser the visitor is using. If it's MSIE, then document.all is true, so ❶ and ❷ execute. ❶ creates a big string (window.document.all.divOne.style), which names the div we want to move, and ❷ evaluates that string, setting the_div to point to the div we want to move. ❸ and ❹ do the same thing for people who are visiting the page with Netscape. Once we've set the_div to point to the div we want to move, ❺ actually moves it.

Making an Animated Race with eval()

Figure 13-13 shows you a much longer but much more fun example of eval()—a race between three numbers. Clicking on the "Start the race" link starts the numbers racing across the page. When one crosses the invisible finish line, the race ends and the text box at the top of the page announces the winner. Figure 13-14 shows you what the screen looks like before the race starts.

```
<html><head><title>Numbers Race</title>
<script language = "JavaScript">
<!--
❶ var the_timers = new Array();
function startRace()
{
    window.document.the_form.winner.value = "AND THEY'RE OFF!";
    moveNumber('numberOne');
    moveNumber('numberTwo');
    moveNumber('numberThree');
}
function stopRace()
{
❷    clearTimeout(the_timers['numberOne']);
    clearTimeout(the_timers['numberTwo']);
    clearTimeout(the_timers['numberThree']);
}
function moveNumber(the_number)
{
    var the_div, div_string, time_out_string;
❸    var loop_speed = 100;  // how fast the numbers move
    var distance = 10;  // how far the numbers move
    var finish_line = 400;  // where the race ends
    if (document.all)
    {
❹      the_div_name = "document.all.divOne.style";
❺      the_div = eval(the_div_name);
    } else if (document.layers) {
        div_string = "window.document." + the_number;
        the_div = eval(div_string);
```

Figure 13-13: Using eval with setTimeout() to simulate a race

```
        } else {
            alert("sorry, this only works in 4.0 browsers");
            return;
        }
❻  the_div.left = parseInt(the_div.left) + Math.floor(Math.random()*distance);
❼  if (parseInt(the_div.left) > finish_line)
      {
❽        if (window.document.the_form.winner.value.indexOf("WINNER") == -1) {
            window.document.the_form.winner.value = "THE WINNER IS: " + the_number + " !!!";
            window.document.the_form.winner.value += " (reload the page for a new race).";
            stopRace();
         }
      } else {
❾        time_out_string = "moveNumber('" + the_number + "');";
❿        the_timers[the_number] = setTimeout(time_out_string, loop_speed);
      }
   }
}
// -->
</script>
</head>
<body>
<h1>Numbers Race</h1>
<form name = "the_form">
<input type="text" name = "winner" size = "60" value="">
</form>
<p>
<div id = "numberOne" style="position:absolute; top:150; left:100;">
<img src="one.jpg">
</div>
<div id = "numberTwo" style="position:absolute; top:200; left:100;">
<img src="two.jpg">
</div>
<div id = "numberThree" style="position:absolute; top:250; left:100;">
<img src="three.jpg">
</div>
<br>
<a href="#" onClick="startRace(); return false;">Start the race</a>
<br>
<a href="#" onClick="stopRace(); return false;">Stop the race</a>
<p>
</body>
</html>
```

Figure 13-13 (continued): Using eval with setTimeout() to simulate a race

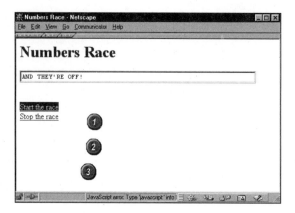

Figure 13-14: A numbers race

This is a pretty long and advanced example, so take it slowly. The body of the page is simple. It has a form, which holds the announcement text box; three divs, one for each number; and two links, one to start the race and another to stop it.

Clicking on the start link calls the function startRace(), puts "AND THEY'RE OFF!" in the announcement box, and starts each div moving with the moveNumber() function.

The moveNumber() function contains a timing loop for each div (❾ and ❿—see page 281). Each time through the loop, the div moves a little bit. If one div crosses the finish line before any other div, the text box announces the winner and stops the race.

The moveNumber() Function

First of all, ❸ defines a couple of variables that let you change the functions without having to understand exactly how they work. For example, to move the finish line down the page, you would just change the value of the finish_line variable. After you've defined these variables, the function figures out which div to use (this relies on techniques I've already covered). If a visitor views the page with MSIE, ❹ creates the name of the div we want to move, and ❺ sets the variable the_div to point to that div.

Once the_div is set, ❻ moves it a random distance and ❼ checks to see if it has crossed the finish line. If it has, the race is over. The div announces that it has won and stops the race by calling the stopRace() function. In a close race, there's a small chance that a second div might cross the finish line before the code in stopRace() finishes running. ❽ makes the div check the announcement box before announcing that it has won. If another div has already finished, the announcement box contains the words "THE WINNER IS…"

If the div has not crossed the finish line, it needs to keep moving. ❾ creates a string that the setTimeout() in ❿ calls. If the div is numberOne, ❾ sets time_out_string to moveNumber('numberOne');. Look closely at ❾ and its quotation marks. Because we want to call the moveNumber() function with the string numberOne, we have to make sure to use single quotes. Once we've created time_out_string, ❿ calls the setTimeout() using that string, which calls the moveNumber() function again in 100 milliseconds (❸). When the function calls moveNumber()again, the div again moves to the right and checks to see if it's won. This loop continues until cancellation of the setTimeout() for that div (that is, when the script calls the stopRace() function).

The setTimeout()

Since we have three divs, each one running in its own timed loop, each loop needs its own name. One way to keep track of the three timed loops is with an array, as done here. The array the_timers created at ❶ keeps track of the timed loop for each div.

To stop the div called numberOne from moving, we can cancel its timed loop with this line:

```
clearTimeout(the_timers['numberOne']);
```

This works because when ❿ calls the setTimeout() on the div named number_one, it sets the_timers['numberOne'] equal to the timeout. Canceling the timeout with clearTimeout() stops the moveNumber() function from running again on that div, which means the div won't move anymore. This is the hardest part of this example—if you understand what I'm talking about, you have a great grip on JavaScript. If you don't get it, take a closer look. Imagine there's only one div. If you still don't understand, take a break and look at it again later. Sometimes that's the best thing to do.

An Alternative to eval()

Figure 13-13 used the eval() function to get a pointer to a div using the div's name. JavaScript's div associative arrays provide an alternative to using eval(). For example, instead of writing

```
the_div_name = "document.all.divOne.style";
the_div = eval(the_div_name);
```

as in lines ❹ and ❺, I could have written the following:

```
the_div = document.all["divOne"].style;
```

The previous line assigns the_div to point to the div named divOne in the all array. In Netscape, the line looks like this:

```
the_div = document.layers["divOne"];
```

This line looks up the div named divOne in JavaScript's layers array. The eval() or div arrays are equivalent methods, both often used.

Hierarchical Menus

I'll close this chapter by showing you how to build a basic hierarchical menu with DHTML. Not too many sites use hierarchical menus because the code is difficult to write. This section will give you the basic idea behind how they work, but if you really want to put hierarchical menus on your site, I suggest visiting http://www.webreference.com/dhtml/hiermenus/—a huge, multipart tutorial on hierarchical menus.

The hierarchical menu in Figure 13-15 has three links: Dogs, Cats, and Birds. Mousing over Dogs causes a submenu to pop up with the name of several dogs. Clicking on one of those links sends the browser to a Web page about that kind of dog.

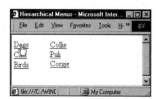

Figure 13-15: A hierarchical menu

Figure 13-16 shows the code that drives this hierarchical menu. I've already covered everything you must know to understand this code, so take a look and see if you can figure out how it works before reading my explanation.

```
<html><head><title>Hierarchical Menus</title>
<script language = "JavaScript">
<!--
❶ var div_array = new Array("divOne", "divTwo", "divThree");
   function changeDiv(the_div, the_change)
   {
❷    if (document.all)
       {
           div_string = "window.document.all." + the_div + ".style";
       } else if (document.layers) {
           div_string = "window.document." + the_number;
       } else {
           alert("sorry, this only works in 4.0 browsers");
           return;
       }
❸    the_div = eval(div_string);
❹    the_div.visibility = the_change;
   }
   function closeAll()
   {
❺    for (var loop=0; loop < div_array.length; loop++)
       {
❻        changeDiv(div_array[loop], "hidden");
       }
   }
   // -->
   </script>
   </head>
   <body>
❼ <div id="top_border" style="position:absolute; top:0; left:5;">
   <a href="#" onMouseOver="closeAll();"><img src="long_spacer.gif"border=0></a>
   </div>
❽ <div id="top1" style="position:absolute; top:20; left:5;z-index:1">
   <a href="#"
       onMouseOver="closeAll(); changeDiv('divOne','visible');">Dogs</a>
   </div>
   <div id="top2" style="position:absolute; top:40; left:5;z-index:1">
   <a href="#"
   onMouseOver="closeAll(); changeDiv('divTwo','visible');">Cats</a>
   </div>
   <div id="top3" style="position:absolute; top:60; left:5;z-index:1">
   <a href="#"
```

Figure 13-16: A basic hierarchical menu

```
            onMouseOver="closeAll(); changeDiv('divThree','visible');">Birds</a>
        </div>
        <div id="bottomBorder" style="position:absolute; top:80; left:5;">
        <a href="#" onMouseOver="closeAll();"><img src="long_spacer.gif"border=0></a>
        </div>
        <div id="rightBorder" style="position:absolute; top:5; left:150;">
        <a href="#" onMouseOver="closeAll();"><img src="tall_spacer.gif"border=0></a>
        </div>
  ❾    <div id="divOne" style="position:absolute; top:20; left:80; visibility:hidden">
        <a href="#">Collie</a><br>
        <a href="#">Puli</a><br>
        <a href="#">Corgie</a><br>
        </div>
        <div id="divTwo" style="position:absolute; top:40; left:80; visibility:hidden">
        <a href="#">Siamese</a><br>
        <a href="#">Manx</a><br>
        <a href="#">Calico</a><br>
        </div>
        <div id="divThree" style="position:absolute; top:60; left:80; visibility:hidden">
        <a href="#">Parakeet</a><br>
        <a href="#">Finch</a><br>
        <a href="#">Canary</a><br>
        </div>
        </body>
        </html>
```

Figure 13-16 (continued): A basic hierarchical menu

Line-by-Line Analysis of Figure 13-16

A hierarchical menu has a div for each menu option. The nine divs in Figure 13-16 include one div for each top-level menu element (❽), one for each sub-menu (❾), one for the top border of the menu (❼), one for the bottom border, and one for the right border. Each time a visitor mouses over one of the main menu options, only the submenu matching the link most recently moused over is shown. If the visitor mouses over Cats, making the list of cats visible, and then mouses over Dogs, the closeAll() function hides the cats submenu and changeDiv() displays the dogs submenu. Mousing over the top, bottom, or right border closes all the submenus.

The closeAll() Function

The closeAll() function loops through the array of divs defined at ❶. Each time through the loop at ❺, closeAll() calls the changeDiv() function to hide one of the divs.

The changeDiv() Function

The changeDiv() function takes two parameters: the name of a div to change, and whether to make the div hidden or visible. The if-then-else statement starting at ❷ does the now-familiar task of figuring out how to refer to the div we want to change. ❸ then uses eval() to turn the string created in the if-then-else statement into a pointer to the appropriate div. ❹ changes the visibility of the div to visible or hidden, depending on the second parameter of changeDiv().

The Borders

Notice that the menu's top border is a long invisible GIF (❼). The code in ❼ dictates that mousing over this invisible GIF hides all submenus. Together with the blank GIFs on the bottom and right of the menus, these GIFs make sure the submenu vanishes if the visitor's mouse leaves the menu area completely.

Figure 13-16 offers a basic example of how you might implement a hierarchical menu. To see how Microsoft wrote its hierarchical menus, visit http://www.microsoft.com/library/toolbar/toolbar.js. If your browser asks you to save or run the file, choose to save it, then open the file with a word processing program. The file is about 670 lines long, and packed with JavaScript magic.

Summary

DHTML is the topic of several excellent books—what we've discussed here should just whet your appetite. But you have learned a few DHTML basics, including these:

- How to use divs to create blocks of HTML.

- How to add styles to divs.

- How to make divs, along with the HTML they contain, visible or invisible.

- How to move divs.

- How to animate divs with timed loops.

- How to use the eval() function to force JavaScript to interpret a string.

- How to create a basic hierarchical menu.

If you got all that, you shouldn't have any problem with the assignment.

Assignment

Create a DHTML screen saver like the one shown in Figure 13-17. The smiley face in the figure continually bounces around the screen. When it hits one of the walls, it bounces off at a random angle. To make the smiley face move diagonally, change its top and left positions in a timing loop. To get it to bounce off a wall, make it change directions when it hits one side of the screen. Remember, to make the smiley move right, you would add to its left property, and to make it move left, you would subtract from its left property.

Figure 13-17: A screen saver created with JavaScript

14

HOW TO FIX BROKEN CODE

Now that you know how JavaScript works, it's time to practice, practice, practice. But as you've probably realized, when you write JavaScript, you spend about half your time *debugging*— finding and fixing mistakes you've made. When you write a program that works the first time you try it, break out the champagne—it's a rare occasion.

Because you'll spend so much time fixing mistakes (according to numerous studies, the average programmer spends 50 percent of his or her programming time figuring out what's wrong with the code), one of the best skills you can learn is how to debug your scripts. This chapter covers a few debugging tips and safe coding practices that will make this process easier.

Debugging Techniques

The more you program JavaScript, the more you'll understand the sometimes opaque error messages JavaScript gives you—and the fewer errors you'll introduce in your code. Programming is definitely a skill that improves dramatically over time, and learning how to debug efficiently is one of the biggest components of that process. This section covers some common debugging tips and techniques to decrease the number of bugs in your scripts and help you figure out why your program isn't doing what you want, including:

- How to use and interpret your browser's JavaScript bug detector.

- How to print out variables in various ways.

- How to watch for common mistakes.

- What to think about before you start coding.

Your Browser's Built-in Bug Detector

If you've been trying the examples and doing the assignments as we've gone along, you've no doubt encountered your browser's bug detector. When you've made a coding mistake, running your code in the browser often results in a window that describes the error. Some browsers, such as MSIE 5.0 and up, warn you by putting an error icon at the bottom left corner of the window. Clicking on the error icon opens a window that describes the error. Other browsers, like Netscape 4.0, may not show errors at all but instead have a console that displays errors. To see the console, type `javascript:` in the location box of your browser.

Sometimes you may find the JavaScript error messages helpful, other times they may seem confusing. All you can do is read the message to see if you understand it. If not, try some of the following debugging techniques.

Printing Variables

Much of the debugging process involves discovering where the bug is in the first place. Unfortunately, finding the little pests isn't always easy. The most tried-and-true debugging method is to use alerts or similar statements to print out what's going on in your script.

Figure 14-1 lists two functions. In one, if you enter random names in the prompt boxes, you'll see the greeting ahoy palloi. If you enter Dave in the first prompt box and Thau in the second one, you're supposed to get the message howdy partner. However, running the functions won't work because one of them contains an error.

Running theGreeting() doesn't result in any JavaScript syntax errors, but the function works incorrectly. If you enter Dave in the first prompt box and Thau in the second one, you get the ahoy palloi message rather than howdy partner. In this simple example, you may discover the error easily just by looking at the JavaScript. However, as your scripts get more complicated, you'll find it harder to locate errors by eyeballing your code.

```
function getName()
{
    var first_name = prompt("what's your first name?","");
    var last_name = prompt("what's your last name?","");
    var the_name = first_name + " " + last_name;
}


function theGreeting()
{
    var the_name = getName();
    if (the_name == "Dave Thau")
    {
        alert("howdy partner!");
    } else {
        alert("ahoy palloi!");
    }
}
```

Figure 14-1: Find the error

If JavaScript doesn't catch your error and you can't figure it out by looking at the script, try printing out the variables. The easiest way to do this is to use an alert() to print out a variable, as in Figure 14-2:

```
function getName()
{
    var first_name = prompt("what's your first name?","");
    var last_name = prompt("what's your last name?","");
    var the_name = first_name + " " + last_name;
❶  alert("in getName, the_name is: " + the_name);
}
function theGreeting()
{
    var the_name = getName();
❷  alert("after getName, the_name = " + the_name);
    if (the_name == "Dave Thau")
    {
        alert("howdy partner!");
    } else {
        alert("ahoy palloi!");
    }
}
```

Figure 14-2: Using alert() to print out variables

After you enter the names dave and thau at the prompts in getName(), the alert at ❶ says "in getName, the_name is: dave thau." That looks fine, so you can be pretty sure nothing's wrong up to the point of ❶. However, the alert at ❷ says "after getName, the_name = undefined." That means the script has a problem somewhere between ❶ and ❷—the_name is correct just before get-Name() exits, but it's wrong after theGreeting(). Because getName() gets the right answer but theGreeting() fails to receive that answer from getName(), the problem probably lies in the way the script passes the answer from getName() to theGreeting().

Sure enough, that's the problem. The getName() function figures out the name but never returns it. We need to put return the_name at the end of the function.

Debugging Beyond Alerts

Putting alert boxes in your code is a good debugging tool, but it's also annoying to have to press the OK button every other line. One solution is to write your debugging messages to another window or text area inside a form.

Another trick that can make your debugging experience more pleasant involves using a variable to set different levels of debugging, such as none, brief, and extreme. The brief level prints a few debug messages along the way, extreme prints a ton of debugging messages, and the none option doesn't print any messages. Figure 14-3 lists some code that uses a variable to determine what kind of debugging you want to do.

Figure 14-3 uses a function called doError() to handle its debugging. For example, ❷ passes a debugging message to doError(); the doError() function then decides what to do with this message based on how ❶ sets the debug variable. If it sets debug to brief, ❸ puts the debugging message in an alert box. Using alerts is handy when you want to check variables in just a few places and you don't mind pressing OK in each alert box. However, if you want to look at a lot of debugging messages simultaneously, it's more helpful to set the debug variable to extreme (❹). Finally, when you're ready to show your code to the world, just set debug to none to prevent the debugging messages from appearing at all.

Setting a debug variable like the one in Figure 14-3 saves you the hassle of having to find and remove multiple debugging statements. Depending on how you set debug, you can even use document.write() to show or hide the textarea you're using to display the debug message. That way, you can show the textarea while debugging the script, then hide it when you're ready to let visitors see your JavaScript.

```
❶ var debug = "none";
   function getName()
   {
       var first_name = prompt("what's your first name?","");
       var last_name = prompt("what's your last name?","");
       var the_name = first_name + " " + last_name;

❷     doError("in getName, the_name is: " + the_name);
   }
   function theGreeting()
   {
       var the_name = getName();
       doError("after getName, the_name = " + the_name);
       if (the_name == "Dave Thau")
       {
           alert("hello partner!");
       } else {
           alert("ahoy palloi!");
       }
   }
   function doError(the_message)
   {
❸     if (debug == "brief")
       {
           alert(the_message);
❹     } else if (debug == "extreme") {
           window.document.the_form.the_text.value += the_message + "\n";
       }
   }
```

Figure 14-3: Using a debug variable

Common Programming Mistakes

Most people, especially when they start out with scripting, make simple syntactic mistakes. It takes a long time to stop forgetting to close quotes, curly braces, and parentheses, but luckily modern browsers have JavaScript bug detectors that detect such errors for you. This section covers a few common mistakes many browsers won't catch.

Incorrect Variable or Function Names

The JavaScript bug detector often misses incorrect capitalization and pluralization of variable and function names, a common and annoying error. You'll greatly reduce the occurrence of such mistakes if you stick to one convention for naming variables and functions. For instance, I name my variables in all lowercase and with underscores replacing spaces (my_variable, the_date, an_example_variable), and I use in-caps notation for functions (addThreeNumbers(), writeError(), and so on. See the section on naming functions in Chapter 6 for more information). I avoid pluralizing anything because it's easy to forget which variables you've made plural.

Accidentally Using Reserved Words

You can't use words reserved for JavaScript as variables. For example, you can't name a variable if because JavaScript uses if. Though it's not likely you'd name a variable if, you might want to use a variable called, for example, document. Unfortunately, document is a JavaScript object, so using it as a variable would wreak all kinds of havoc.

Even more unfortunately, different browsers reserve different words, so there's no complete list of words to eschew. The safest course of action is to avoid words used in JavaScript and in HTML. If you're having problems with a variable and you can't figure out what's wrong, you may be running into such a problem—try renaming the variable.

Use Two Equal Signs in Logical Tests

Some browsers catch the equal-sign error, some don't. This very common mistake is extremely difficult to detect if the browser doesn't find it for you. Here's an example:

```
var the_name = prompt("what's your name?", "");
if (the_name = "thau")
{
    alert("hello thau!");
} else {
    alert("hello stranger.");
}
```

This code shows you the hello thau! alert box regardless of what you type in the prompt because only one equal sign appears in the if-then statement. The equal sign sets the_name equal to thau. This extremely insidious bug will drive you batty. For your own sanity's sake, concentrate on not making mistakes like this. Your psychiatrist will thank you.

Accidentally Quoting Variables or Forgetting to Quote Strings

This one gets me time and time again. The only way JavaScript knows the difference between a variable and a string is that strings have quotes around them and variables don't. Here's an obvious error:

```
var the_name = 'Ishmael';
alert("the_name is very happy");
```

The above code yields an alert box that says the_name is very happy even though the_name is a variable. Once JavaScript sees quotes around something, it simply treats it like a string. Putting the_name in quotes stops JavaScript from looking up the_name in its memory.

Here's a less obvious variation of this bug, which we saw in Chapter 9 (page 191):

```
function wakeMeIn3()
{
    var the_message = "Wake up!  Hey!  Hey!  WAKE UP!!!!";
    setTimeout("alert(the_message);", 3000);
}
```

The problem here is that you're telling JavaScript to execute alert(the_message) in three seconds—but three seconds from now the_message won't exist because you've exited the wakeMeIn3() function (the function itself defines the_message variable). Here's the solution to this problem:

```
function wakeMeIn3()
{
    var the_message = "Wake up!";
    setTimeout("alert('" + the_message + "');", 3000);
}
```

When you pull the_message out of the quotes, the setTimeout() schedules the command alert("Wake up!");, which is the result you want.

Fixing Bugs

Once you've found where your bugs are, you need to fix them—and you have multiple options for this, both good and bad. This section covers a few things you should do when getting rid of bugs.

Copy Your Program First

Some bugs are really hard to get rid of. In fact, sometimes in the process of eradicating a little bug that's driving you nuts, you end up destroying your entire program. This happens a lot, so saving your program before you start to debug is the best way to ensure that a bug doesn't get the best of you.

Fix One Bug at a Time

If you have multiple bugs, fix one and test your fix before moving to the next bug. Fixing a lot of bugs at once increases the risk of adding even more bugs.

Beware of Voodoo Coding

Sometimes you know a bug exists, but you don't really know why. Let's say you have a variable called index and for some reason index is always 1 less than you think it should be. At this point you can do two things. You can sit there for a while and figure out *why* index is 1 less than it should be, or you can just shrug, add 1 to index before using it, and move on. The latter method is called voodoo programming. When you start thinking "What the hell? Why is index 2 instead of 3 here? Well . . . I'll just add 1 for now and fix it later," you're engaging in voodoo programming.

Voodoo programming may work in the short term, but eventually it will doom you. It's like sweeping dust under a rug. The problem resurfaces— either you get yet another weird error you can't figure out, or the next poor soul cursed to look at your code will find it extremely hard to understand.

Don't practice voodoo coding.

Look for Similar Bugs

In some ways, the ability to cut and paste code is the worst thing that ever happened to programmers. Often you'll write some JavaScript in one function, then cut and paste it into another function. If the first function had a problem, you have now created problems in *two* functions. I'm not saying you shouldn't cut and paste code—but keep in mind that bugs have a way of multiplying, so if you find one bug, look for similar bugs elsewhere in your code. One bug that typically crops up several times in every JavaScript is misspelled variable names. If you misspell the_name as teh_name in one place, chances are you've done it someplace else too.

If All Else Fails

You're sitting there staring at a bug and you just can't figure out what's going on or how to fix it. Or maybe you can't even find the bug in the first place. The best thing to do is walk away from your computer. Go read a book and take a stroll around the corner. Get a tasty beverage. Do something— anything—but don't think about the program or the problem. This technique is called *incubation* and it works amazingly well. After you've had a little break and relaxed a bit, try finding the bug again. Often you'll approach the problem in a new, more fruitful way. Incubation works because it breaks you out of a dysfunctional mindset.

If It Still Doesn't Work . . .

Ask for help. Sometimes you get stuck in your own contorted thought patterns, and you need someone who hasn't thought about the problem to find the hole in your logic. In structured coding environments, programmers periodically review each other's code. Code review not only helps iron out bugs, but also results in better code. Don't be afraid to show other people your JavaScripts. You'll become a better JavaScripter.

Good Coding Practices

The key to good programming is to write programs for people, not for computers. If you keep in mind that someone else will probably be reading your JavaScript, you'll write much clearer code. The clearer it is, the less likely you are to encounter mistakes. Clever coding is cute, but the clever coder gets the bug.

It is also helpful to write comments *before* you start writing any code. Doing this ensures you've thought about the problem instead of just diving in. Once you've written the comments, you can write the code under them. Here's an example of writing a function this way.

Step 1: Write the Comments

```
//function beKind()
//  beKind asks for a user's name, chooses a random
//  affirmation, and returns an alert box with the name and the
//  kind words.
function beKind()
{
    //  first construct a list of affirmations
    //

    //  next get the user's name
    //

    //  then choose a random affirmation
    //

    //  finally return the personalized kindness
    //
}
```

Step 2: Fill In the Code

```
//function beKind()
//  beKind asks for a user's name, chooses a random
//  affirmation, and returns an alert box with the name and the
//  affirmation.
function beKind()
{
    //  first construct a list of affirmations
    //
    var the_affirmation_list = new Array();
    the_affirmation_list [0] = "you are a great coder!";
    the_affirmation_list [1] = "your JavaScript is powerful!";
    the_affirmation_list [2] = "you finished the whole JavaScript book!";

    //  next get the user's name
    //
    var the_name = prompt("what's your name?", "");

    //  then choose a random affirmation
    //
    var the_number =  Math.floor(Math.random() * 5);
    var the_affirmation = the_affirmation_list[the_number];

    //  finally return the personalized kindness
    //
    alert("Congratulations " + the_name + " " + the_affirmation);
}
```

Commenting not only forces you to think before you code, it also makes the task of coding seem a lot easier. Instead of facing one huge task, you've already broken it down into easily coded sections.

Summary

Now that you've mastered the basics of JavaScript, it's time to start writing some complicated scripts of your own. This chapter should help you figure out the problems that inevitably arise when writing even simple scripts. The key point is to *think* before you code. Having a clear idea of how your script will work before you write it will cut down tremendously on your rewriting and bug fixing.

Now Go Forth and Code

Congratulations! You now know everything you need to start a career as an official JavaScripter. All that remains is lots and lots of practice. View source on every page that catches your fancy, and keep looking at the free JavaScript directories listed in Chapter 1.

If you've made it this far, you've learned a lot of JavaScript, but this book hasn't by any means covered every detail of this huge subject—so leaf through Appendix B to get a feel for the other JavaScript functions and objects at your disposal. If you're going to do a lot of JavaScripting, get a good JavaScript reference book, like David Flanigan's *JavaScript: The Definitive Guide* (O'Reilly & Associates). But most important, experiment freely and push the boundaries of what you've learned here. Now go forth and code!

BEYOND THE BROWSER: PLUG-INS, ACTIVEX, MAKING MUSIC, AND JAVA

Although Web browsers are great programs, they can't do everything. Luckily, Netscape and Microsoft have written their browsers so other programs can run inside Web pages. For example, most browsers can run QuickTime movies, even though they don't have Apple's QuickTime video player built in. Netscape and MSIE can also handle Macromedia's Flash, which runs animations; ActiveX, which runs programs specific to Microsoft Windows; and Java, a programming language from Sun.

Plug-ins and ActiveX

Netscape and Microsoft Internet Explorer interact with external programs using *plug-ins*—pieces of software other companies have built to allow their programs to exchange information with browsers. Web pages generally invoke plug-ins using the <embed> tag. For example, to put a QuickTime movie called "my_vacation.mov" on your Web page, you would insert the following HTML:

```
<embed src="my_vacation.mov"> </embed>
```

Unfortunately, not everyone has the QuickTime plug-in installed. Those who don't have it on their machines will get a broken-link icon instead of your movie. You can use JavaScript to avoid the broken-link icon, but it's not at all straightforward because Netscape and Microsoft Internet Explorer deal with plug-ins in vastly different ways.

How Netscape Deals with Plug-ins

Netscape keeps track of plug-ins using arrays called `navigator.plugins` and `navigator.mimeTypes`. However, not all plug-ins do a good job of letting Netscape know what they are, and different versions of Netscape handle the feature a bit differently, so using these arrays can be difficult.

How MSIE Deals with Plug-ins

Microsoft Internet Explorer also has these arrays, but they're always empty. To check which plug-ins or ActiveX components someone has, you must use Visual Basic, a Microsoft-proprietary language similar to JavaScript that works only in Microsoft Internet Explorer for PCs. If you're using Microsoft Internet Explorer on a Macintosh, there's no way to check for plug-ins.

Use a Plug-in Detection Library

Writing a cross-browser plug-in detector is not an easy task. Luckily, several free plug-in detection libraries can do the work for you. I recommend Webmonkey's at http://hotwired.lycos.com/webmonkey/reference/javascript_code_library/wm_pluginbot/ (it's also on the included CD-ROM under libraries/plugins/). Take a look to see the coding fun you're missing by not writing the plug-in detector yourself.

Making Music with Plug-ins

Some of the very first plug-ins designed for browsers played music. Netscape uses a plug-in called LiveAudio to manipulate sounds, and Microsoft Internet Explorer uses the ActiveMovie Control.

Netscape's LiveAudio

LiveAudio comes packaged with Netscape 3 and up, so you probably have it if you're using a Netscape browser. To use LiveAudio to manipulate a sound, first include the sound in a Web page using the embed tag:

```
<embed name="beep" src="beep.aiff" hidden = "true" autostart = "false" mastersound> </embed>
```

The `mastersound` feature lets JavaScript affect the sound and setting the `autostart` feature to `true` plays the sound when the page first loads. If you have a plug-in such as QuickTime or Shockwave that actually shows something on the page, set the `hidden` feature to `false`. Because the above line is dealing with sounds, there's no reason to show the plug-in in the window.

LiveAudio provides several JavaScript methods for controlling sounds. Table A-1 lists some common ones.

Table A-1: Common LiveAudio methods

Name	Description
play()	Plays the loaded sound—this option can be true, false, or the number of times to loop.
stop()	Stops the sound.
setVol()	Sets the volume percentage (0 to 100), as in setVol(45).
fade_from_to()	Gradually changes from one volume to another (0 to 100), as in fade_from_to(25, 76).

Figure A-1 shows you the JavaScript that sets a sound's volume and controls the sound from a form.

```
<html><head><title>LiveAudio</title>
<script language = "JavaScript">
<!-- hide me
function setAndPlay(the_volume)
{
❶    var the_sound = window.document.beep;
❷    the_sound.setvol(the_volume);
❸    the_sound.play();
}

function fadeAndPlay(start_vol, stop_vol)
{
     var the_sound = window.document.beep;
❹    the_sound.fade_from_to(start_vol, stop_vol);
     the_sound.play();
}

// hide me -->
</script>
</head>
<body>
<p>
❺ <EMBED name="beep" src="dooropen.aiff" hidden = "true" AUTOSTART = TRUE MASTERSOUND></EMBED>
<form name="the_form">
Set Volume (0-100): <input type = "text" name="vol">
❻ <input type="button" value="play"
onClick="setAndPlay(document.the_form.vol.value); return false;"><br>
Play with Fader:
```

Figure A-1: Playing Sounds with Netscape's LiveAudio

```
    From (0-100): <input type="text" name="start_vol"><br>
    To (0-100): <input type ="text" name="stop_vol"><br>
❼  <input type="button" value="play" onClick="fadeAndPlay(document.the_form.start_vol.value,
    document.the_form.stop_vol.value); return false;"><br>
    </form>
    </body>
    </html>
```

Figure A-1 (continued): Playing Sounds with Netscape's LiveAudio

❺ loads the beep sound, and the form's contents manipulate the sound when the visitor uses the buttons at ❻ or ❼. The button at ❻ sends the volume to the function setAndPlay(). ❶ finds the sound called beep in the window's document and sets the variable the_sound to point to it. ❷ sets the volume of the sound to the value ❻ passes to the function, and ❸ actually plays the sound.

The second button in the form works similarly. Clicking on the button at ❼ calls the fadeAndPlay() function, which finds the sound, uses the fade_from_to() method to set the starting and ending volume, and plays the sound with the play() method.

NOTE *This example may not work in all versions of Netscape. For more on LiveAudio, you can check Netscape's documentation at http://developer.netscape.com/docs/manuals/js/ client/jsguide/liveaud.htm.*

Microsoft's ActiveMovie Control

Microsoft's alternative to LiveAudio is the ActiveMovie Control (AMC) ActiveX component, which comes with MSIE 4.0 and up. To play a sound in AMC, use this HTML:

```
<object id="mySound" width=0 height=0 classid="CLSID:05589FA1-C356-11CE-BF01-00AA0055595A">
<param name="FileName" value="dooropen.wav">
<param name="AutoStart" value="-1">
</object>
```

You add ActiveX components to your page with the <object> tag. Every ActiveX component has a classid you must get from the component manufacturer. The classid for AMC is the monstrous thing you see in the <object> tag above. Giving the <object> tag an ID allows us to refer to it later with JavaScript.

Between the `<object>` tags, you can list parameters that affect the tag with the `<param>` tag. In the example above, I've set the FileName parameter to the name of the music file to play, and the AutoStart parameter to -1, which means I want the sound to play when the page loads. If I didn't want the sound to start right away, I'd have set AutoStart to 0. Although I didn't use it above, the PlayCount parameter comes in quite handy: Setting it to 0 makes the sound loop play forever, and setting it to another number makes it play that many times.

AMC lets you manipulate its objects using JavaScript. The code in Figure A-2, for example, shows how to use JavaScript to lower sound volume:

```
    <html><head><title>Thau Sound</title>
    </head>
    <body>
❶  <object id="the_sound" width=0 height=0 classid="CLSID:05589FA1-C356-11CE-BF01-00AA0055595A">
    <param name ="FileName" value="dooropen.wav">
❷  <param name ="AutoStart" value ="-1">
❸  <param name="PlayCount" value ="0">
❹  </object>
    <form>
    <input type="button" value="turn down the volume!"
❺   onClick="the_sound.Volume = the_sound.Volume - 200;">
    </form>
    </body>
    </html>
```

Figure A-2: Lowering sound volume with AMC

In this straightforward example, the `<object>` tag in ❶ sets the component's id to my_sound and lets the browser know it's an AMC. The FileName parameter in ❷ sets the name of the sound file; the AutoStart parameter in ❸ tells the browser to start the sound when the page loads; and the PlayCount parameter in ❹ tells the browser to loop the sound continuously.

The JavaScript kicks in at ❺: Every time a user clicks the button there, JavaScript lowers the volume, stored in the_sound.Volume. ❺ lowers the volume by subtracting 200 from it. In AMC, 0 is the loudest you can get, and −10,000 is the quietest level.

The AMC component has dozens of other properties. To learn more about it, visit Microsoft's http://www.microsoft.com/Train_Cert/ffie3/author/actvmult.htm or check out Webmonkey's tutorial on AMC at http://hotwired.lycos.com/webmonkey/97/45/index2a.html.

JavaScript and Java

As mentioned in Chapter 1, you can embed Java applets in Web pages and use JavaScript to control them. I won't cover Java at all—it's a complicated language in its own right—but you should know how JavaScript can control Java applets. If you'd like to learn more about Java, I suggest you pick up *Just Java 2* by Peter van der Linden (Prentice Hall, 1998).

Figure A-3 is a screen shot taken from the Java Boutique's site, http://javaboutique.internet.com/Flame/. This page contains a free Java applet that sets a string of text on fire. Once the text burns up, it reappears and gets burned again.

Once you've downloaded the applet, you can call it with this HTML:

❶ `<applet code="flame.class" name="flame">`
❷ `<param name="text" value="JavaScript Is Great!">`
`<param name="link" value="http://book_of_javascript.tripod.com/">`
`</applet>`

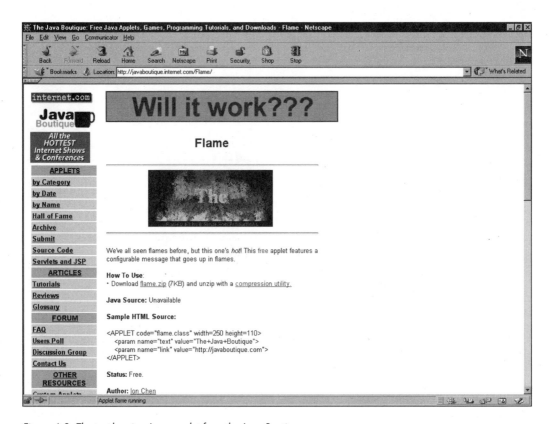

Figure A-3: The text-burning Java applet from the Java Boutique

As explained on the Java Boutique site, this applet takes two parameters: the text to display and the page to link if a visitor clicks on it. To change the text, just change the value of the parameter named text in ❷.

You can always use JavaScript to start or stop a Java applet. We can stop the words from burning up using this line:

```
<a href="#" onClick="window.document.flame.stop(); return false;">put out the fire!</a>
```

This script refers to this applet as `window.document.flame` because the applet above was named flame in ❶. To stop the applet, use the `stop()` method as shown above. To restart the applet, use the `start()` method:

```
<a href="#" onClick="window.document.flame.start(); return false;">start the fire!</a>
```

Some applets are written so JavaScript can change how they work. If someone had written the flame applet above so you could use JavaScript to change the words that appeared, you would write this to do so:

```
<a href="#" onClick="window.document.flame.text='something new';  return false;">change the text to something new!</a>
```

NOTE *The javaboutique flame applet does not let you change its text with JavaScript. The above is only a hypothetical example.*

The directions that come with a Java applet let you know whether you can change its workings via JavaScript. There are plenty of free applets available on the Web. Some good resources are:

http://www.jars.com

http://www.gamelan.com

http://javaboutique.internet.com

Summary

This appendix has touched on a few extensions to JavaScript: plug-ins, ActiveX, and Java. Very few sites use JavaScript to manipulate these extensions, but this technique can be very impressive when done well. For a list of more plug-ins, check out BrowserWatch's Plug-In Plaza at http://browserwatch.internet.com/plug-in.html, or take a look at http://www.plugins.com.

REFERENCE TO JAVASCRIPT
OBJECTS AND FUNCTIONS

This reference covers all objects and functions currently part of JavaScript in the various versions of Netscape and Microsoft Internet Explorer. Each entry appears with the earliest version of Netscape (NS) and Microsoft Internet Explorer (IE) that supports it. For example, an entry listed with NS 3, IE 3 will work in Netscape 3, Internet Explorer 3, and newer versions of those browsers. If I used an entry in this book or consider it an important function, I define and illustrate it with an example. For the less common JavaScript functions and objects, I provide brief descriptions and list the browsers that support them.

The reference capitalizes object entries and lists them with their methods, properties, and handlers (properties come first, in alphabetical order, followed by methods and then handlers). Because certain browsers support some but not all of an object's properties, methods, and handlers, I list each item with the earliest browser versions that support it.

Object properties can be read-only or read-write. If a property is read-write, JavaScript can look up and change its value. However, JavaScript *can't* change a read-only property—JavaScript can only look up the value of that property. For example, JavaScript changes (writes to) the src property of an image in an image swap:

```
window.document.my_image.src = "happy.gif";
```

JavaScript can also look it up (read it):

```
var the_gif_showing = window.document.my_image.src;
```

JavaScript can *only* look up the height property of the image, though:

```
var the_image_height = window.document.my_image.height;
```

Unless stated otherwise, the properties in this glossary are read-write.

Netscape 4.0 introduced a security feature called *signed scripts*. These can perform special tasks other scripts can't do—such as set a Web page permanently as the topmost window on your screen. I will point out the methods and properties that only work in Netscape with a signed script. For more information on how to sign your scripts, see http://developer. netscape.com/library/documentation/signedobj/signtool/.

Although this reference tries to be as complete as possible, the newer browsers have literally hundreds of browser-specific methods and properties, and new ones are added with each new browser version. The most complete references may be gotten straight from the horses' mouths:

Microsoft Internet Explorer   http://msdn.microsoft.com/workshop/ c-frame.htm?/workshop/author/default.asp

Netscape   http://developer.netscape.com/tech/javascript/ index.html

alert()   [NS 2, IE 3]

Displays a dialog box with one button labeled OK and a message specified by the function's parameter.

Example:

```
alert("hello world");
```

Creates a dialog box with the words hello world and an OK button. The browser window is frozen until the user clicks the OK button.

Anchor

All anchors on a page are stored in the document's anchor array: window.document.anchors[].

Example:

```
<a name="some_name"></a>
```

PROPERTIES

name	NS 4, IE 4	The anchor tag's name.
text	NS 4	The anchor's text.
x	NS 4	The anchor tag's horizontal position in pixels.
y	NS 4	The anchor tag's vertical position in pixels.

Applet

Refers to a Java applet. All applets on a page are stored in the JavaScript array `window.document.applets[]`.

METHODS

start()   NS 2, IE 3   Starts a Java applet.

Example:

```
window.document.applets[0].start();
```

Tells the first Java applet on a Web page to start.

stop()   NS 2, IE 3   Stops a Java applet.

Example:

```
window.document.applets[0].stop();
```

Tells the first Java applet on a Web page to stop.

Area

An HTML tag that describes a clickable region inside a client-side image map. Area tags are stored in the JavaScript array `window.document.links[]`; an area is treated just like a link object (see Link).

Array

A list of information. There are two ways to create an array:

```
var the_array = new Array();
var the_array = new Array(element_one, element_two, element_three...);
```

You can look up or change elements in an array using their position number (numbering starts with 0):

```
the_array[0] = "thau!";
window.document.writeln(the_array[0] + " wrote this book.");
```

PROPERTIES

length   NS 3, IE 3   The number of elements in an array.

Example:

```
var my_array = new Array("eenie", "meenie", "miney", "moe");
var number_of_things = my_array.length;
```

The variable number_of_things holds the value 4 because there are four elements in the array.

METHODS

join()   NS 3, IE 3   Creates a string from an array. Each element in the array will be listed in the string and separated by a space, unless some other element is listed as a parameter to join.

Example:

```
var my_array = new Array("eenie", "meenie", "miney", "moe");
var my_string = my_array.join(":");
```

The variable my_string contains eenie:meenie:miney:moe.

reverse()   NS 3, IE 3   Returns a copy of an array with the elements reversed.

Example:

```
var my_array = new Array("eenie", "meenie", "miney", "moe");
var new_array = my_array.reverse();
```

The variable new_array contains an array with the elements moe, miney, meenie, and eenie, in that order.

sort()   NS 3, IE 4   Returns an array with the elements of another array sorted in alphabetical order. If the name of a function is listed as a parameter to sort, that function will sort the elements as follows:

- If the function returns a value less than 0, the first element is smaller than the second.
- If the function returns a value greater than 0, the second element is smaller than the first.
- If the function returns 0, do not change the order of the elements.

Examples:

```
var my_array = new Array("eenie", "moe", "miney", "meenie");
var sorted_array = my_array.sort();
```

The variable sorted_array contains the elements eenie, meenie, miney, moe in that order.

```
var my_array = new Array(1, 12, 2);
var sorted_array = my_array.sort(numericalSorter);
function numericalSorter(element_one, element_two)
{
    return element_one - element_two;
}
```

The variable sorted_array contains the elements 1, 2, 12, in that order.

LESS COMMON METHODS

concat()	NS 4, IE 4	Concatenates many elements into one array.
pop()	NS 4	Returns the last element of an array and deletes that element from the array.
push()	NS 4	Appends a value to the end of an array.
shift()	NS 4	Returns the first element of an array and shifts the other elements to replace it.
slice()	NS 4, IE 4	Creates a new array by taking a piece out of this array.
splice()	NS 4	Replaces or deletes parts of an array or puts something in the middle.
toString()	NS 2, IE 3	Converts an array into a comma-separated string.
unShift()	NS 4	Appends a value to the start of an array.

Button

The button form element.

PROPERTIES

name	NS 2, IE 3	The name of a button. Note that name is *not* the text that shows up in the button on the Web page (see the value property).

Example:

```
<input type="button" name="happy" onClick="alert(this.name);">
```

Creates a button that, when clicked, calls an alert with the word happy in it.

value	NS 2, IE 3	The text that appears in a button when it shows up on a Web page.

Example:

```
<input type="button" value="click me" onClick="this.value='stop clicking me!';">
```

When the user clicks this button, the words on the button change from click me to stop clicking me!

HANDLERS

onClick   NS 2, IE 3   Gets triggered when a visitor clicks on the button.

Checkbox

The checkbox form element.

PROPERTIES

checked   NS 2, IE 3   A checkbox's checked property is true if a visitor has selected the checkbox and false otherwise. Setting the property to true will cause the checkbox to act as if a visitor had selected the box.

Example:

```
if (window.document.my_form.the_checkbox.checked == true)
{
    alert("thanks for clicking on the checkbox!");
}
```

This if-then statement calls an alert box if a visitor has checked the checkbox named the_checkbox in the form named my_form.

name   NS 2, IE 3   The name of a checkbox.

Example:

```
<input type="checkbox" name="happy" onClick="alert(this.name);">
```

Calls an alert with the word happy in it.

value   NS 2, IE 3   The value of a checkbox.

Example:

```
<input type="checkbox" value="priceless" onClick="alert(this.value);">
```

Calls an alert with the word priceless in it.

HANDLERS

onClick   NS 2, IE 3   Gets triggered when a visitor clicks on the checkbox.

clearInterval() (NS 4, IE 4)

Cancels an interval set by setInterval(). JavaScript commands may execute repeatedly every n milliseconds. See setInterval() for more information.

clearTimeout() (NS 2, IE 3)

Cancels a timeout set by setTimeout(). See setTimeout() and Chapter 9 for more information on timeouts.

Example:

```
clearTimeout(my_timeout);
```

Cancels a timeout named my_timeout.

confirm() (NS 2, IE 3)

Creates a dialog box with two buttons, OK and Cancel, and text specified by the function's parameter. Clicking on OK results in the function returning a value of true and clicking on Cancel results in a false value.

Example:

```
if (confirm("are you feeling happy?"))
{
    alert("clap your hands!");
} else {
    alert("don't worry!");
}
```

This example calls up a dialog box with the text are you feeling happy? along with an OK button and a Cancel button. Clicking on OK causes the function to return true, executing the first part of the if-then-else statement with an alert box showing the words clap your hands! Clicking on Cancel causes the function to return false, triggering the else clause of the if-then-else statement and calling an alert box showing the words don't worry!

Date

This object represents dates; you can create it in several ways:

```
var the_date = new Date();
var the_date = new Date("month dd, yyyy");
var the_date = new Date("month dd, yyyy hh:mm:ss");
var the_date = new Date(yy, mm, dd);
var the_date = new Date(milliseconds);
```

Here month is the name of the month (January, February, and so on), dd is a two-digit day (01 to 31), yyyy is a four-digit year (0000 to 9999), and so on. If you create a date object without anything in the parentheses, JavaScript will assume you mean the current date and time according to the computer that's running the JavaScript.

The date object has numerous methods for getting and setting the date. Except where noted, the methods work for all JavaScript-enabled browsers.

METHODS FOR GETTING THE DATE AND TIME

Here are the standard methods to get the date and time (supported by NS 2, IE 3 except where noted).

getDate()	Returns the day of the month as an integer from 1 to 31.
getDay()	Returns the day of the week as an integer where 0 is Sunday and 1 is Monday.
getFullYear()	Returns the year as a four-digit number (only in NS 4, IE 4).
getHours()	Returns the hour as an integer between 0 and 23.
getMinutes()	Returns the minutes as an integer between 0 and 59.
getMonth()	Returns the month as an integer between 0 and 11 where 0 is January and 11 is December.
getSeconds()	Returns the seconds as an integer between 0 and 59.
getTime()	Returns the current time in milliseconds where 0 is January 1, 1970, 00:00:00.

Example:

```
var the_date = new Date();
var the_hours = the_date.getHours();
```

If the clock on the computer running the JavaScript thinks it's 8 p.m., the_hours contains the number 20.

METHODS FOR GETTING THE UTC DATE AND TIME

The following methods (NS 4, IE 4) return dates and times in *UTC time* (Greenwich Mean Time).

getUTCDate()	Returns the day of the month as an integer from 1 to 31.
getUTCDay()	Returns the day of the week as an integer where 0 is Sunday and 1 is Monday.
getUTCFullYear()	Returns the year as a four-digit number.
getUTCHours()	Returns the hour as an integer between 0 and 23.
getUTCMinutes()	Returns the minutes as an integer between 0 and 59.

getUTCMonth()	Returns the month as an integer between 0 and 11 where 0 is January and 11 is December.
getUTCSeconds()	Returns the seconds as an integer between 0 and 59.

THE PROBLEMATIC GETYEAR() METHOD

The getYear() method should return the number of years since 1900, but its behavior differs from browser to browser. Some browsers perform as advertised—for example, returning 110 if the year is 2010. Others, however, equate getYear() with getFullYear(), returning 2010 if the year is 2010. Due to these cross-browser discrepancies, it's best to adjust the date provided by getYear() as follows:

```
var the_date = new Date();
var the_year = the_date.getYear();
if (the_year < 1000)
{
    the_year = the_year + 1900;
}
```

This code always results in the_year containing the correct four-digit year.

METHODS FOR SETTING THE DATE AND TIME

The methods below change the contents of a date object (NS 2, MS 3, except where noted):

setDate()	Sets the day of the month as an integer from 1 to 31.
setFullYear()	Sets the year as a four-digit number (only in NS 4, IE 4).
setHours()	Sets the hour as an integer between 0 and 23.
setMinutes()	Sets the minutes as an integer between 0 and 59.
setMonth()	Sets the month as an integer between 0 and 11 where 0 is January and 11 is December.
setSeconds()	Sets the seconds as an integer between 0 and 59.
setTime()	Sets the current time in milliseconds where 0 is January 1, 1970, 00:00:00.
setYear()	Sets the year—uses two digits if the year is between 1900 and 1999, four digits otherwise.

Example:

```
var the_date = new Date();
the_date.setHours(22);
the_date.setYear(2012);
```

The date object called the_date thinks it's 10 p.m. in the year 2012.

METHODS FOR SETTING THE UTC DATE AND TIME

The following methods (NS 4, IE 4) are just like the ones above, except the dates and times set by the methods are adjusted to reflect *UTC time,* which is the same as Greenwich Mean Time.

setUTCDate()	Day of the month as an integer from 1 to 31.
setUTCFullYear()	Sets the year as a four-digit number.
setUTCHours()	Sets the hour as an integer between 0 and 23.
setUTCMinutes()	Sets the minutes as an integer between 0 and 59.
setUTCMonth()	Sets the month as an integer between 0 and 11 where 0 is January and 11 is December.
setUTCSeconds()	Sets the seconds as an integer between 0 and 59.

Example:

```
var the_date = new Date();
the_date.setUTCHours(10);
```

If the computer is one time zone to the west of Greenwich, England, the_date will now think it's 9 a.m. UTC.

CONVERTING DATES TO STRINGS

These methods turn the date stored in a date object into a string.

toGMTString()	Returns the date adjusted to reflect Greenwich Mean Time (NS 2, IE 3).
toUTCString()	The suggested method for newer browsers (NS 4, IE 4).

Document

The document of a window holds all the HTML elements of the Web page in that window.

PROPERTIES

applets[]	NS2, IE 3	An array storing the applets in the document. See Applet for more information.
bgColor	NS2, IE 3	The background color of a page. The value can be the name of a color or a hexadecimal triplet.

Example:

```
window.document.bgColor = "#000000";
```

This line makes the background of a page black.

cookie	NS 2, IE 3	The HTML cookie associated with this document. See Chapter 12 for more information on cookies.
forms[]	NS 2, IE 3	An array that stores all of a document's forms. See the form object for more information.
images[]	NS 2, IE 3	An array that stores all of a document's images. See the image object for more information.
lastModified	NS 2, IE 3	A read-only string that stores the date when a user most recently changed the document.

Example:

```
window.document.writeln("last changed on: " + window.document.lastModified);
```

This line writes the date of the last time the page was modified.

links[]		An array storing all of a document's hyperlinks. See the Link object for more information.
referrer	NS 2, IE 3	A read-only string containing the domain name of the hyperlink that led to this page.

Example:

```
window.document.writeln("thanks for coming from " + window.document.referrer);
```

Writes thanks for coming from www.nostarch.com if a hyperlink from the No Starch Press Web site led to the page.

title	NS 2, IE 3	Contains the document's title.

Example:

```
window.document.title = "Presto Chango";
```

Changes the title of the page to *Presto Chango*.

LESS COMMON PROPERTIES

activeElement	IE 4	A reference to the currently active input element.
all	IE 4	All of the HTML elements in the window.
anchors[]	NS 4, IE 4	An array of all the document's anchor tags (<a name="something"></a>).
charset	IE 4	The character set currently used.
children	IE 4	All of the document's direct properties.

classes	NS 4	All of the CSS styles defined in the HEAD of the page.
defaultCharset	IE 4	The default character set.
domain	NS 3, IE 4	The domain from which this page came (for example, nostarch.com).
embeds[]	NS 3, IE 4	An array of objects on the page using the <EMBED> tag.
expando	IE 4	If set to false, this prevents you from adding new properties to objects.
fgColor	NS 2, IE 3	Set or read the font color; can't be used to change the color once drawn.
height	NS 4	The height of the document in pixels.
linkColor	NS 2, IE 3	Set or read the color of links not followed; doesn't change drawn colors.
parentWindow	IE 4	The window that contains the document.
plugins[]	NS 3, IE 4	Same as embeds[]—an array holding all the <EMBED> tags.
readyState	IE 4	Describes the loading status of the document.
URL	NS 3, IE 4	The URL of the document.
vlinkColor	NS 2, IE 3	The color of visited links; can't be changed once you write the link.

METHODS

write(), writeln()	NS 2, IE 3	Writes to a Web page. The only difference between these two methods is that writeln() appends a line break at the end of whatever is written.

Example:

```
window.document.writeln("Wassup?!");
```

Writes Wassup?! to a Web page.

LESS COMMON METHODS

clear()	NS 2, IE 3	Deprecated method used to clear a document. Don't use this method—it may vanish in future JavaScript versions.
close()	NS 2, IE 3	Use close() when you've finished writing to the document (optional). Sometimes, due to browser bugs, writing to a Web page using document.write() won't actually complete that action unless you execute document.close() after executing document.write().

elementFromPoint(x,y)	IE 4	Returns a reference to the HTML element that is at x,y.
getSelection()	NS 4	Returns the text selected in a document.
open()	NS 2, IE 3	Use open() if you want to clear the contents of a Web page before writing to it using write() or writeln(). If you use document.open(), use document.close() when you're done writing to the page.

Elements[]   [NS 2, IE 3]

An array in the Form object that stores all the elements (buttons, checkboxes, radio buttons, and so on) of a form. See the Form object for more information.

escape()   [NS 2, IE 3]

Formats a string so it conforms to URL encoding. Generally used for setting cookies. See Chapter 12 for more information.

Example:

```
var encoded_string = escape("a string safe for cookies");
```

The variable encoded_string now holds a%20string%20safe%20for %20cookies because the escape function replaces spaces with %20. See also unescape().

eval()   [NS 2, IE 3]

Evaluates a string.

Example:

```
var the_sum = eval("2 + 3");
```

The variable the_sum will equal 5 because eval() forces JavaScript to evaluate the string "2 + 3".

Event

The Event object describes an event that just happened: a mouse click, a cursor movement, and so on. Netscape 4 and Internet Explorer both introduced the Event object but implemented it very differently. The Netscape properties marked below with an asterisk only work for signed scripts (see http://developer.netscape.com/library/documentation/signedobj/signtool/ for more information on signed scripts).

PROPERTIES (NS 4)

data*   Information about a DragDrop event.

height   The height of a resized window.

layerX   The event's horizontal pixel coordinate on a layer.

layerY   The event's vertical pixel coordinate on a layer.

modifiers   The modifier keys (ALT, CTRL, and so on) held down during an event.

pageX   The event's horizontal pixel coordinate on the Web page.

pageY   The event's vertical pixel coordinate on the Web page.

screenX   The event's horizontal pixel coordinate on the screen.

screenY   The event's vertical pixel coordinate on the screen.

target   The object in which the event occurred.

type   The type of event.

which   Which key or mouse button the user pressed to trigger the event.

width   The page's width after resizing.

x   See layerX.

y   See layerY.

PROPERTIES (IE 4)

AltKey   True if the user pressed the ALT key during the event,
                 false otherwise.

button   Which mouse button the user clicked to trigger the event.

cancelBubble Stops the event from triggering all the objects in which it
                 happened.

clientX   The event's horizontal pixel coordinate on the Web page.

clientY   The event's vertical pixel coordinate on the Web page.

ctrlKey   True if the user pressed the CTRL key during the event,
                 false otherwise.

fromElement The HTML element out of which the mouse is moving.

keyCode   The key pressed to trigger the event.

screenX   The event's horizontal pixel coordinate on the screen.

screenY   The event's vertical pixel coordinate on the screen.

shiftKey   True if the user pressed SHIFT during the event, false otherwise.

srcElement   The object in which the event occurred.

toElement   The HTML element into which the mouse is moving.

type   The type of event.

FileUpload

The `FileUpload` form element lets a visitor choose a file on the computer to submit to a CGI script along with the form. Use the syntax `<input type="file">`.

PROPERTIES

name	NS 2, IE 3	The name of the `FileUpload` field.
value	NS 3, IE 4	The read-only file name selected.

METHODS

blur()	NS 2, IE 3	Removes the cursor from the `FileUpload` element.
focus()	NS 2, IE 3	Moves the cursor to the `FileUpload` element.
select()	NS 2, IE 3	Selects the text inside the `FileUpload` element.

HANDLERS

onBlur	NS 2, IE 3	Called when the user removes the cursor from the field.
onChange	NS 2, IE 3	Triggered when a visitor changes the contents of the field.
onFocus	NS 2, IE 3	Called when the user puts the cursor into the field.

Form

Every form on a Web page has a Form object. The `window.document.forms[]` array stores all of a Web page's form objects.

PROPERTIES

Each type of form element—button, checkbox, fileupload, hidden, password, radio, reset, select, submit, text, and textarea—has its own object listing in the glossary. See that object for more information.

action	NS 2, IE 3; read-only in IE 3	Triggers a specified CGI script when a user submits the form.

Example:

```
if (user == "expert")
{
    window.document.the_form.action = "expert_script.cgi";
} else {
    window.document.the_form.action = "basic_script.cgi";
}
```

If the user is considered an expert, the above sets the form to run expert_script.cgi when he or she submits the form.

elements[]   NS 2, IE 3   An array of the elements of this form.

Example:

```
window.document.form_name.elements[0].checked = true;
```

will set the checked value of the first element of the form named form_name to true.

encoding   NS 2, IE 3; read-only in IE 3   How the information in the form is encoded when it's sent to a CGI script. It's almost always "application/x-www-form-urlencoded" and there's almost never a reason to change it.

length   NS 2, IE 3   The number of elements in a form.

Example:

```
var number_elements = window.document.the_form.length;
```

method   NS 2, IE 3; read-only in IE 3   Specifies how a form sends information (via either POST or GET) to the CGI script listed in the action tag.

Example:

```
window.document.the_form.method = "GET";
```

name   NS 2, IE 3   Looks for a form by name if you need to locate it.

Example:

```
window.document.form_name
```

Indicates the form named form_name.

target   NS 2, IE 3; read-only in IE 3   The target property in a form tells the form where to write the results of the form's CGI script. If the target specifies a window that does not exist, a new window opens.

Example:

```
var target_window = window.open("blank.html","my_target");
window.document.the_form.target = "my_target";
```

The first line opens a window with the name my_target. The second line tells the form named the_form that the CGI script it runs should return its results to the window named my_target.

METHODS

reset()	NS 3, IE 4	Resets the elements of a form. Acts as if a visitor clicked on a reset button.

Example:

```
window.document.the_form.reset();
```

submit()	NS 2, IE 3	Submits the form. Acts as if a visitor clicked on a submit button except that the onSubmit handler is not called when the submit() method is invoked.

HANDLERS

onReset	NS 2, IE 3	Triggered when a form is reset.
onSubmit	NS 2, IE 3	Triggered when a form is submitted. Executing return false inside a submit handler stops submission of the form to the CGI script.

Example:

```
<FORM onSubmit="if (formNotDone(this)) {return false;})">
```

This calls the function formNotDone() on the form. If the function returns true, the if-then statement returns false and the form is not submitted. Note: formNotDone() is not a built-in JavaScript function. See Chapter 11 for more information on form validation.

Hidden

An invisible form element that can store values on a Web page without the visitor seeing them; useful for sending secret information to a CGI script.

PROPERTIES

name	NS 2, IE 3	The name of a hidden element.

Example:

```
window.document.the_form.my_hidden.value = "a nice person";
```

Will set the value of the hidden element named my_hidden to a nice person. If the form is subsequently sent to a CGI script, the value will be passed along.

value   NS 2, IE 3   The value of a hidden element (see the previous example).

History

The history of URLs visited by the visitor's browser.

PROPERTIES

length   NS 2, IE 4   The number of URLs in the history list.

PROPERTIES REQUIRING A SIGNED SCRIPT (NS 4)

current   The URL of the current document.

next   The URL of the history array's next document.

previous   The URL of the history array's previous document.

METHODS

back()   NS 2, IE 3   Returns to the previous page (like clicking on the browser's back button).

Example:

```
history.back();
```

forward()   NS 2, IE 3   Advances to the next page (like clicking on the browser's forward button).

Example:

```
history.forward();
```

go()   NS 2, IE 3   Takes one parameter: the number of URLs to advance (positive values) or go back (negative values). In IE 3, the parameter can only be -1, 0, or 1.

Example:

```
history.go(-2);
```

HTMLElement   **[NS 4, IE 4]**

All HTML elements (images, links, forms, and form elements) are considered objects in the newer browsers. Internet Explorer has a passel of additional properties and methods for each of these elements, and both browsers have an expanded set of handlers. The IE 4 properties and methods are listed below, followed by the handlers the two browsers support.

PROPERTIES (IE 4)

all[]	The array holding all the elements the element contains.
children[]	The array holding the direct children of this element.
className	The value of the element's CLASS attribute.
document	A reference to the element's document.
id	The element's ID.
innerHTML	HTML text inside the element, not including the start and end tags.
innerText	Normal text (the text excluding all the HTML tags) inside the element.
lang	The element's lang attribute. Used by Microsoft Internet Explorer to determine how to display language-specific characters. See http://msdn.microsoft.com/workshop/author/dhtml/reference/language_codes.asp for a list of language codes.
offsetHeight	The element's height.
offsetLeft	The horizontal position of the element in pixels, relative to the containing element.
offsetParent	A reference to the element that contains this element.
offsetTop	The vertical position of the element in pixels, relative to the containing element.
offsetWidth	The width of the document.
outerHTML	The HTML text of the element, including the start and end tags.
outerText	The text of the whole document.
parentElement	A reference to the element that contains this element.
sourceIndex	The array position of this element in the all[] array.
style	The element's CSS style information.
tagName	The type of element.
title	The element's title attribute.

METHODS (IE 4)

contains()	Determines whether this element contains the element specified in the parameter.
getAttribute()	Gets the value of an attribute specified in the parameter.
insertAdjacentHTML()	Inserts HTML into the document near this element.
insertAdjacentText()	Inserts text into the document near this element.
removeAttribute()	Removes the attribute specified in the parameter.
scrollIntoView()	Scrolls the page until this element is visible.
setAttribute()	Sets the value of an attribute. First parameter is the attribute, second is the value.

HANDLERS (NS 4, IE 4)

onClick	**onMousedown**
onDblclick	**onMousemove**
onHelp	**onMouseout**
onKeydown	**onMouseover**
onKeypress	**onMouseup**
onKeyup	

Image

JavaScript stores images in the `images` array of the `document` object. A user may create a new image object as follows:

```
var new_image = new Image();
```

The above creates a new image and sets its `src` property to a GIF or JPG, then preloads that file. See Chapter 4 for more information about images and preloading.

PROPERTIES

border NS 3, IE 4 A read-only property containing the size of the border around the image.

Example:

```
var the_border_size = window.document.my_image.border;
```

complete NS 3, IE 4 A read-only property that is true if the image has completely downloaded and false otherwise.

Example:

```
if (window.document.pretty_bird.complete)
{
    alert("you should now see a pretty bird");
}
```

hspace	NS 3, IE 4	A read-only property containing the number of pixels to the left and right of the image.
height	NS 3, IE 4	A property (read-only in NS) that stores the height of an image in pixels.

Example:

```
var image_height = window.document.the_image.height;
```

lowsrc	NS 3, IE 4	The image to show on a low-resolution monitor.

Example:

```
window.document.the_image.lowsrc = "small_image.gif";
```

name	NS 3, IE 4	The name of an image; JavaScript can use this to identify the image.

Example:

```
<img src="sad.gif" name="my_image">
```

If this appears on your Web page, the following JavaScript swaps sad.gif with happy.gif:

```
window.document.my_image.src = "happy.gif";
```

The name of the image, my_image, identifies which image to swap.

src	NS 3, IE 4; read-only in IE 3	The name of the file containing the image to show.

Example:

```
window.document.my_image.src = "happy.gif";
```

Swaps the image contained in the file happy.gif into the image named my_image.

| **vspace** | NS 3, IE 4 | A read-only property containing the number of pixels to the left and right of the image. |
| **width** | NS 3, IE 4 | A property (read-only in NS) that stores the width of an image in pixels. |

Example:

```
var image_width = window.document.the_image.width;
```

isNaN() [NS 3, IE 4]

Returns true if the parameter is not a number, false otherwise.

Example:

```
var zip_code = "none of your business";
if (isNaN(zip_code))
{
    alert("please provide something that at least looks like a zip code!");
}
```

Since zip_code contains a string, isNaN() returns true, triggering the alert.

Layers [NS 4]

Netscape formerly used the layers object for Dynamic HTML, but the Layer tag is now deprecated (see the Style object and Chapter 13 for more information on DHTML). Layers are stored in the layers[] array, which is part of the document object in Netscape. Because layers have been deprecated, I will just list the properties and methods here.

PROPERTIES

above	**left**	**src**
background	**name**	**top**
below	**pageX**	**visibility**
bgColor	**pageY**	**window**
clip	**parentLayer**	**x**
document	**siblingAbove**	**y**
hidden	**siblingBelow**	**zIndex**

METHODS

captureEvents()	moveBy()	releaseEvents()
handleEvents()	moveTo()	resizeBy()
load()	moveToAbsolute()	resizeTo()
moveAbove()	offset()	routeEvents()
moveBelow()		

Link

The hypertext link object: <A HREF=""></A>

PROPERTIES

hash   NS 2, IE 3   The part of the URL following a hash mark (#).

Example:

```
window.document.my_link.hash = "where_to_go";
```

This sets the link to go to the anchor named where_to_go when clicked.

host   NS 2, IE 3   The host name and the port of the href.

Example:

```
window.document.my_link.host = http://www.feedmag.com:80/
```

Sets the link to go to http://www.feedmag.com:80/ when clicked.

hostname   NS 2, IE 3   The domain of the link's HREF.

Example:

```
window.document.my_link.hostname = "www.nostarch.com";
```

href   NS 2, IE 3   The link's full path.
pathname   The path and file name of the HREF (the URL minus the domain information).

Example:

```
window.document.my_link.pathname = "some_directory/index.html;"
```

port   NS 2, IE 3   The port of the HREF URL.

Example:

```
window.document.my_link.port = 80;
```

protocol   NS 2, IE 3   The protocol of the HREF URL.

Example:

```
window.document.my_link.protocol = "http:";
```

search   NS 2, IE 3   The part of a URL following a question mark (?).

Example:

```
window.document.my_link.href = "http://www.hotbot.com/";
window.document.my_link.search = "stuff_after_question_mark";
```

Makes the HREF of the my_link:

```
http://www.hotbot.com/?stuff_after_question_mark
```

HANDLERS

onClick	NS 2, IE 3
onMouseOut	NS 3, IE 4
onMouseOver	NS 2, IE 3

Location

The location object controls the URL shown in the browser window.

PROPERTIES

hash   NS 2, IE 3   The part of the URL following a hash mark.

Example:

```
window.location.hash = "where_to_go";
```

This will cause the browser to jump to the position of the current page which has the anchor `<a name="where_to_go"></a>`.

host   NS 2, IE 3   The host name and port of a URL.

Example:

If the URL is http://www.feedmag.com:80/index.html, the host is www.feedmag.com:80.

hostname   NS 2, IE 3   The domain of the URL shown in the browser.

Example:

```
if (window.location.hostname == "www.nostarch.com")
{
    alert("welcome to No Starch Press");
}
```

href   NS 2, IE 3   The full path of the page shown. Changing href causes the browser to load the specified page.

Example:

```
window.location.href = "http://www.nostarch.com/index.html";
```

Loads the page index.html from the No Starch Press Web site.

pathname   The path and file name shown in the browser window (the URL minus the domain information).

Example:

```
var the_path = window.location.path;
```

The variable the_path will hold index.html if the window is currently showing http://www.nostarch.com/index.html.

port   NS 2, IE 3   A URL's port.

Example:

If the URL is http://www.feedmag.com:80/index.html, the port will be 80.

protocol   NS 2, IE 3   A URL's protocol.

Example:

If the URL is http://www.feedmag.com:80/index.html, the protocol will be http.

search   NS 2, IE 3   The part of a URL following a question mark.

Example:

If the URL is http://www.webmonkey.com/index.html?hello_there,

```
var the_search = window.location.search;
```

the variable the_search will contain hello_there.

METHODS

reload()   NS 3, IE 4   Reloads the page.

Example:

```
window.location.reload();
```

Will act as if a visitor clicked on the reload or refresh button in the browser.

replace()   NS 3, IE 4   This method takes one parameter, a URL to load into the browser window. The page shown when replace() is called is removed from the browser's history and replaced with the new page. This means clicking on the back button after the new page has replaced the currently shown page won't result in revisiting the current page. It's as if you're telling the browser to forget the currently shown page.

Example:

```
window.location.replace("http://www.npr.com");
```

Math   *[NS 2, IE 3 except where noted]*

The math object contains numerous properties and methods. Except where noted, all of these properties and methods work in NS 2, IE 3, and more recent browsers, and all the properties are read only. Because most of the methods and properties are self-explanatory, I will give few examples. I'll round all numbers to the sixth decimal point.

PROPERTIES

E	Euler's constant (2.718282).
LN2	Natural log of 2 (0.693147).
LN10	Natural log of 10 (2.302585).
PI	Pi (3.141592).
SQRT2	Square root of 2 (1.414214).

METHODS

abs()   The absolute value. *Example:* `var ab_value = Math.abs(-10);` sets ab_value to 10.

acos()   The arc cosine in radians.

asin()   The arc sine in radians.

atan()   The arc tangent in radians.

ceil()		The integer greater than or equal to the number passed. *Example:* var the_ceiling = Math.ceil(9.5); sets the_ceiling to 10.
cos()		The cosine.
exp()		The value of E to the power passed.
floor()		The integer lower than or equal to the number passed.
log()		The natural log.
max()		Takes two numbers and returns the higher number. *Example:* var the_higher = Math.max(10,11); sets the_higher to 11.
min()		Takes two numbers and returns the lower number.
pow()		Takes two numbers and returns the first to the power of the second. *Example:* two_cubed = Math.pow(2,3); sets two_cubed to 8 (2 to the third power).
random()	NS 3, IE 3	Creates a random number between 0 and 1.
round()		Rounds a number up if the decimal value is greater than or equal to .5 and rounds it down otherwise.
sin()		The sine of a number.
sqrt()		The square root of a number.
tan()		The tangent of a number.

Navigator

The Navigator object lets JavaScript know what type of Web browser your visitor is using.

PROPERTIES

appName	NS 2, IE 3	The manufacturer of the browser: Netscape, Microsoft Internet Explorer, Opera, and so on.

Example:

```
if (navigator.appName == "Netscape")
{
    window.location = "netscape_index.html";
}
```

The above sends a visitor to a page called netscape_index.html if he or she is using Netscape.

appVersion	NS 2, IE 3	A string representing the version of the browser. It's not useful unless interpreted with the parseFloat() function.

Example:

```
if (parseFloat(navigator.appVersion) < 2)
{
    alert("isn't it time to upgrade?");
}
```

LESS COMMON PROPERTIES

appCodeName	NS 2, IE 3	The browser's code name.
language	NS 4	The language the browser's in.
platform	NS 4, IE 4	The browser's operating system.
systemLanguage	IE 4	The operating system's language.
userAgent	NS 2, IE 3	Generally a string composed of appCodeName and appVersion.
userLanguage	IE 4	The language the browser's in.

Number   *[NS 3, IE 4]*

The Number object has some helpful read-only properties.

PROPERTIES

MAX_VALUE	The highest integer possible given the configuration of the browser and the computer it's on.
MIN_VALUE	The lowest integer possible given the configuration of the browser and the computer it's on.
NaN	Not a number. Results if a mathematical operation fails (Math.sqrt(-1) for example). Can be tested with the isNaN() function.

Example:

```
if (isNaN(Math.sqrt(-1)))
{
    alert("Get real!  You can't take the square root of -1!");
}
```

NEGATIVE_INFINITY	A value smaller than Number.MIN_VALUE. You know no number will ever be less than this value.
POSITIVE_INFINITY	A value bigger than Number.MAX_VALUE. No number will ever exceed this value.

Option

The option object refers to an option in a select element of a form—either a pull-down menu or scrollable list. All the options of a select element are stored in the options[] array of that element.

PROPERTIES

selected   NS 2, IE 3   True if the option has been selected, and false otherwise.

Example:

```
if (window.document.the_form.the_pulldown.options[0].selected == true)
{
    var the_option_text = window.document.the_form.the_pulldown.option[0].text;
    alert("thanks for picking " + the_option_text);
}
```

text   NS 2, IE 3   The text associated with an option. See the above example.

parseInt()   [NS 2, IE 3]

Converts a string to an integer as long as the first character is a number. If the first character is not a number, parseInt() returns NaN (not a number). If the string is a number followed by letters, parseInt() grabs the first set of numbers in the string.

Example:

```
var the_string = "123abc456";
var the_numbers = parseInt(the_string);
```

The variable the_numbers contains 123.

parseFloat()   [NS 2, IE 3]

Converts a string to a floating-point number as long as the first character is a number. If the first character is not a number, parseFloat() returns NaN (not a number). If the string is a number followed by letters, parseFloat() grabs the first set of numbers in the string.

Example:

```
var the_string = "3.14etc";
var the_numbers = parseFloat(the_string);
```

The variable the_numbers contains 3.14.

Password

The password form element, like the text form element, allows a visitor to type a line of text into a form. In a password element, however, asterisks or bullets replace the letters to hide the contents from view. The element is represented like this in HTML: `<input type="password">`.

PROPERTIES

name   NS 2, IE 3   The name of the password field.

value   NS 2, IE 3   The text that appears in the password field.

Example:

```
<input type="password" onChange="alert(this.value);">
```

When a visitor enters a password into this field and presses return, whatever he or she typed gets sent to the alert() function.

METHODS

blur()   NS 2, IE 3   Removes the cursor from the password element.

Example:

```
window.document.my_form.the_password.blur();
```

focus()   NS 2, IE 3   Moves the cursor to the password element.

Example:

```
window.document.my_form.the_password.focus();
```

The above line puts the cursor inside the password element named the_password. Unless the focus is changed, the next characters typed go into the_password.

select()   NS 2, IE 3   Selects the text inside the password element.

Example:

```
window.document.my_form.the_password.select();
```

HANDLERS

onBlur   NS 2, IE 3   Called when a visitor removes the cursor from the password element.

Example:

```
<input type="password" onBlur="alert('don\'t forget your password!');">
```

onChange   NS 2, IE 3   Triggered when a visitor changes the contents of the field and then clicks out of the field or presses return.

Example:

```
<input type="password" onChange="thanks for the password!">
```

onFocus   NS 2, IE 3   Called when the cursor is put into the password field.

Example:

```
<input type="password" onFocus="window.open('instruct.html','inst')";>
```

The above opens a window when a visitor clicks inside the password field.

prompt()

A dialog box that has OK and Cancel buttons, a place for a message to the visitor, and a box into which the visitor may type a reply. The prompt() function returns the visitor's reply and takes two parameters: a message that appears above the input area, and a default value to put in the input area. If the visitor clicks on Cancel, prompt() returns the value null.

Example:

```
var the_name = prompt("what's your name?", "your name here");
if (the_name == null)
{
    the_name = prompt("come on!  what's your name?","please.....");
}
```

This calls up a prompt box asking visitors for their name. The words your name here appear as default text in the input area. If a visitor presses Cancel, the if-then statement asks for the name one more time.

Radio

The radio button form element. Radio buttons given the same name are considered a set and are stored in an array with the set's name. A visitor can select only one radio button of the set at any given time. If a Web page has five radio buttons named favorite_color, the second radio button in the set is referred to as:

```
window.document.the_form.favorite_color[1]
```

PROPERTIES

checked   NS 2, IE 3   A radio button's checked property is true if a visitor has selected the radio button, and false otherwise. Setting the property to true causes the radio button to act as if a visitor selected the button.

Example:

```
if (window.document.the_form.favorite_color[3].checked == true)
{
    alert("I like that color too!");
}
```

This if-then statement calls an alert box if a visitor selects the fourth radio button named favorite_color.

name   NS 2, IE 3   A radio button's name.

value   NS 2, IE 3   The value of a radio button.

HANDLERS

onClick   NS 2, IE 3   Triggered when a visitor clicks on the radio button.

Reset

The reset button is a form element that clears a form's entries.

PROPERTIES

name   NS 2, IE 3   A reset button's name. The name is *not* the text that shows up in the button when it appears on a Web page (see the value property).

Example:

```
<input type="reset" name="happy" onClick="alert(this.name);">
```

Calls an alert with the word happy in it.

value   NS 2, IE 3   A read-only property containing the text that appears in a reset button when it appears on a Web page.

Example:

```
<input type="reset" value="click me" onClick="alert(this.value);">
```

Clicking on this button results in an alert box with the words click me inside.

HANDLERS

onClick   NS 2, IE 3   Triggered when a visitor clicks on the reset button.

Screen

The screen object contains a number of read-only properties that provide information about the computer screen used to view a Web page.

PROPERTIES

availHeight   NS 4, IE 4   The available height of the screen, in pixels. Excludes the taskbar in Windows systems and any other permanent screen elements.

Example:

```
var screen_height = screen.availHeight;
```

availWidth	NS 4, IE 4	The available width of the screen in pixels. Excludes any permanent screen elements along the right or left side of the screen.
height	NS 4, IE 4	The height of the screen in pixels.
width	NS 4, IE 4	The width of the screen in pixels.
availLeft	NS 4	The horizontal position of the leftmost available pixel on the screen.
availTop	NS 4	The vertical position of the topmost available pixel on the screen.
colorDepth	NS 4, IE 4	The number of colors on the screen (bits per pixel in IE, natural log in NS).
pixelDepth	NS 4	Bits per pixel.

Select

The select form element can either be a pull-down menu or a scrollable list. The items in it are called the options of the select and are stored in the select element's options[] array.

PROPERTIES

length	NS 2, IE 3	The number of options in the select.
name	NS 2, IE 3	A select object's name.
options[]	NS 2, IE 3	The array containing the select's options. See the Option object for more information about options.
selectedIndex	NS 2, IE 3	Contains the selected option's array position in a select element. If no item has been selected, selectedIndex is -1. If more than one option has been selected, selectedIndex contains the position of the first option. To determine all the options selected, use a loop to look at the selected property of each Option object. See the Option object for more information.

Example:

```
var option_number = window.document.the_form.the_select.selectedIndex;
if (selected_option_number != -1)
{
    var option_text = window.document.the_form.the_select.options[option_number].text;
    alert("thanks for choosing " + option_text);
}
```

The above determines which option (if any) has been selected, and presents an alert box with the selected option's text.

HANDLERS

onChange	NS 2, IE 3	Triggered when a visitor selects or deselects an option.

Example:

```
<select onChange="alert(this.options[selectedIndex].text + ' is a good choice');">
<option>Cat
<option>Dog
</select>
```

Selecting Cat or Dog triggers the select's onChange, resulting in an alert box commending the visitor on his or her choice.

setInterval()   *[NS 4, IE 4]*

Executes JavaScript statements in repeated intervals. Takes two parameters: the JavaScript statements to execute, and the number of milliseconds between each execution. The function returns a reference to the interval so that clearInterval() may cancel it.

Example:

```
var the_interval = setInterval("alert('stop procrastinating!');", 10000);
```

Creates an interval that calls up an alert box every 10 seconds.

setTimeout()   [NS 2, IE 3]

Executes JavaScript statements once after a specified amount of time. Takes two parameters: the JavaScript statements to execute, and the number of milliseconds in the future to execute the statements. The function returns a reference to the timeout so that clearTimeout() may cancel it.

Example:

```
var the_timeout = setTimeout("alert('stop procrastinating!');", 10000);
```

Creates a timeout that calls up an alert box in 10 seconds.

String

Strings are sets of characters between quotes. See Chapter 11 for more information on strings.

PROPERTIES

length   NS 2, IE 3   The number of characters in a string.

Example:

```
var the_string = "hello";
var the_length = the_string.length;
```

The above code sets the_length to 5.

METHODS

anchor()   NS 2, IE 3   Takes a name as a parameter and returns an anchor
                                    tag with the string as the text of the link.

Example:

```
var the_string = "Information about Fish";
var the_anchor = the_string.anchor("fish_info");
window.document.writeln(the_anchor);
```

Writes `<A NAME="fish_info">Information about Fish</A>` to a Web page.

bold() NS 2, IE 3 Puts the string between `<B>` and `</B>` tags.

Example:

```
var the_string = "something really important";
window.document.writeln(the_string.bold());
```

Writes `<B>something really important</B>` to a Web page.

charAt() NS 2, IE 3 Takes a number as a parameter and returns the character in that position of the string. Returns null if there is no character.

Example:

```
var the_string = "rabbit";
var the_first_char = the_string.charAt(0);
```

Sets the_first_char to r because r is in position 0 of the string.

fontcolor() NS 2, IE 3 Takes the name of a color or a hexidecimal triplet as a parameter and encloses the string between `<FONT COLOR="the_color">` and `</FONT>` tags.

Example:

```
var the_string = "pretty";
window.document.writeln(the_string.fontcolor("pink"));
```

Writes `<FONT COLOR="pink">pretty</FONT>` to a Web page.

fontsize() NS 2, IE 3 Takes an integer as a parameter and encloses the string between `<FONT SIZE="the_size">` and `<FONT>` tags.

Example:

```
var the_string = "cheese";
window.document.writeln(the_string.fontsize(48));
```

Writes `<FONT SIZE="48">cheese</FONT>` to a Web page.

indexOf()　　NS 2, IE 3　　Can take one or two parameters. The first parameter is a substring to search for within the string. The second parameter is an optional integer that dictates where in the string to start searching. If the string contains the substring, `indexOf()` returns the position of the substring within the string. If the string does not contain the substring, `indexOf()` returns -1.

Example:

```
var the_string = "The Waldorf Astoria";
var wheres = the_string.indexOf("Waldo");
```

Sets wheres to 4 because the W in Waldo is in position 4 in the string.

italics()　　NS 2, IE 3　　Puts the string between <I> and </I> tags.

Example:

```
var the_string = "tower";
window.document.writeln(the_string.italics());
```

Writes <I>tower</I> to a Web page.

lastIndexOf()　　NS 2, IE 3　　Returns the position of the last occurrence of a substring in a string. Like `indexOf()`, it can take one or two parameters. The first is the substring to search for and the second is where in the string to start searching.

Example:

```
var the_string = "The last word.";
var last_space = the_string.lastIndexOf(" ");
```

The above sets last_space to 8.

link()　　NS 2, IE 3　　Takes a URL as a parameter and creates a hyperlink with the string as the text of the link and the URL as the contents of the HREF element.

Example:

```
var the_string = "News For Geeks";
window.document.writeln(the_string.link("http://www.slashdot.org"));
```

Writes `<A HREF="http://www.slashdot.org">News for Geeks</A>` to a Web page.

split()   NS 3, IE 4   Splits a string into an array along a substring passed as a parameter.

Example:

```
var the_string = "Jan,Feb,Mar,Apr,May,Jun,Jul,Aug,Sep,Oct,Nov,Dec";
var the_months = the_string.split(",");
```

The above code creates an array called the_months, which has Jan in position 0, Feb in position 1, and so on.

substr()   NS 4, IE 4   Extracts a substring from a string. Takes two parameters: the position of the first character of the substring and the length of the substring. Similar to the substring() method below.

Example:

```
var the_string = "core";
var the_extract = the_string.substr(1, 2);
```

The above sets the_extract to or because o is in position 1 in the string and is 2 letters long.

substring()   NS 2, IE 3   Extracts a substring from a string. Takes two parameters: the position of the first character of the substring and the position of the character after the last character in the substring. Similar to the substr() method above except it works in more browsers and takes a different second parameter.

Example:

```
var the_string = "core";
var the_extract = the_string.substr(1, 3);
```

The above example sets the_extract to or because o is in position 1 of the string and e, the letter after the last character in or, is in position 3.

toLowerCase()   NS 2, IE 3   Converts a string to lowercase.

Example:

```
var the_string="WHITTLE ME";
window.document.writeln(the_string.toLowerCase());
```

The above writes whittle me to a Web page.

toUpperCase()   NS 2, IE 3   Converts a string to uppercase.

Example:

```
var the_string = "something very important";
window.document.writeln(the_string.toUpperCase());
```

The above writes something very important to a Web page.

LESS COMMON METHODS

big()	NS 2, IE 3	Puts the string between <BIG> and </BIG> tags.
blink()	NS 2, IE 3	Too evil to mention (try it if you really want to know).
charCodeAt()	NS 4, IE 4	Just like charAt().
concat()	NS 4, IE 4	Appends the parameter to the string.
fixed()	NS 2, IE 3	Puts the string between <TT> and </TT> tags.
fromCharCode()	NS 4, IE 4	Creates a string out of numeric Unicode.
match()	NS 4, IE 4	Finds one or more regular expressions (regexp)—outside this book's scope.
replace()	NS 4, IE 4	Uses regexp to replace part of a string with something else.
search()	NS 4, IE 4	Uses regexp to find the position of a substring.
slice()	NS 4, IE 4	Extracts a substring from a string.
small()	NS 2, IE 3	Puts the string between <SMALL> and </SMALL> tags.
sub()	NS 2, IE 3	Puts the string between _{and} tags.
sup()	NS 2, IE 3	Puts the string between ^{and} tags.

Style   **[NS 4, IE 4]**

The object that represents a Cascading Style Sheet (CSS). As discussed in Chapter 13, you can use CSS in combination with JavaScript to animate a Web page in many ways. Netscape and IE refer to a Style object with styleid as follows:

Netscape	`window.document.styleid`
IE	`window.styleid.style`

Style sheets are often attached to <DIV> HTML tags as follows:

```
<DIV ID="mystyle" STYLE="position:absolute;top:100;left:100;">
Here's a style sheet!
</DIV>
```

The above gives DIV an id of mystyle and positions the text between the <DIV> and </DIV> tags 100 pixels from the left and 100 pixels from the top of the screen.

All the properties of a Style object are read-write. For more information about those properties, pick up a good book on CSS or Dynamic HTML.

PROPERTIES (NS 4, IE 4)

backgroundColor	fontFamily	paddingBottom
backgroundImage	fontSize	paddingLeft
borderBottomWidth	fontStyle	paddingRight
borderColor	fontWeight	paddingTop
borderLeftWidth	left	textAlign
borderRightWidth	lineHeight	textDecoration
borderStyle	listStyleType	textIndex
borderTopWidth	marginBottom	textTransform
clear	marginLeft	top
color	marginRight	visibility
display	marginTop	zIndex

PROPERTIES (IE ONLY)

background	borderTopColor	overflow
backgroundAttachment	borderTopStyle	pageBreakAfter
backgroundPosition	borderWidth	pageBreakBefore
backgroundPositionX	clip	pixelHeight
backgroundPositionY	cssText	pixelLeft
backgroundRepeat	cursor	pixelTop
border	filter	pixelWidth
borderBottom	font	posHeight
borderBottomColor	fontVariant	position
borderBottomStyle	height	posLeft
borderLeftColor	letterSpacing	posTop
borderLeftStyle	listStyle	posWidth
borderRight	listStyleImage	styleFloat
borderRightColor	listStylePosition	verticalAlign
borderRightStyle	listStyleType	width
borderTop	margin	

borderWidths()	Takes four parameters: top, right, bottom, left. Sets the `borderTopWidth`, `borderRightWidth`, `borderBottomWidth`, and `borderLeftWidth` properties.
margins()	Takes four parameters: top, right, bottom, and left. Sets the `marginTop`, `marginRight`, `marginBottom`, and `marginLeft` properties.
paddings()	Takes four parameters: top, right, bottom, left. Sets the `paddingTop`, `paddingRight`, `paddingBottom`, and `paddingLeft` properties.

Submit

The submit button sends an onSubmit event to the form that contains it.

PROPERTIES

name	NS 2, IE 3	The name of the button. Note that the name is not the text that shows up in the button when it appears on a Web page (see the value property).
value	NS 2, IE 3	A read-only property containing the text in a submit button when it appears on a Web page.

HANDLERS

onClick	NS 2, IE 3	Triggered when a visitor clicks on the submit button. JavaScript inside an onClick handler will occur before JavaScript that appears inside an onSubmit handler in the containing form.

Text

The text form element allows a visitor to type a line of text into a form.

PROPERTIES

name	NS 2, IE 3	The name of the text field.
value	NS 2, IE 3	The text typed in the text field.

METHODS

blur()	NS 2, IE 3	Removes the cursor from the text element.

Example:

```
window.document.my_form.the_text.blur();
```

focus()	NS 2, IE 3	Moves the cursor to the text element.

Example:

```
window.document.my_form.the_text.focus();
```

This example puts the cursor inside the text element named the_text. Unless the focus is changed, the next characters typed go into the_text.

select()	NS 2, IE 3	Selects the text inside the text element.

Example:

```
window.document.my_form.the_text.select();
```

HANDLERS

onBlur	NS 2, IE 3	Called when the cursor is removed from the text element.

Example:

```
Name: <input type="text" onBlur="alert('hello ' + this.value);">
```

onChange	NS 2, IE 3	Triggered when a visitor changes the contents of the field and then clicks out of the field or presses return.

Example:

```
<input type="text" onChange="thanks for filling this out!">
```

onFocus	NS 2, IE 3	Called when a visitor puts the cursor into the text field.

Example:

```
<input type="text" onFocus="window.open('instruct.html','inst')";>
```

The above opens a window when a visitor clicks inside the text field.

Textarea

The textarea form element allows a visitor to type several lines of text. The textarea's properties, methods, and handlers are the same as those for the Text object.

this ***[NS 2, IE 3]***

A term that refers to the object in which it appears.

Example:

```
<input type = "checkbox" name = "riddle_me" onClick="alert(this.name)">
```

Here, this refers to the checkbox named riddle_me because that's where this appears. The alert box will have the text riddle_me inside.

unescape() ***[NS 2, IE 3]***

Decodes a string encoded with escape().

Example:

```
var decoded_string = unescape("a%20string%20safe%20for%20cookies");
```

The variable decoded_string now holds a string safe for cookies because the unescape function replaces each %20 with a space. See also escape().

var ***[NS 2, IE 3]***

A term used the first time a variable is named.

Example:

```
var a_new_variable = "I feel good!";
```

window

The Window object is either a browser window or a frame.

PROPERTIES

closed   NS 3, IE 4   This read-only property is true if a window has been closed and false if it is still open. The window referenced is generally created using the window.open() method described below.

Example:

```
if (my_window.closed == false)
{
    my_window.location = "http://www.hits.org";
}
```

This example makes sure the window named my_window has not been closed before sending a visitor to http://www.hits.org.

document	NS 2, IE 3	The Document object of the window. See the Document object for more information.
frames[]	NS 2, IE 3	The array of frames stored in a window. Each frame is considered another Window object.

Example:

```
window.frames[0].document.writeln("hello!");
```

The above writes the word hello into the document of the first frame in the window's frame set.

history	NS 2, IE 3	The History object of a window. See the History object for more information.
location	NS 2, IE 3	The Location object of a window. See the Location object for more information.
name	NS 2, IE 3	The name of a frame or window. The frame set provides the name of a frame. The name of a window is the second parameter in the window.open() method.

Example:

```
var first_frame_name = window.frames[0].name;
```

onerror	NS 3, IE 4	The name of a function to trigger when there's a JavaScript error. The function must take three parameters: the error message, the URL of the document in which the error occurred, and the line of the error.

Example:

```
function alertError(the_message, the_url, the_line)
{
    var the_string = "warning will robinson! " + the_message;
    the_string += " occurred on line " + the_line " of " + the_url;
}
window.onerror = window.alertError;
```

Now, whenever there is a JavaScript error, an alert will pop up with the contents of that error.

opener	NS 3, IE 3	A reference back to the window or frame that opened the current window.

Example:

```
window.opener.location = "http://www.nostarch.com";
```

This example changes the URL shown in the window that opened the current window.

parent   NS 2, IE 3   A reference back to the window in which the current frame was declared.

Example:

```
parent.frames[1].location = "http://www.aclu.org";
```

The above changes the URL of the second frame in a frame set when called by another frame in the same frame set.

self   NS 2, IE 3   A reference to the current window or frame. The same as window.

Example:

```
self.location = "http://www.npr.org";
```

status   NS 2, IE 3   The contents of the window's status bar.

Example:

```
window.status = "don't forget to smile!";
```

top   NS 2, IE 3   The topmost window in a window hierarchy. Helpful when your JavaScript is in a deeply nested frame and you want it to affect the whole Web page.

Example:

```
window.location = "http://www.theonion.com";
top.location = "http://www.theonion.com";
```

When executed inside a frame, the first line changes the URL of the frame to www.theonion.com and the second line changes the URL of the entire Web page.

LESS COMMON PROPERTIES

ClientInformation	IE 4	Same thing as the Navigator object.
InnerHeight	NS 4	The height of the display area of the Web page. Only signed scripts can make this smaller than 100 pixels.
InnerWidth	NS 4	The width of the display area of the Web page. Only signed scripts can make this smaller than 100 pixels.
locationbar	NS 4	True if the location bar is showing. Signed scripts can change this value.
menubar	NS 4	True if the menu bar is showing. Signed scripts can change this value.
offscreenBuffering	NS 4, IE 4	Setting this to true may reduce flicker in DHTML animations.
outerHeight	NS 4	The height of the window. Only signed scripts can make this smaller than 100 pixels.
outerWidth	NS 4	The width of the window. Only signed scripts can make this smaller than 100 pixels.
pageXOffset	NS 4	How far to the right the screen has scrolled in pixels. Read-only.
pageYOffset	NS 4	How far down the screen has scrolled in pixels. Read-only.
screenX	NS 4	The horizontal coordinate of the left side of the window.
screenY	NS 4	The vertical coordinate of the top of the window.
scrollbars	NS 4	True if the scrollbars are showing. Signed scripts can change this value.
statusbar	NS 4	True if the status bar is showing. Signed scripts can change this value.
toolbar	NS 4	True if the toolbar is showing. Signed scripts can change this value.

METHODS

blur()	NS 3, IE 4	Sends a window behind all the other windows on the screen.

Example:

```
window.blur();
```

open()	NS 2, IE 3	Opens a new window and returns a reference to it. Takes three parameters: the URL of the window to open, the target name of the window, and a comma-delimited list of features the window should have. Some of the features, such as width and height, must have values assigned to them. If the third parameter is left out, the new window contains the same features as the window that opened it.

Example:

```
var little_window =
window.open("http://www.ebay.com","little_window","height=50,width=50,resizable");
```

The above code opens up a small resizable window holding eBay's Web site.

FEATURES

The list below contains all the features a window may have and which browsers allow which features. The first list contains the window features that work in Netscape 2, Microsoft Internet Explorer 3, and more recent versions of these browsers.

copyhistory	Copies the history of the current window to the window being opened (that is, it enables the use of the back button in the new window).
directories	The directory buttons.
height	The height of the new window.
location	The location bar (where URLs may be typed).
menubar	The menu (File, Edit..., always present on a Macintosh).
resizable	Makes the window resizable (Macintosh windows are always resizable).
scrollbars	Provides scrollbars when the content of the window exceeds the window size.
status	Shows the status bar.
toolbar	The toolbar (back, forward, and so on).
width	The width of the window.

The following list contains features that only work in Netscape 4.0 and up. Certain features, noted by an asterisk, require that Netscape sign your script.

alwaysLowered*	Always puts this window behind others on the screen.
alwaysRaised*	Always puts this window above others on the screen.
dependent	Closes the new window when the opening window closes.
hotkeys	Disables keyboard shortcuts except Quit.

innerHeight	The height of the window's content region.	
innerWidth	The width of the window's content region.	
outerHeight	The total height of the window.	
outerWidth	The total width of the window.	
screenX	How far from the left side of the screen the window appears.	
screenY	How far from the top of the screen the window appears.	
scroll()	NS 3, IE 4	Takes two parameters: the position of the horizontal scroll bar and the position of the vertical scroll bar. The positions are roughly equal to the number of pixels on the page.
titlebar*	Set titlebar=no to hide the title bar.	
z-lock*	Puts the window below all other browser windows.	

Example:

```
window.scroll(100,500);
```

The above moves the scroll bars so that the part of the screen 100 pixels from the left border and 500 pixels from the top of the screen appears at the upper left corner of the screen.

scrollBy()	NS 4, IE 4	Takes two parameters: the number of pixels to scroll the window horizontally and vertically. Use negative numbers to move the scroll bars to the left or up.

Example:

```
window.scrollBy(50,-100);
```

The above scrolls the window 50 pixels to right and 100 pixels up.

LESS COMMONLY USED METHODS

back()	NS 4	Goes back a page (like clicking on the browser's back button).
find()	NS 4	Searches in the document for the string passed as the parameter.
forward()	NS 4	Goes forward a page (like clicking on the browser's forward button).
home()	NS 4	Goes to the home page (like clicking on the browser's home button).
moveBy()	NS 4, IE 4	Moves the window a specified number of pixels horizontally and vertically. NS 4 script must be signed to move the window off the screen.

moveTo()	NS 4, IE 4	Moves the window to a certain X, Y position relative to the upper left corner of the browser window. NS 4 script must be signed to move the window off the screen.
print()	NS 4	Prints the current Web page (like clicking on the browser's print button).
setHotkeys()	NS 4	Signed scripts can change this value to allow or disallow keyboard shortcuts.
setResizable()	NS 4	Signed scripts can change the resizable value to true or false.
stop()	NS 4	Stops loading the Web page (like clicking on the browser's stop button).
setZoptions()	NS 4	Signed scripts can set a window to alwaysRaised, alwaysLowered, or z-lock.

HANDLERS

Window handlers go inside the <BODY> tag of the Web page.

onBlur	NS 3, IE 4	Triggered when the window is no longer topmost on the screen.

Example:

```
<BODY onBlur="window.close();">
```

This window closes itself if the user selects another window.

onError	NS 3, IE 4	Triggered when a JavaScript error occurs.

Example:

```
<BODY onError="alert('warning! JavaScript error!');">
```

onFocus	NS 3, IE 4	Triggered when the user selects the window.

Example:

```
<BODY onFocus="alert('Nice to see you again.');">
```

onLoad	NS 2, IE 3	Triggered when the page, including all its images, has completely loaded.

Example:

```
<BODY onLoad="startThauScript();">
```

The above calls the function startThauScript() when the page has fully loaded.

onResize   NS 4, IE 4   Triggered when the visitor has resized the page.

Example:

```
<BODY onResize="alert('hey, that tickles.');">
```

onUnload   NS 2, IE 3   Triggered when a visitor is about to leave the page. This occurs even when the browser holding the page is closed, when the visitor clicks on a link, or when the visitor reloads the page.

Example:

```
<BODY onUnload="alert('sorry to see you go!');">
```

ANSWERS TO ASSIGNMENTS

Here are solutions to the assignments I've given at the end of each chapter. The scripts and images used in the solutions may be found on the CD-ROM in the corresponding chapter folders. The JavaScript listed below contains comments where I think explanation is necessary. If your solution works and is not much longer than mine, you've done a good job.

Chapter 1

No assignment.

Chapter 2

```
<html>
<head>
<title>Write the Date</title>
<script language="JavaScript">
<!-- hide me

// get the date information
//
var today = new Date();
var the_day = today.getDate();
var the_month = today.getMonth();
var the_hour = today.getHours();
```

```
var the_minutes = today.getMinutes();
var the_seconds = today.getSeconds();

// correct for the month starting from zero
//
the_month = the_month + 1;

// create the string you want to print
//
var the_whole_date = the_month + "/" + the_day + " ";
var the_whole_time = the_hour + ":" + the_minutes + ":" + the_seconds;
// show me -->
</script>
</head>
<body>
Right now it's:

<script language="JavaScript">
<!-- hide me

// write the date
//
document.write(the_whole_date);
document.write(the_whole_time);

// show me -->
</script>
</body>
</html>
```

Chapter 3

```
<html><head><title>Chapter 3 Assignment</title></head>
<body>
<script language="JavaScript">
<!-- hide me from old browsers
// get the visitor's name
//
var the_name = prompt("what's your name?", "");
// if the name is thau, dave, pugsly or gomez
// send the visitor to sesamestreet.com,
```

```
// otherwise, send him or her to the New York Times.
if ((the_name == "thau") || (the_name == "dave") ||
(the_name == "pugsly") || (the_name=="gomez"))
{
    window.location = "http://www.sesamestreet.com/";
} else {
    window.location = "http://www.nytimes.com/";
}
// end hiding comment -->
</script>
</body>
</html>
```

Chapter 4

```
<html><head><title>Swapping Two Images</title>
<script language = "JavaScript">
<!--
// function swapTwo() takes the name of the image file to load
// into the Web page images named image_one and image_two
function swapTwo(swap_image)
{
    window.document.image_one.src = swap_image;
    window.document.image_two.src = swap_image;
}

// -->
</script>
</head>
<body>
Mouse Over These<br>
<img src="orange.gif" onMouseOver="swapTwo('orange.gif');">
<img src="blue.gif" onMouseOver="swapTwo('blue.gif');">
<img src="green.gif" onMouseOver="swapTwo('green.gif');">
<p>
To Change These<br>
<img src="blue.gif" name="image_one">
<img src="blue.gif" name="image_two">
</body>
</html>
```

Chapter 5

This assignment needs two HTML files: one that opens the little window (index.html), and one that contains the HTML that appears in the little window when it's opened (image_page.html). Make sure these two HTML files are in the same directory.

index.html

```
<html>
<head>
<title>Remote Image Swap</title>
<script language="JavaScript">
<!-- Hide the javascript from old browsers
// open the little window with the page image_page.html. Call the little
// window the_window
//
var the_window = window.open("image_page.html","the_window","width=100,height=100");
// end the hiding comment -->
</script>
</head>
<body>
<h1>Play with a little window</h1>
<a href="#" onClick="the_window.document.the_image.src='sad_face.gif';">make him sad</a><br>
<a href="#" onClick="the_window.document.the_image.src='happy_face.gif';">make him
happy</a><br>
</body>
</html>
```

image_page.html

```
<html><head><title>Little Window</title></head>
<body>
<img name="the_image" src="happy.gif">
</body>
</html>
```

Chapter 6

```
<html><head><title>Chapter 6 Assignment</title>
<script language="JavaScript">
<!--
// function fancySwap() takes three parameters:
// 1. the Web page image that's getting swapped out
// 2. the file name of an image to swap into the Web page image
// 3. a URL to open into a new window.
//
function fancySwap(the_image, new_image, the_url)
{
    the_image.src = new_image;
    var my_window = window.open(the_url, my_window, "height=300,width=150");
}
// -->
</script>
</head>
<body>
<a href="#"
   onMouseOver="fancySwap(window.document.apple,'hilight_apple.gif','http://www.apple.com/');"
   onMouseOut="window.document.apple.src='normal_apple.gif';">
<img src="normal_apple.gif" name="apple" border="0">
</a>
<a href="#"
   onMouseOver="fancySwap(window.document.sun, 'hilight_sun.gif','http://www.sun.com/');"
   onMouseOut="window.document.sun.src='normal_sun.gif';">
<img src="normal_sun.gif" name="sun" border="0">
</a>
<a href="#"
   onMouseOver="fancySwap(window.document.monkey,'hilight_monkey.gif','http://www.webmonkey.com/');"
   onMouseOut="window.document.monkey.src='normal_monkey.gif';">
<img src="normal_monkey.gif" name="monkey" border="0">
</a>
</body>
</html>
```

Chapter 7

```
<html><head><title>Multiclock</title>
<script language="JavaScript">
<!--
// function updateReadout() takes one parameter, the time zone to
// convert the time to. The parameter can be either newyork, sanfran or tokyo.
// The function determines the time for that timezone and then sets the
// value of a text field to that time.
function updateReadout(the_zone)
{
    // get the current UTC time
    //
    var now = new Date();
    var the_hours = now.getUTCHours();
    var the_minutes = now.getUTCMinutes();
    var the_seconds = now.getUTCSeconds();

    // adjust for selected time zone
    //
    if (the_zone == "newyork")
    {
        the_hours = the_hours - 4;
    } else if (the_zone == "sanfran") {
        the_hours = the_hours - 7;
    } else if (the_zone == "tokyo") {
        the_hours = the_hours + 9;
    }

    // now fix the hours if over 24 or under 0
    //
    if (the_hours < 0)
    {
        the_hours = the_hours + 24;
    } else if (the_hours > 24) {
        the_hours = the_hours - 24;
    }

    // put zeros in front of minutes and seconds if necessary
    the_minutes = formatTime(the_minutes);
    the_seconds = formatTime(the_seconds);

    // now put the time in the text box
    var the_time = the_hours + ":" + the_minutes + ":" + the_seconds;
```

```
        window.document.clock_form.readout.value = the_time;
    }
// function formatTime() takes a number as a parameter.
// if that number is less than 10, it puts a 0 in front
// of it for formating purposes.
//
function formatTime(the_time)
{
    if (the_time < 10) {
        the_time = "0" + the_time;
    }

    return the_time;
}
// by looping through a set of radio buttons, function updateClock()
// checks to see which timezone has been selected by the viewer. Once it
// determines the selected time zone, it calls updateReadout().
//
function updateClock() {
    var selected_zone = "";
    if (window.document.clock_form.zones[0].checked == true) {
        selected_zone = window.document.clock_form.zones[0].value;
    } else if (window.document.clock_form.zones[1].checked == true) {
        selected_zone = window.document.clock_form.zones[1].value;
    } else if (window.document.clock_form.zones[2].checked == true) {
        selected_zone = window.document.clock_form.zones[2].value;
    } else if (window.document.clock_form.zones[3].checked == true) {
        selected_zone = window.document.clock_form.zones[3].value;
    }
    updateReadout(selected_zone);
}

// hide me -->
</script>
</head>
<body>
<form name="clock_form">
<input type="text" name = "readout">
<input type="button" value="update" onClick="updateClock();"><br>
San Francisco <input type="radio" name = "zones" value = "sanfran"
    onClick="updateReadout('sanfran');" checked><br>
New York <input type="radio" name = "zones" value = "newyork"
    onClick="updateReadout('newyork');"><br>
London <input type="radio" name = "zones" value = "london"
    onClick="updateReadout('london');"><br>
Tokyo <input type="radio" name = "zones" value = "tokyo"
```

```
      onClick="updateReadout('tokyo');"><br>
</form>
</body>
</html>
```

Chapter 8

```
<html><head><title>Histogram</title>
<script language = "JavaScript">
<!--
// function getNumbers()
// gets a number of bars to draw and the length
// of those bars. Calls the drawSquares() function
// to actually draw the bars to the Web page
//
function getNumbers()
{
  // create a new array
  //
  var the_values = new Array();

  // find out how many bars the person wants
  //
  var how_many = prompt("How many bars?","");

  // now loop that many times, asking for a value
  // each time and loading that value into the array
  //
  for (var loop=0; loop < how_many; loop++)
  {
    var value = prompt("How long is this bar? (1-10)","");
    the_values[loop] = value;
  }

  // now loop through the array and print out the bars
  //
  for (var loop=0; loop < how_many; loop++)
  {
    drawSquares(the_values[loop]);
  }
}

// function drawSquares()
```

```
// takes a number of squares to draw, and then draws them to
// the web page
//
function drawSquares(the_number)
{
    for (var loop=0; loop < the_number; loop++)
    {
        window.document.write("<img src='square.gif'>");
    }
    window.document.write("<br>");
}


// -->
</script>
</head>
<body>
<a href="#" onClick="getNumbers(); return false;">draw the histogram</a>
</body>
</html>
```

Chapter 9

This solution is very much like Figure 9-12. The only addition is the link around the image which clears the timeout when moused over and restarts the slideshow when the mouse moves off.

```
<html>
<head>
<title>A Timed Slide Show</title>
<script language = "JavaScript">
<!-- hide me
// preload the images
var the_images = new Array();
the_images[0] = new Image();
the_images[0].src = "one.jpg";
the_images[1] = new Image();
the_images[1].src = "two.jpg";
the_images[2] = new Image();
the_images[2].src = "three.jpg";
var the_timeout;
var index = 0;
// function rotateImage()
// this function swaps in the next image in the_images array and
// increases the index by 1. If the index exceeds the number of
```

```
    // images in the array, index is set back to zero.
    // setTimeout is used to call the function again in one second.
    function rotateImage()
    {
        window.document.my_image.src = the_images[index].src;
        index++;
        if (index >= the_images.length)
        {
            index = 0;
        }
        the_timeout = setTimeout("rotateImage();", 1000);
    }
    // show me -->
</script>
</head>
<body>
<a href = "#"
    onMouseOver = "clearTimeout(the_timeout);"
    onMouseOut = "rotateImage();">
<img name = "my_image" src="one.jpg"></a>
<form>
<input type = "button" value = "start the show"
        onClick = "clearTimeout(the_timeout); rotateImage();">
<input type = "button" value = "stop the show"
        onClick = "clearTimeout(the_timeout);">
</form>
</body>
</html>
```

Chapter 10

This assignment requires three HTML files because it uses frames. The first page, index.html, lays out the frameset. The second page, home-work-nav.html, contains the contents of the top frame, including the JavaScript. The third page, blank.html, is just a blank page which appears in the lower frame.

index.html

```
<html><head><title>My Browsers</title></head>
<frameset rows="50%,*">
<frame src = "homework-nav.html" name = "nav">
<frame src = "blank.html" name = "contents">
</frameset>
</html>
```

homework-nav.html

This page contains the image map and the form. Clicking on an area in the image map or submitting the form loads a URL into the lower frame. Notice the use of this in the form's onSubmit.

```
<html><head><title>nav</title></head>
<body>
<table border=0>
<tr><td>
Type a URL below, or
<br>
click on an area of the map.
<form onSubmit="parent.contents.location=this.the_url.value; return false;">
<input type="text" name="the_url">
</form>
</td>
<td>
<img src="src/left.gif" name="left" isMap useMap="#left">
</td>
</tr>
</table>
<MAP name="left">
<AREA coords="9,23,41,42" shape="RECT" href="#"
target="thePicture"
onClick = "parent.contents.location = 'http://www.whitehouse.gov/'; return false;"
onmouseOver="window.document.left.src='src/us.gif';"
onMouseOut="window.document.left.src='src/left.gif';">
<AREA coords="26,42,75,64" shape="RECT" href="#"
target="thePicture"
onClick = "parent.contents.location = 'http://www.whitehouse.gov/'; return false;"
onmouseOver="window.document.left.src='src/us.gif';"
onMouseOut="window.document.left.src='src/left.gif';">
<AREA coords="28,65,55,78" shape="RECT" href="#"
target="thePicture"
onClick = "parent.contents.location = 'http://www.mexico.gov/'; return false;"
onmouseOver="window.document.left.src='src/mexico.gif';"
onMouseOut="window.document.left.src='src/left.gif';">
</MAP>
</body>
</html>
```

blank.html

```
<html><head><title>blank</title></head>
<body>
</body>
</html>
```

Chapter 11

Like the Chapter 10 assignment, this assignment requires three HTML files because is uses frames. The first page, index.html, lays out the frameset. The second page, homework-nav.html, contains the contents of the top frame, including the JavaScript. The third page, blank.html, is just a blank page which appears in the lower frame.

index.html

```
<html><head><title>My Browsers</title></head>
<frameset rows="50%,*">
<frame src = "homework-nav.html" name = "nav">
<frame src = "blank.html" name = "contents">
</frameset>
</html>
```

homework-nav.html

```
<html><head><title>nav</title>
<script language="JavaScript">
<!-- hide me
// function domainCheckAndGo()
// this function makes sure a URL is legal. If it is, it
// sends the visitor to that URL.
function domainCheckAndGo(the_url)
{
  // split the URL into two parts, along the //
  // there should be two parts to it, the protocol (for example, http:)
  // and the address
  var first_split = the_url.split('//');
  if (first_split.length != 2)
  {
```

```
    alert("sorry, there must be one // in a domain name");
    return false;
}
// now check to see if the URL is legal - see the alerts in the
// if-then statement to see what the if statement is checking.
// if any of the conditions are violated, the script calls
// up an alert box explaining
// the error and then uses return to exit the function
// without changing the URL in the bottom frame.
if ((first_split[0] != 'http:') && (first_split[0] != 'https:'))
{
    alert("sorry, the domain must start with http:// or https://");
    return false;
}
if (the_url.indexOf(' ') != -1)
{
    alert("sorry, domains can't have spaces");
    return false;
}
// get everything after the http://
//
var two_slashes = the_url.indexOf('//');
var all_but_lead = the_url.substring(two_slashes+2, the_url.length);
var domain_parts = all_but_lead.split('.');
if (domain_parts.length < 2)
{
    alert("sorry, there must be at least two parts to a domain name");
    return false;
}
// loop through all the parts of the domain, making sure
// there's actually something there - for example,
// http://i.am.happy...com is not legal
// because there are three dots in a row.
for (var loop=0; loop < domain_parts.length; loop++)
{
    if (domain_parts[loop] == '')
    {
        alert("sorry, there must be some text after each .");
        return false;
    }
}
// if we've made it this far, the URL must be legal,
//so, load the URL into the frame.
parent.contents.location=the_url;
}
```

```
// end hiding -->
</script>
</head>
<body>
<table border=0>
<tr><td>
Type a URL below, or
<br>
click on an area of the map.
<form onSubmit="domainCheckAndGo(this.the_url.value); return false;">
<input type="text" name="the_url">
</form>
</td>
<td>
 <img src="src/left.gif" name="left" isMap useMap="#left">
</td>
</tr>
</table>
<MAP name="left">
<AREA coords="9,23,41,42" shape="RECT" href="#"
target="thePicture"
onClick = "parent.contents.location = 'http://www.whitehouse.gov/'; return false;"
onmouseOver="window.document.left.src='src/us.gif';"
onMouseOut="window.document.left.src='src/left.gif';">
<AREA coords="26,42,75,64" shape="RECT" href="#"
target="thePicture"
onClick = "parent.contents.location = 'http://www.whitehouse.gov/'; return false;"
onmouseOver="window.document.left.src='src/us.gif';"
onMouseOut="window.document.left.src='src/left.gif';">
<AREA coords="28,65,55,78" shape="RECT" href="#"
target="thePicture"
onClick = "parent.contents.location = 'http://www.mexico.gov/'; return false;"
onmouseOver="window.document.left.src='src/mexico.gif';"
onMouseOut="window.document.left.src='src/left.gif';">
</MAP>
</body>
</html>
```

....

blank.html

....

```
<html><head><title>blank</title></head>
<body>
</body>
</html>
```

....

Chapter 12

```
<html><head><title>One Shot Survey</title>
<script language="JavaScript">
<!-- hide me
// this is from the webmonkey cookie library www.webmonkey.com
//
function WM_readCookie(name) {
    if(document.cookie == '') { // there's no cookie, so go no further
     return false;
    } else { // there is a cookie
     var firstChar, lastChar;
     var theBigCookie = document.cookie;
     firstChar = theBigCookie.indexOf(name);      // find the start of 'name'
     var NN2Hack = firstChar + name.length;
     if((firstChar != -1) && (theBigCookie.charAt(NN2Hack) == '=')) {
         firstChar += name.length + 1; // skip 'name' and '='
         lastChar = theBigCookie.indexOf(';', firstChar); //
         if(lastChar == -1) lastChar = theBigCookie.length;
         return unescape(theBigCookie.substring(firstChar, lastChar));
     } else { // If there was no cookie of that name, return false.
         return false;
     }
    }
} // WM_readCookie

// function setCookie() sets a cookie named was_here to expire far
// in the future.
//
function setCookie()
{
    var the_future = new Date("December 31, 2023");
    var the_cookie_date = the_future.toGMTString();

    var the_cookie = "was_here=yes;expires=" + the_cookie_date;
    document.cookie = the_cookie;
}

// function checkFirst() checks if the was_here cookie
// has been set. If it hasn't, the alert pops up and the
// cookie is set using setCookie();
//
function checkFirstTime()
{
    var the_date = WM_readCookie("was_here");
```

```
        if(the_date == false)
        {
            alert("welcome newtimer!");
            setCookie();
        }
    }
    // end hide me ->
    </script>
    </head>
    <body>
    <h1>My Page</h1>
    <script language="JavaScript">
    <!-- hide me
    checkFirstTime();
    // end hide -->
    </script>
    Don't you just love this page?
    </body>
    </html>
```

Chapter 13

```
<HTML>
<HEAD>
<TITLE>Bouncing Happy Face</TITLE>
<script language="javascript">
<!-- hide me
// set the direction
//
var x_motion = "plus";
var y_motion = "plus";

// set the borders
//
var top_border = 100;
var bottom_border = 200;
var left_border = 100;
var right_border = 300;

// this function moves the face 5 pixels to the right.
// if it's too far to the right, it moves it back to the left
// border
```

```
function moveSmile()
{
    var the_smile;

    if (navigator.appName == "Netscape")
    {
    the_smile = document.smile;
    } else {
    the_smile = smile.style;
    }

    if (x_motion == "plus")
    {
    the_smile.left = parseInt(the_smile.left) + 5;
    } else {
    the_smile.left = parseInt(the_smile.left) - 5;
    }

    if (y_motion == "plus")
    {
    the_smile.top = parseInt(the_smile.top) + 5;
    } else {
    the_smile.top = parseInt(the_smile.top) - 5;
    }

    if (parseInt(the_smile.left) > right_border)
    {
    x_motion = "minus";
    } else if (parseInt(the_smile.left) < left_border) {
    x_motion = "plus";
    }

    if (parseInt(the_smile.top) > bottom_border)
    {
    y_motion = "minus";
    } else if (parseInt(the_smile.top) < top_border) {
    y_motion = "plus";
    }

    theTimeOut = setTimeout('moveSmile()', 100);
}

// show me-->
</script>
</HEAD>
```

```
<BODY BGCOLOR="#FFFFFF">
<form>
<input type="button" value="make happiness bounce"
    onClick="moveSmile();">
<input type="button" value="stop that smiley!"
onClick="clearTimeout(theTimeOut);">
</form>
<div id="smile" style="position:absolute; left:100; top:100;">
<img src="happy_face.gif" width="130" height="75">
</div>
</BODY>
</HTML>
```

Chapter 14

No assignment.

ABOUT THE CD-ROM

The CD-ROM contains all the code examples from each chapter, archived copies of each site mentioned, and lots of script libraries, demos, and freeware. Each chapter has its own folder with the example scripts and relevant images from that chapter, as well as the answer to the chapter's assignment. Here's a rundown of the other folders.

/demos

This folder contains three demo versions of retail software:

Macromedia Dreamweaver 3.0   An HTML editor that can generate simple JavaScripts like image roll-overs and simple animations.

Adobe GoLive Cyberstudio 4.0   A good HTML editor that can generate JavaScript in version 5.0.

Jshop 2.1   A JavaScript-based shopping-cart program.

/freeware

The creators of these fully functional PC programs offer them for free. The freeware catalog file in this directory provides detailed explanations of each program.

Webflex (webflex.zip)	A free HTML editor.
Nethtml (nethtml.zip)	Another free HTML editor (this one written entirely in JavaScript).
Winhotpot (winhotpot.zip)	Web authoring tools for educators.
Omentree (omentree.zip)	A JavaScript-based hierarchical menu system.
JSCalendar (jscalendar.zip)	A JavaScript-based calendar.

/libraries

This folder contains free JavaScript libraries of complicated JavaScript applications you can cut and paste into your Web pages.

/cookies	JavaScript that can read and write cookies for long-term storage of information.
/form validation	Scripts that make sure visitors are filling out your forms correctly.
/plugin detection	Scripts that determine whether a visitor's browser can handle Flash before they actually run the Flash code.
/preload	A good preload script for loading all the images a page needs so image swaps go smoothly.

/sites

The HTML (including JavaScript) and images of all the sites discussed in the book.

INDEX

of mortgage rates, *116*

capitalization
    event names, 139
    function names, 95, 293–294
    HTML specifications for, 69
    in if-then statements, 37
    in-caps notation, 95
    JavaScript built-in object names, 25
    of strings with toUpperCase(), 238
    variable names, 16, 293–294
    of while, 149

Cascading Style Sheets (CSS), 267–271, 347

CGI scripting, 5–6, 139, 221, 323

charAt(), 226, 229–231, 344

checkboxes
    about, 120
    code for, *119, 148, 151*–152
    events handled by, *135*
    naming, 154
    properties of, 130
    reading and setting, 130–132
    screenshots, *119, 144, 149*

Checkbox (form element), 314

checked (Boolean), 120, 130

checked (property) of Checkbox, 130, 148, 314

checked (property) of Radio, 340

Classic Wine Investors Web site, 244–245
    screenshots, *244, 245*

clearInterval(), 315

clearTimeout(), 172, 173–175, 178, 283, 315

clocks
    12-hour, 31
    building with timing loops, 179–181
    code and screenshots, *141, 179–180*
    on NASA's Web site, 181–186
    showing time in different cities, 141

closed (property) of generic objects, 105

closed (property) of window, 351–352

colon (:), 248

comma and space, coding, 30

comments
    code with, *9*
    importance of, 9
    and older browsers, 10
    why write first when coding, 297–298

comment tags (!-- and //--), 10–11, 30

complete (property) of Image, 328–329

confirm(), 315

cookies
    about, 245, 246
    access to, 253
    adding more than one piece of information to, 248
    on Classic Wine Investors Web site, 244–245
    code for, *247, 249, 250–251, 252, 254, 255*
    expiration date for, 251–253
    libraries for, 255
    multiple, 254, 255
    properties of, 248, 253–*254*
    resetting, 248–251
    setting, 246–*247*
    setting the path of, 253
    and shopping carts, 258–259
    viewing, 245
    from Web sites with multiple domains, 253

credit card numbers, verifying, 226, 233

CSS (Cascading Style Sheets), 267–271, 347

curly brackets ({})
    after function names, 95
    when and where to place, 46, 69
    in while loops, 149

pull-down menus (*continued*)
    screenshots, *117, 120, 137*

THE NO B.S. GUIDE TO
RED HAT LINUX 6.x

by BOB RANKIN

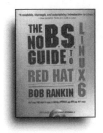

This book is a thorough yet concise guide to installing Red Hat Linux 6.*x* and exploring its capabilities. Author Bob Rankin (*The No B.S. Guide to Linux*, No Starch Press) provides easy-to-follow instructions for installing and running Red Hat 6.*x*. Through examples and helpful illustrations, the author guides readers through these topics and more:

- Installation—in ten easy steps!

- How to use and configure GNOME—the new Linux GUI

- How to write Bash or Perl scripts and use the Bash shell

- How to connect to the Internet with SLIP/PPP and how to run the Apache Web server for Linux

- How to access DOS files and run Windows programs under Linux

The CD-ROM contains Red Hat Linux 6.2—one of the most popular Linux distributions available. It's easy to install and requires minimal configuration—you'll be up and running in a snap!

BOB RANKIN is a programmer and nationally recognized expert on the Internet. He is a columnist for *Boardwatch Magazine* and a contributor to several computer publications. His books include *Dr. Bob's Painless Guide to the Internet* (1996) and *The No B.S. Guide to Linux* (1997).

402 pp., paperback, $34.95 w/CD-ROM
ISBN 1-886411-30-1

STEAL THIS COMPUTER BOOK: WHAT THEY WON'T TELL YOU ABOUT THE INTERNET

by WALLACE WANG

"*A delightfully irresponsible primer.*" — *Chicago Tribune*

"*If this book had a soundtrack, it'd be Lou Reed's 'Walk on the Wild Side.'*"
— *InfoWorld*

"*An unabashed look at the dark side of the Net — the stuff many other books gloss over.*" — *Amazon.com*

Steal This Computer Book explores the dark corners of the Internet and reveals little-known techniques that hackers use to subvert authority. Unfortunately, some of these techniques, when used by malicious hackers, can destroy data and compromise the security of corporate and government networks. To keep your computer safe from viruses, and yourself from electronic con games and security crackers, Wallace Wang explains the secrets hackers and scammers use to prey on their victims. Discover:

- How hackers write and spread computer viruses
- How criminals get free service and harass legitimate customers on online services like America Online
- How online con artists trick people out of thousands of dollars
- Where hackers find the tools to crack into computers or steal software
- How to find and use government-quality encryption to protect your data
- How hackers steal passwords from other computers

WALLACE WANG is the author of several computer books, including *Microsoft Office 97 for Windows for Dummies* and *Visual Basic for Dummies*. A regular contributor to *Boardwatch* magazine (the "Internet Underground" columnist), he's also a successful stand-up comedian. He lives in San Diego, California.

340 pp., paperback, $19.95
ISBN 1-886411-21-2

THE LINUX PROBLEM SOLVER

by BRIAN WARD

- Hands-on, practical guide solves kernel issues

- Helps solve hundreds of problems

A must-have for intermediate to advanced users who already have Linux up and running. Solves technical problems related to printing, networking, back-up, crash recovery, and compiling or upgrading a kernel. Quick and concise in approach, with over 100 problem boxes that help to solve specific problems in addition to those discussed throughout the book.

CD-ROM: Supports the book's contents with configuration files and numerous programs not included in many Linux distributions.

BRIAN WARD is a Unix systems programmer, and is the author of the "Linux Kernel HOWTO," widely circulated on the Internet. A Unix network administrator, he has worked with Linux since 1993. He is currently pursuing a Ph.D. in computer science at the University of Chicago.

350 pp. w/CD-ROM, $34.95 ($54.00CDN)
ISBN 1-886411-35-2

Phone:
1 (800) 420-7240 OR
(415) 863-9900
MONDAY THROUGH FRIDAY,
9 A.M. TO 5 P.M. (PST)

Fax:
(415) 863-9950
24 HOURS A DAY,
7 DAYS A WEEK

E-mail:
SALES@NOSTARCH.COM

Web:
HTTP://WWW.NOSTARCH.COM

Mail:
NO STARCH PRESS
555 DE HARO STREET, SUITE 250
SAN FRANCISCO, CA 94107
USA

Distributed to the book trade by Publishers Group West

UPDATES

This book was carefully reviewed for technical accuracy, but it's inevitable that some things will change after the book goes to press. Visit the Web site for this book at **http://www.nostarch.com/js_updates.htm** for updates, errata, and other information.

CD-ROM LICENSE AGREEMENT FOR *THE BOOK OF JAVASCRIPT*

Read this Agreement before opening this package. By opening this package, you agree to be bound by the terms and conditions of this Agreement.

This CD-ROM (the "CD") contains programs and associated documentation and other materials and is distributed with the book entitled *The Book of JavaScript* to purchasers of the book for their own personal use only. Such programs, documentation and other materials and their compilation (collectively, the "Collection") are licensed to you subject to terms and conditions of this Agreement by No Starch Press, having a place of business at 555 De Haro Street, Suite 250, San Francisco, CA 94107 ("Licensor"). In addition to being governed by the terms and conditions of this Agreement, your rights to use the programs and other materials included on the CD may also be governed by separate agreements distributed with those programs and materials on the CD (the "Other Agreements"). In the event of any inconsistency between this Agreement and any of the Other Agreements, those Agreements shall govern insofar as those programs and materials are concerned. By using the Collection, in whole or in part, you agree to be bound by the terms and conditions of this Agreement. Licensor owns the copyright to the Collection, except insofar as it contains materials that are proprietary to third party suppliers. All rights in the Collection except those expressly granted to you in this Agreement are reserved to Licensor and such suppliers as their respective interests may appear.

1. Limited License. Licensor grants you a limited, nonexclusive, nontransferable license to use the Collection on a single dedicated computer (excluding network servers). This Agreement and your rights hereunder shall automatically terminate if you fail to comply with any provision of this Agreement or the Other Agreements. Upon such termination, you agree to destroy the CD and all copies of the CD, whether lawful or not, that are in your possession or under your control. Licensor and its suppliers retain all rights not expressly granted herein as their respective interests may appear.

2. Additional Restrictions. (A) You shall not (and shall not permit other persons or entities to) directly or indirectly, by electronic or other means, reproduce (except for archival purposes as permitted by law), publish, distribute, rent, lease, sell, sublicense, assign, or otherwise transfer the Collection or any part thereof or this Agreement. Any attempt to do so shall be void and of no effect. (B) You shall not (and shall not permit other persons or entities to) reverse-engineer, decompile, disassemble, merge, modify, create derivative works of, or translate the Collection or use the Collection or any part thereof for any commercial purpose. (C) You shall not (and shall not permit others persons or entities to) remove or obscure Licensor's or its suppliers' or licensor's copyright, trademark, or other proprietary notices or legends from any portion of the Collection or any related materials. (D) You agree and certify that the Collection will not be exported outside the United States except as authorized and as permitted by the laws and regulations of the United States. If the Collection has been rightfully obtained outside of the United States, you agree that you will not reexport the Collection, except as permitted by the laws and regulations of the United States and the laws and regulations of the jurisdiction in which you obtained the Collection.

3. Disclaimer of Warranty. (A) The Collection and the CD are provided "as is" without warranty of any kind, either express or implied, including, without limitation, any warranty of merchantability and fitness for a particular purpose, the entire risk as to the results and performance of the CD and the software and other materials that is part of the Collection is assumed by you, and Licensor and its suppliers and distributors shall have no responsibility for defects in the CD or the accuracy or application of or errors or omissions in the Collection and do not warrant that the functions contained in the Collection will meet your requirements, or that the operation of the CD or the Collection will be uninterrupted or error-free, or that any defects in the CD or the Collection will be corrected. In no event shall Licensor or its suppliers or distributors be liable for any direct, indirect, special, incidental, or consequential damages arising out of the use of or inability to use the Collection or the CD, even if Licensor or its suppliers or distributors have been advised of the likelihood of such damages occurring. Licensor and its suppliers and distributors shall not be liable for any loss, damages, or costs arising out of, but not limited to, lost profits or revenue; loss of use of the Collection or the CD; loss of data or equipment; cost of recovering software, data, or materials in the Collection; the cost of substitute software, data, or materials in the Collection; claims by third parties; or other similar costs. (B) In no event shall Licensor or its suppliers' or distributors' total liability to you for all damages, losses, and causes of action (whether in contract, tort or otherwise) exceed the amount paid by you for the Collection. (C) Some states do not allow exclusion or limitation of implied warranties or limitation of liability for incidental or consequential damages, so the above limitations or exclusions may not apply to you.

4. U.S. Government Restricted Rights. The Collection is licensed subject to RESTRICTED RIGHTS. Use, duplication, or disclosure by the U.S. Government or any person or entity acting on its behalf is subject to restrictions as set forth in subdivision (c)(1)(ii) of the Rights in Technical Data and Computer Software Clause at DFARS (48 CFR 252.227-7013) for DoD contracts, in paragraphs (c)(1) and (2) of the Commercial Computer Software Restricted Rights clause in the FAR (48 CFR 52.227-19) for civilian agencies, or, in the case of NASA, in clause 18-52.227-86(d) of the NASA Supplement to the FAR, or in other comparable agency clauses. The contractor/manufacturer is No Starch Press, 555 De Haro Street, Suite 250, San Francisco, CA 94107.

5. General Provisions. Nothing in this Agreement constitutes a waiver of Licensor's, or its suppliers' or licensors' rights under U.S. copyright laws or any other federal, state, local, or foreign law. You are responsible for installation, management, and operation of the Collection. This Agreement shall be construed, interpreted, and governed under California law. Copyright © 2000 No Starch Press. All rights reserved. Reproduction in whole or in part without permission is prohibited.